INTERDISCIPLINARITY AND LANGUAGES

CONTEMPORARY STUDIES
IN DESCRIPTIVE LINGUISTICS

VOL. 30

Edited by

DR GRAEME DAVIS & KARL A. BERNHARDT

PETER LANG
Oxford • Bern • Berlin • Bruxelles • Frankfurt am Main • New York • Wien

Francisca Suau-Jiménez and
Barry Pennock-Speck (eds)

INTERDISCIPLINARITY AND LANGUAGES

CURRENT ISSUES IN RESEARCH, TEACHING, PROFESSIONAL APPLICATIONS AND ICT

PETER LANG
Oxford • Bern • Berlin • Bruxelles • Frankfurt am Main • New York • Wien

Bibliographic information published by Die Deutsche Nationalbibliothek
Die Deutsche Nationalbibliothek lists this publication in the Deutsche National-bibliografie; detailed bibliographic data is available on the Internet at http://dnb.d-nb.de.

A catalogue record for this book is available from the British Library.

Library of Congress Cataloging-in-Publication Data:

Suau Jiménez, Francisca.
Interdisciplinarity and languages : current issues in research, teaching, professional applications and ICT / Francisca Suau-Jiménez and Barry Pennock-Speck.
p. cm. – (Contemporary studies in descriptive linguistics; 30)
Includes bibliographical references and index.
ISBN 978-3-0343-0283-8 (alk. paper)
1. Language and languages–Study and teaching–Technological innovations. 2. Interdisciplinary approach in education. I. Pennock-Speck, Barry, 1954- II. Title.
P53.855.S83 2011
407–dc22
2011007336

ISSN 1660-9301
ISBN 978-3-0343-0283-8

Hochfeldstrasse 32, CH-3012 Bern, Switzerland
info@peterlang.com, www.peterlang.com, www.peterlang.net

Printed in Germany

Contents

List of Figures vii
List of Tables ix
Acknowledgements xi
Preface xiii

CARMEN VALERO-GARCÉS AND DENIS SOCARRÁS-ESTRADA

1 Development and Assessment of an Aptitude Test for Interpreters: Using Labs for Interpreting Training 1

MARÍA LUISA PÉREZ-CAÑADO

2 The Use of ICT in the European Higher Education Area: Acting upon the Evidence 21

CHELO VARGAS-SIERRA

3 Translation-oriented Terminology Management and ICTs: Present and Future 45

FRANCISCO YUS

4 Relevance Equations of Effective Internet Communication 65

BEATRIZ GALLARDO-PAÚLS AND VERÓNICA MORENO-CAMPOS

5 Linguistic Models in Learning Innovation Theories: Linear Approaches versus Interactive Practices 87

FRANÇOISE SALAGER-MEYER

6 Interdisciplinarity and Languages for Specific Purposes in Latin America 107

ISABEL GARCÍA-IZQUIERDO

7 Investigating Professional Languages through Genres 125

MIGUEL ÁNGEL CANDEL-MORA

8 Computer-assisted Translation and Terminology Management: Tools and Resources 145

JOSÉ RAMÓN GÓMEZ-MOLINA

9 Developing Intercultural Communicative Competence through Video-web Communication in the NIFLAR Project 161

VICTORIA GUILLÉN-NIETO

10 When Humanities and Information and Communications Technology Merge 185

Notes on Contributors 209

Index 215

List of Figures

Figure 1.	Accuracy vs Speed of response vs Stress	15
Figure 2.	Screenshot of the methodology questionnaire	26
Figure 3.	Total number of participants	27
Figure 4.	Materials and resources (students)	30
Figure 5.	Materials and resources (teachers)	31
Figure 6.	Gentt Corpus	133
Figure 7.	Personal Information. Profile	134
Figure 8.	Search Corpus	135
Figure 9.	Advanced Search	135
Figure 10.	Superimposed panels	136
Figure 11.	Subcorpus creation	137
Figure 12.	Subcorpus Management	137
Figure 13.	Genre Tree Management	138
Figure 14.	Double Tree	139
Figure 15.	Genre Template	140
Figure 16.	Corpus Report	141
Figure 17.	Adobe Connect platform	164
Figure 18.	Carrying out the task *Gente con corazón*	174
Figure 19.	Hofstede's value dimension scores for Spain and the UK	191
Figure 20.	Visionaire's main screen. Setting designed by draftsman Facundo Ferré Luparia. 'It's a Deal!', 2010	199
Figure 21.	Example of an animation. Setting and characters designed by draftsman Facundo Ferré Luparia. 'It's a Deal!', 2010	201

Figure 22. Elia and George Watts negotiating at TAW Ltd in London. Setting and characters designed by draftsman Facundo Ferré Luparia. 'It's a Deal!, 2010 203

List of Tables

Table 1. Vocabulary exercise 10

Table 2. Synonyms and antonyms exercise 11

Table 3. Reliability of the questionnaire 25

Table 4. Differences between students and teachers in materials and resources 32

Table 5. Tasks in the Jaén-Dallas telecollaboration project 36–37

Table 6. A fragment of a GPS translation memory (English-Spanish) 54

Table 7. Intercultural communicative tasks in video-web communication 168–171

Table 8. Evaluation of the interaction 176–177

Table 9. Evaluating the impact of video-web communication on motivation 178

Table 10. How do participants evaluate the interaction tasks? 179

Table 11. Hypothetical correlation of culture-specific values with language-specific behaviour (Guillén-Nieto, Pernías-Peco, Vargas-Sierra, & Williams 2009; Guillén-Nieto 2009a) 195–196

Acknowledgements

We would like to thank our colleagues from the Instituto Interuniversitario de Lenguas Modernas Aplicadas (IULMA) at the University of Valencia for its academic and financial support, without which the publication of this book would not have been possible.

Preface

This volume provides a state-of-the-art view of research into interdisciplinarity, language and Information and Communication Technologies (ICTs), with an overview of teaching proposals within a university context. Interdisciplinarity is understood here as how language expresses the discourse and lexis of specialised knowledge in science, technology and the professions. Language helps in the creation of these different fields and constitutes a strategic tool that, if harnessed correctly, will facilitate competitiveness on an international level, in order to boost technological, scientific, economic and educational growth. Interdisciplinarity, together with language and ICTs, constitute our focus here. Teachers, translators and other experts in the field of linguistics in educational institutions need to take into account all three when dealing with the real needs of industry, commerce and the professions. The contributions deal with themes that are crucial to the demands of modern society: intercultural business communications, one of the most challenging areas of specialised discourse and commerce; ICT and specialised translation, a current issue of utmost relevance; terminology applied to translation; language acquisition and communication in virtual environments; training interpreters through ICT; exploring the commercial needs of language industries; corpus-based research and ICT applications in specialised dictionaries; university e-learning courses; and, finally, the state of research on specialised languages in Latin America.

In their chapter, 'Development and Assessment of an Aptitude Test for Interpreters: Using Labs for Interpreting Training', Carmen Valero-Garcés and Denis Socarrás-Estrada give a detailed account of an assessment instrument they have created for interpreters. They detail the scales and grading method that should be applied, the reliability and validity of the test, and the kinds of exercises to be used in the test. They state that, on the basis of their results, the tests constitute a useful instrument to measure the ability of students to develop the skills and knowledge needed.

In her contribution, 'The Use of ICT in the European Higher Education Area: Acting upon the Evidence', María Luisa Pérez-Cañado describes three pedagogical innovation projects developed at the University of Jaén from both a quantitative and qualitative perspective. Within the new higher education landscape that has come about due to the move toward European Convergence in higher education, she suggests that ICTs should have an increasingly significant role in teaching at tertiary level.

Chelo Vargas-Sierra describes, in her chapter, 'Translation-oriented Terminology Management and ICTs: Present and Future', different aspects of terminology management and a computerised workbench, all with regard to translation-oriented terminology. Future developments with regard to translators' workstations and their relation to terminology work are put forward.

In his chapter, 'Relevance Equations of Effective Internet Communication', Francisco Yus analyses user-to-user internet communication from a Relevance Theory point of view. He analyses nine sample relevance equations and claims that any relevance equation that we apply to internet communication should include an analysis of aspects that generate alterations in the eventual validity of such an equation.

Beatriz Gallardo-Paúls and Verónica Moreno-Campos revise, in 'Linguistic Models in Learning Innovation Theories: Linear Approaches versus Interactive Practices', what the teaching and learning dimension that university educational innovation based on ICTs has to offer. They focus on the dominant linguistic model associated with teaching in higher education and the need to choose a model that is compatible with truly interactive teaching practices.

Françoise Salager-Meyer, in 'Interdisciplinarity and Languages for Specific Purposes in Latin America', looks at the genesis of the ESP movement in Latin America and provides a state-of-the-art revision of the research and teaching problems that have been and still are of concern to most LSP practitioners throughout Latin American. Her chapter concludes with a description of an ongoing project between the Latin American and Caribbean countries, on the one hand, and the European Union, on the other.

Through 'Investigating Professional Languages through Genres', Isabel García-Izquierdo, from the Gentt Group, reflects on the research currently being conducted on specialised languages, with particular attention being given to the needs of interlinguistic communication. She proposes a genre-based approach (as redefined in recent studies carried out in the fields of linguistics, rhetoric and translation studies) to carry out research in this field.

In 'Computer-assisted Translation and Terminology Management: Tools and Resources', Miguel Ángel Candel-Mora proposes the use of several tools and resources that are essential for professional translators. He describes the rebirth of machine translation, new advances in statistical machine translation and provides an overview of computer-assisted translation (CAT tools) and translation-oriented terminology management in the last ten to fifteen years. He analyses why they have become important resources in both research and professional practice alike.

In 'Developing Intercultural Communicative Competence through Video-web Communication in the NIFLAR Project', José Ramón Gómez-Molina gives an account of the e-learning of Spanish as a Foreign Language in which students from the MA in Hispanic Studies (pre-service teachers) from the University of Valencia and students of Spanish as a Foreign Language from the University of Utrecht (Holland) have participated using a video-web communication virtual environment. He discusses the role of telecollaboration, the design of interactive tasks, interaction among participants, and the research that is being performed using quantitative and qualitative criteria, in order to analyse the learning outcomes and the problems and advantages that one might encounter in this and similar communicative environments.

Finally, in her chapter, 'When Humanities and Information and Communications Technology Merge', Victoria Guillén-Nieto gives an account of the interdisciplinary COMINTER-SIMULNEG project, in which the insights of applied linguistics are synthesised with those of social anthropology and ICT with a practical agenda in mind: (a) designing a pragmatic model for the analysis of intercultural communication between Spaniards and Britons in business settings and (b) constructing a graphic adventure for the purpose of developing intercultural communicative competence in business settings.

– FRANCISCA SUAU-JIMÉNEZ AND BARRY PENNOCK-SPECK
March 2011

CARMEN VALERO-GARCÉS AND DENIS SOCARRÁS-ESTRADA

1 Development and Assessment of an Aptitude Test for Interpreters: Using Labs for Interpreting Training

1. Introduction

The main aims of our study are to describe in detail the assessment instrument we have created, its theoretical foundations based on previous studies of an interdisciplinary group of scholars, and the main preliminary results arrived at according to our perspectives.

1.1 What is an aptitude test?

A quick search in some dictionaries and websites yields these general answers which could be consider as applicable:

- A standardized test designed to measure the ability of a person to develop skills or acquire knowledge.[1]
- Any of various tests given to measure abilities: as manual dexterity, visual acuity, reasoning, or verbal comprehension, and used to assist in the selection of a career.[2]

1 Aptitude test. (n.d.). *The American Heritage Dictionary of the English Language*, 4th edn. Accessed 1 March 2010 from Dictionary.com website, <http://dictionary.reference.com/browse/aptitude test>.

2 Aptitude test. (n.d.). Dictionary.com Unabridged. <http://dictionary.reference.com/browse/aptitudetest> accessed 1 March 2010.

- An occupation-oriented test for evaluating intelligence, achievement, and interest.[3]

1.2 Where do we want to apply the test?

The aptitude test application is a milestone in the Master of Arts in Intercultural Communication, Interpreting and Translation in Public Services, opened as an official degree at the University of Alcala (UAH) in 2006. It is currently taught in nine language pairs: German-, Arabic-, Bulgarian-, Chinese-, French-, English-, Polish-, Rumanian-, and Russian-Spanish. It lasts one academic year that corresponds to sixty ECTS-credits, equivalent to 1,500–1,800 hours of study in the European Union. It aims at training specialists to liaise between institutions and their increasing amount of clients with a limited Spanish proficiency. It is divided into three modules: one in intercultural communication, another one in translation and interpreting (T&I) in healthcare settings and the last one in T&I in legal-administration settings. It also includes an internship in institutions where public services are offered; and finally the preparation of a research project or master thesis.

A high percentage (42.3%) of our candidate / students in the language pair English-Spanish for the academic year (2009–2010) hold a recently obtained degree in (T&I). The other important major part (30.8%) of the candidates hold a degree in Studies in Language and Literature (either Spanish or English). Only (26.9%) of the students have previous studies not directly related to languages; some of them have a bilingual or near bilingual level, others have a high proficiency level in both languages they are going to be trained in.

3 <http://www.answer.com> accessed November 2009.

2. Background

This research starts by reviewing some of the authors who have recently written about training, mainly evaluating and assessing interpreters. We will mention below some researchers who have helped the development of the aptitude testing, wisely summarized by Russo (2009).

We agree with Sawyer (2004: 5) that high quality education is [supposed to be] based upon sound assessment. But more recently, Jacobson (2009: 49) has concluded that the assessment of interpreting performance is an area of research that is still in its infancy. The following data might prove he was right. Ulrych (2005) reported on a questionnaire sent to sixty-five institutions of higher education, located mainly in Europe and North America out of which forty-one answered. Only 50% of them administered an entrance exam. That finding suggests that either standardized instruments to assess interpreters did not exist there at that moment or some institutions were still reluctant to accept the reliability and validity of the existing tests. Therefore the need to develop an instrument adapted to assess candidate's aptitudes for the integral professional formation is what we intend to provide based on our local needs.

Hatim & Mason (1997) made it clear that in interpreter assessment, we have to distinguish between evaluating quality and evaluating performance and we totally agree with that idea which is very applicable to our context – public service interpreting and translating. Jacobson (2009: 51–60) has also identified an important weakness in interpreting studies stating that most of the published research has benefitted little from cross-pollination between disciplines. He has underlined the need to use concepts derived from interactional sociolinguistics and conversation analysis, to develop a more comprehensive approach to assessing interpreter performance.

Developing an assessment instrument requires analysing four main factors: the competences and skills to be assessed; the scales and grading method to be applied; the reliability and validity of the test; and the different kind of exercises to be used in the test. Below we will review how other researchers approached these topics in previous works.

2.1 *Competences and skills*

We claim that the main strength a future language professional must have is his/her mother tongue competence. Lang (1994) reported that one of the problems for trainee translators was not so much foreign language competence as mother tongue competence and also that this problem was more widespread than they initially believed, when making reference to a joint training project. More than a decade later Nord (2005: 210–212) states that it is still a frequent complaint that translation students have an insufficient command of their own native language.

Besides mother tongue competence, there is an array of other competences and skills an interpreting professional should have. But there is not yet an established standard set of parameters to measure a candidate's skills. The current situation still remains as Pochhacker (2004) depicted it: 'in tests for interpreting skills, there's little systematic information on parameters ... It is largely left to the professional judgement of the examiner(s)' (as cited in Salaets & Vermeerbergen 2009).

Although Jacobson (2009: 67) sounds a bit sceptic when referring to the standardization of the interpreter corresponding competencies, a certain consensus has existed among authors when defining those competencies. We will cite just a few of them below.

Longley (1989) says that their tests to select candidates included: linguistic knowledge, performance under stress and reaction time to verbal stimuli (cited in Jiménez & Pinazo 2002: 83).

Baker (1991: 119) had already mentioned some of the most relevant features oral interpreting requires: extremely good listening skills, immediate recall, and an ability to convert meaning from one language to another on the spot, while relating to both users and controlling the process as necessary.

And another thing is very clear according to Kalina (1994) when she states that interpreters should know about both the theoretical framework and the cognitive process required for their activity.

Among the personal qualities and abilities for liaison interpreting, Gentile et al. (1996: 65ff) suggest language skills, cultural competence, interpreting techniques, memory skills and professional ethics as the main components of an interpreter's competence (cited in Pöchhacker 2004: 166).

Schjoldager (1996) proposes the following assessment criteria simply explicated as 'ideal interpreting': comprehensibility; language; coherence and plausibility; loyalty; intertextual level; intratextual level; macrolevel language; macro-level communication; professionality; and attitude.

And although Schaeffner (2000: 146) is characterizing translators, we will adopt her set of competencies as initially valid and very useful for our purposes, taking into account that we will be educating interpreters-translators. For her, the process of translation involves at least the following specific competences:

- Linguistic competence of the languages concerned
- Cultural competence
- Textual competence
- Domain / subject specific competence
- (Re)search competence; and
- Transfer competence

Pöchhacker (2004: 180–186) also includes these competencies in the profile of professional interpreters: general knowledge, cognitive skills (analysis, attention and memory) and personality traits (stress tolerance and intellectual curiosity). As required for dialogue interpreting: note-taking, whispered simultaneous interpreting, and intercultural communication; turn-taking and role performance.

Salaets and Vermeerbergen (2009) group competence into three main areas:

- Knowledge: general, specialized, deontological, L1 and L2
- Skills: interpreting, communicative, research
- Attitude: reliability, loyalty, *professionality*, critical attitude

The main objective of some online tests, such as the one designed by Kent University,[4] is to assess the following main areas: memory, attention, focus, speed, language, spatial reasoning, problem solving, fluid intelligence, stress, and reaction time.

4 <http://www.kent.ac.uk/careers/psychotests.htm> accessed November 2009.

The admission criteria of the European Master's in Translation (EMT) network, into which our master course entered on 15 September 2009, raising the standard requirements to a very high limit, states:

> Candidates should hold a recognised university degree or equivalent and have an excellent command of his/her mother tongue; have an in-depth knowledge of his/her working languages; and be well-informed about the economic, social and cultural background of the countries in which his/her working languages are used. S/he should have: a good power of concentration; an ability to grasp varied and often complex issues swiftly; a high degree of motivation and intellectual curiosity; an inclination to show initiative and imagination; an ability to work consistently and under pressure, both independently and as a member of a team; a readiness to accept advice and an ability to give feedback.

2.2 *Scales and grading*

Nord (1997: 76f) raises an important point to bear in mind when stating that the grading of cultural and linguistic errors depend on the influence they have on the function of the target text (cited in Nord 2005: 219).

For interpreter testing, Sawyer (2004: 105) uses three types of scales:

- Nominal (pass / fail)
- Ordinal (high pass / pass / borderline fail / fail // greater than / less than (the level of the attributes are not equidistant)
- Interval (the distances between the levels are equal)

For the same purpose, Jacobson (2009: 61–62) uses four levels of achievement: Superior, Advanced, Fair and Poor.

Pochhacker (2009) used a numerical scoring system for his SynCloze test giving two points for each completion, with one-point deductions for 1) grammar mistakes; 2) lack of coherence; 3) faulty collocation; and 4) amendments. Response times were measured using standard audio software and the values were added to the plain scores as a *speed bonus*.

2.3 Reliability and validity

According to Sawyer (2004: 93), and we completely agree, a central concern should be the need to conduct reliability and validity studies and to foster greater awareness of the role of professional judgement in assessment practices.

Gipps (1994: 67) states that reliability is a prerequisite for test validity [as it is not sufficient, therefore, it does not imply validity]. Parallel forms: same test has multiple versions, different but equivalent with the same degree of difficulty. Inter-rater: different raters give the same score on the same test (cited in Sawyer 2004: 101–102).

Messick (1988: 40) points out at three broad types for evidence of validation: *content*, *criterion* and *construct validity*. The latter being considered the force unifying all types of validity evidence (cited in Sawyer 2004: 96).

Sawyer (2004: 111) states that there does not seem to be consensus among interpreter educators that entry-level testing must show predictive validity. And Jacobson (2009: 67) states that reliability and validity must be established before implementation on a wide scale. This relates back to the need to define and establish the interpreter's role and relevant competencies for particular contexts. Instruments must be validated *a posteriori* via data obtained through assessment of authentic performance.

According to Pöchhacker (2004: 180) while there is considerable consensus regarding the nature and extent of the abilities to be demonstrated on entry into a training program, there is little certainty regarding objective ways of testing candidates for the required knowledge and skills. And Sawyer (2004: 103–104) confirms and supports this by saying that since the evaluation of interpreter performance requires professional judgement, interpreter testing is inherently subjective in nature; and professional judgement alone is an insufficient basis for decision-making. Rather, empirical data may be used to reduce subjectivity.

To summarize the matter Salaets & Vermeerbergen (2009) state that special consideration must be given to those methods that can reduce the negative, undesired consequences of individual rater subjectivity. Test standardization is a means to reduce such unwanted fluctuation in assessment.

2.4 *Approaches to aptitude testing*

The tests developed and applied by Russo (2009) and Pöchhacker (2009) are intended to assess conference interpreters online. They are a very important foundation for the development of an assessment instrument for public service interpreters.

Russo (2009) analyses synonymic substitutions and loss of coherence as significant predictors. She concludes that there is a need for aptitude test replication in other schools. She also argues that interpreting-related cognitive skills and verbal fluency can be both measured and predictive.

Pöchhacker (2009) analyses different approaches from Moser (1978) to Russo & Pippa (2004); and the results of the administration of the assessment instrument to students of both undergraduate and postgraduate levels. The SynCloze test combines a customized auditory cloze exercise with a task requiring high expressional fluency. The scoring method takes into account both the degree of accuracy and the speed of response (Pochhacker 2009). He concludes the SynCloze test to measure aural-oral language use proficiency and basic interpreting-related sub skills is effective.

3. Developing the instrument

Considering all the above studies and the latest tests applied, and taking into account our specific context, we set out to develop our aptitude test. It will help our trainers to assess the student's competence aptitude level thus allowing them to adapt the content of the syllabus to the student's individual characteristics and needs to achieve the high level of performance required from any professional in our field.

Based on Campbell & Hale's (2003) checklist we can describe the main characteristics of our test as follows: the broad area we are going to assess is interpreting in a specific language combination, English-Spanish. The purpose of the assessment instrument is aimed at: measuring aptitude prior to entering a training course and determining placement at a particular starting point in a training course. The competences we want to assess are the following: language, message transfer, speed, accuracy, memory, terminology, and cultural knowledge. The form of the assessment instrument is the following: vocabulary exercise, a synonyms and antonyms exercise, a comprehension and summary exercise, a short consecutive interpreting exercise, a sight translation exercise, and a short interview. The basic approach of the instrument is criterion-referenced, measuring performance against a known criterion. According to Arjona (1984) it is a more meaningful approach; given the need for the interpreter to perform adequately in all situations, they should be judged against a scale of absolute criteria (cited in Sawyer 2004: 115). The kind of result the instrument generates is a qualitative description of performance, and a numerical score based on the objectives. The reporting mechanisms are the following: feedback for the candidates, the instructors, and the department. It will be given in a qualitative way and made available immediately for the department and instructors, and some time later for the students. The validity of the instrument will be based on a holistic approach more than on an analytical one.

We have developed two specific aptitude tests which are administered right before starting the healthcare and the legal-administration settings modules. The content and structure of these tests aim to assess also the students' aptitude with regard to translating in public services. The tests do not have an eliminatory character.

4. The test

It is a specfic battery of tests on legal settings. It was devised in September–October 2009 at the University of Alcala by two interpreter trainers – the authors of this research – and tested by a research group: FITISPos e-Learning. It is an oral / aural test administered in a multimedia lab. It is composed of seven exercises and lasts from forty-five minutes to one hour, depending on the time students take to do the last two exercises. Candidates do not need either to write – except for note-taking – or to operate the computers, just follow the oral instructions and speak when indicated by tones.

Few details are previously given to the students. They are told that there will be continuous language shifts (En-Sp) and that they may take notes during the consecutive interpreting exercise. They are also told that the answer time gaps are rather short, without mentioning the actual length (3 sec.).

It starts with a short fragment of classical music. Then the 'speaker' introduces the test mentioning the title, objectives and assessment areas as well as the different exercises it includes. These are the following:

- Two general / specific language knowledge exercises
- Two comprehension and summary exercises
- A short consecutive interpreting
- A sight translation, and
- A short interview

There is a short fragment (8–10 seconds) of classical music from different composers and of a different degree of intensity before every exercise.

The first exercise is a vocabulary exercise composed of twenty Spanish words and twenty English words which are read/heard alternating languages. The Spanish is spoken by a native speaker, English by a bilingual speaker. All of the forty words are related to a legal setting. Out of those words, 50% are in common use and the other 50% are more specific, thus increasing the level of difficulty. Candidates should provide a word or a short phrase to interpret the terms. The terms belong to different syntactic categories: two verbs; two verbal phrases; seventeen nouns; fifteen noun phrases; and one adverb.

Scoring is carried out by assigning half a point to every word and discounting part of it for functional inaccuracies.

Question	Answer	Question	Answer
1. To Acquit	1. Absolver	1. Catastro	1. Land registry

Table 1 Vocabulary exercise

The second exercise is a synonyms and antonyms exercise composed of sixteen Spanish words and fourteen English words. All of the forty words are related to a legal setting. Out of those words, 50% are in common use and the other 50% are more specific, so increasing the level of difficulty. The synonyms are all read/heard first alternating languages. Candidates are required to provide a synonym (similar or identical) for every term. Then the antonyms are read / heard alternating languages and students are required to provide an antonym for every term. The terms belong to different syntactic categories: seventeen verbs; one verb phrases; nine nouns; one noun phrase; and two adverbs.

The task here is not interpreting the terms, but providing a synonym or antonym. Since the previous exercise is interpreting into the second language and it lasts for a considerable period of time, candidates tend to continue to interpret instead.

Scoring is done by assigning half a point to every word and discounting part of it for functional inaccuracies.

Question	Answer	Question	Answer
Synonym		Antonym	
1. Refutar	1. Rebatir/rechazar	1. Revocar	1. Aprobar/ratificar

Table 2 Synonyms and antonyms exercise

The third exercise is a verbal reasoning exercise consisting of 251 English words about a common topic to (im)migrants (Residence Permit Application in Spain). The first task is a comprehension question with four sentences and three options (true, false or not enough information). The second task is summarizing the listening exercise in sixty seconds to measure comprehension, vocabulary and speaking fluency. The degree of difficulty increases in this exercise with the appearance of dates, acts and laws, not common linguistic borrowings, and informal language examples. Candidates are prompted when to start talking by means of tones.

This exercise analyses a candidate's capacity of concentration and comprehension. The text is related to a very common type of information for all those students who have either lived abroad or are foreigners.

By offering such a short period of time to summarize a listening exercise we are adding pressure and stress. The ones who do not perform well under pressure will rush, make more mistakes and probably not finish the phrases appropriately.

Scoring consists in assigning two points to every sentence; and seven points to the summary. Points are taken off for grammar mistakes, lack of coherence, incompleteness and fluency breakdown.

a) *Say whether the following statements are true, false or there is not enough information. You can speak after the beep.*
b) *Make a summary of the listening in sixty seconds. You can speak after the beep.*

The fourth exercise is a short consecutive interpreting exercise, the first one where interpreting skills are really required, with a short introduction of eighty words and 680 words to be interpreted. The text is a Direct Examination of the proceedings of a trial. Students are instructed to interpret the dialogue using the consecutive mode and may take notes. They are prompted when to start talking by means of tones. The degree of difficulty increases in this exercise mainly because of two reasons; one of the speakers is not a native speaker and hesitates a lot and uses confusing terms. To score the exercise the trainer takes into account omissions, editions, additions, speed of response and accurate renditions; also, rhythm, intonation and the appropriate use of the specific terminology. Twenty points are assigned to this exercise.

Q. Y para que quede claro ¿en el Centro de Maltrato Doméstico, usted trabaja no solo con las víctimas de la violencia doméstica, sino que creo que ha testificado con maltratadores también?
A. Yes. I co-facilitate that group.

The fifth exercise is a cloze exercise made up of 313 words about a topic related to the listening used in exercise three. The exercise is divided into two parts. The first one is a listening exercise in English (about working permit in Spain) consisting of a total of 153 words and ten gaps. The deletions belong to different syntactic categories: one verb; eight nouns; and one adverb.

The second part is a listening exercise in Spanish about a topic related to the previous ones (ways to work in Spain) with 158 words and thirteen gaps. The deletions belong to different syntactic categories: one verb; ten nouns; two adverbs; and one gap which does not need completion, it is only meant to check on students' concentration. The degree of difficulty increases here due to the use of dates, phrases in the second language and the presence of gaps to be anticipated. The short time slot allowed for the subjects to supply an answer also adds not only difficulty, but stress. The second listening exercise is also more difficult since it deals with more specific vocabulary related to governmental guidelines and regulations.

To perform appropriately in this kind of exercise, candidates also need a good memory, concentration, imagination and speed of response. The use of specific terminology in the texts also contributes to the increase in the degree of difficulty.

To score the exercise the trainer will give a point to every correct answer.

Should you lose your employment and have contributed to the Spanish social security system whilst working, you will also be entitled to unemployment (benefit).

El contingente podrá establecer un número de visados para búsqueda de (empleo) dirigidos a hijos o nietos de español de origen.

The sixth exercise is a sight translation exercise with 349 words in the main text and forty-nine words in a supporting footnote. This text is related to the texts used in the previous exercises. The text appears on the student's screen right after they hear the piece of music and the title of the exercise. The degree of difficulty increases here due to the constant use of acronyms; the formal language contrasts with the previous texts that were less formal – as it is part of the documentation used by an official institution – and also as it is a long text after more than forty minutes of interpreting activity.

c) *Read the following text and translate it at sight. You can take some minutes to read it, and then start sight translating when you feel ready.*

The seventh exercise is a short interview consisting of fourteen questions asked in English. Out of the total, six are closed questions, seven are questions requiring specific information, and the last one is an open question to obtain as much information as possible about the students' feelings and impressions on the test. It is used as a qualitative research method to collect ethnographic data as well as feedback on the test.

The questions go from simple to a higher degree of complexity, from stating their personal data to providing information that could show their language competence and intercultural capacity. The questions then go from professional details into personal expectations to end by asking about the test.

a) *Do you consider it is necessary following a Continuing Professional Development program?*

5. Findings

The test was administered to thirteen students of both genders and from three different nationalities and. The average age was 25.2 years.

Knowledge: In general most of the students showed a good level of knowledge both in the general language and in the specific terminology. Students with a degree in Translation and Interpreting (T&I) showed a higher level of knowledge than the rest.

Skills: Students with a degree in T&I were more skilful when dealing with the specialized exercises (interpreting and sight translation) and showed more developed short time memory skills than the rest.

Attitudes: Students with a degree in T&I tried harder to render more complete messages, and were therefore more coherent and comprehensible. They were also more faithful to the original message amending their own errors when necessary.

5.1 Correlation: Accuracy, speed of response and personality trait (stress tolerance)

Accuracy: We have found that students arrive at the lab to sit the test in a typical nervous state. And little by little their level of stress increases. It can be noticed by observing a progression in their own amendments, also the increase in frequency of hesitation markers. Their renditions tend to be less accurate twenty minutes into the test.

Speed of response: They started the test with a very low speed of response but it increased with the rhythm marked by the 'speakers' and with their realization that they knew many of the words / phrases. Students had a similar speed of response compared with their own performance in exercises I) and II). In exercise III) their speed of response augmented. In exercise IV) their speed of response gradually increased, which might be due to their getting used to the vocabulary. In exercise V) their speed of response was much slower, although in the second part they did better. In exercise VI) their speed of rendering was low at the beginning, but it increased towards the middle of the text. And it ended at a medium level. In exercise VII) their speed of response augmented considerably (see Figure 1).

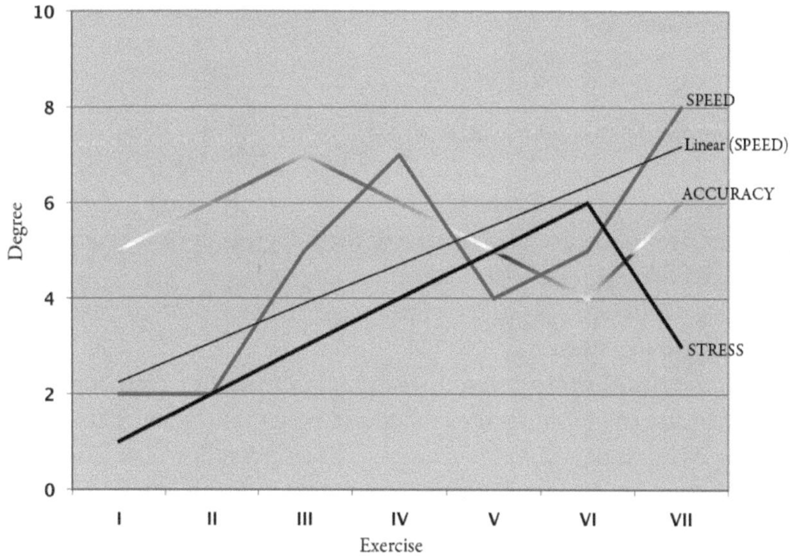

Figure 1 Accuracy vs Speed of response vs Stress

Background education and training: Students who have a degree in (T&I) performed much better than the rest of the candidates. The ones who have a degree in Language and Literature performed better than those who had degrees in non-language related fields.

Gender: Females performed better than the only male in the group. This is not significant since the male testee was working in his B and C working languages while the female subjects were working in their mother tongue and B language.

Age: Not many differences were found since the majority of students were of similar age. There were only two students over twenty-seven years of age. The younger ones performed better than the older ones.

Nationality: The test involved a greater number of Spanish speakers. So, there were more exercises to interpret from English into Spanish. In any case, Spanish speakers performed better than non Spanish speakers.

Mother tongue: Students performed slightly better in the first two exercises in their second language than in their mother tongue. During the rest of the test, students performed better from the B language into their mother tongue.

Professional experience: Few students had any experience, but those with some experience in the profession performed better than those who had never had any.

5.2 *Examination of qualitative feedback*

Students had little professional experience in interpreting and translation apart from practice in class during their degrees, for those who had a degree in T&I.

Most of the Spanish students had not lived more than a year in an English speaking country.

All the students expressed their desire to be in the profession for a long time, and to become professional interpreters and translators in the public service sector and consider that it is necessary following a Continuing Professional Development program.

This was the second aptitude test for the great majority of the students. They had sat another one before starting the interpreting module in healthcare settings. They consider it to be a very difficult but useful test and would like to re-sit it at some time in the future.

6. Conclusions

After a thorough review of the literature on interpreter training and assessment, we have analysed the four main factors required to develop an aptitude test: the competences and skills to be assessed; the scales and grading method to be applied; the reliability and validity of the test; and the different kind of exercises to be used in the test.

A combination of all of the aforementioned competences and skills would be an ideal combination for the professional interpreter-translators we need in our multicultural societies today. Therefore, that set of criteria should be the core of our training and assessment in higher education institutions, although, most of the competences and skills might well be learned and obtained through intensive practice during subsequent training courses.

Based on the preliminary results briefly explained in the Findings section of this study, and after comparing them with the final exam results, we can confirm that the battery of tests designed to measure the ability of our students to develop skills and acquire knowledge has turned out to be a fair predictive instrument. Students with a high level of achievement in the test obtained either a similar or a better level in their final exam, which was a video recorded role-play. Whether the students who have performed better in this test will always be the ones who obtain better results at the end of the master course will depend very much on many other factors; such as their personal interest and motivation, and the work they put in both in the theoretical and practical modules. It will also depend on our trainer's capacity to take advantage of their strengths and to transform the weaknesses shown in the results of this test into drills and other activities which allow students to achieve an optimum level of performance in interpreting in a legal setting.

We encourage other institutions and trainers to replicate this study and kindly share feedback.

6.1 Drawbacks

This instrument needs to be tested for reliability and validity. We intend to administer the test to all the master students at the beginning of the next academic year. Then we will compare the results obtained by different students and marks given by different reviewers.

Also, the application in a lab using all its technology, will allow us to assess a higher number of candidates in a shorter period of time, but that assessment is mainly based on lexicon and not on face-to-face performance. We are considering the idea of using a role-play to assess performance in order to complement this instrument.

7. References

Arjona, E., 'Testing and Evaluation', in M. L. McIntire, ed., *New Dialogs in Interpreter Education. Proceedings of the Fourth National Conference of Interpreter Trainers Convention* (Silver Spring, MD: RID, 1984), 111–138.

Baker, D., *Language Testing: A Critical Survey and Practical Guide* (London: Edward Arnold, 1989).

Campbell, S., and Sandra Hale, 'Translation & Interpreting assessment in the context of educational measurement', in G. Anderman & M. Rogers, eds., *Translation Today Trends and Perspectives* (Clevedon: Multilingual Matters, 2003), 205–224.

Gentile, A., Uldis Ozolins and M. Vasilakakos, *Liaison Interpreting: A Handbook* (Melbourne: Melbourne University Press, 1996).

Gipps, C. V., *Beyond Testing: Towards a Theory of Educational Assessment* (London and Washington, DC: Falmer, 1994).

Hatim, B. and Ian Mason, *The translator as communicator* (London: Routledge, 1997).

Jacobson, H. E., 'Mediated discourse and the role of the interpreter: What Can Be Learned from Foregrounding the Profile of the Mediator?' Paper presented at the meeting of the *American Association of Applied Linguistics* (Costa Mesa, CA, 2007).

Jacobson, H. E., 'Moving beyond words in assessing mediated interaction', in Claudia V. Angelelli and H. E. Jacobson, *Testing an Assessment in translation and Interpreting Studies*. (NL: John Benjamins, 2009).

Jiménez Ivars, A. and D. Pinazo Calatayud, 'Aptitudes necesarias en la formación de intérpretes. Un estudio exploratorio', *Quadern, Revista de traducción* 8 (2002).

Kalina, S., 'Some views on the theory of interpreter training and some practical suggestions', in Mary Snell-Hornby, Franz Pochhacker, and K. Kaindl, eds, *Translation Studies – An Interdiscipline* (Benjamins, 1994), 219–225.

Lang, M. F., 'The problem of mother tongue competence in the training of translators', in Mary Snell-Hornby, Franz Pochhacker, and K. Kaindl, eds, *Translation Studies – An Interdiscipline* (Benjamins, 1994).

Longley, P., 'The use of Aptitude Testing in the Selection of Students for Conference Interpretation Training', in L. Gran and J. Dodds, eds, *The Theoretical and Practical Aspects of Teaching Conference Interpretation* (Udine: Campanotto, 1989), 105–108.

Nord, Christiane, *Translation as a Purposeful Activity* (Manchester: St Jerome, 1997).

Nord, Christiane, 'Training Functional Translators', in Martha Tennent, ed., *Training for the New Millennium* (Amsterdam: Benjamins, 2005).

Pöchhacker, Franz, *Introducing Interpreting Studies* (London/New York: Routledge, 2004).

Pöchhacker, Franz, 'Testing aptitude for interpreting: The SynCloze test', Symposium *Aptitude for Interpreting. Towards Reliable Admission Testing*, Lessius University College (28–29 May 2009).

Russo, Mariachiara, 'Aptitude testing over the years', Symposium *Aptitude for Interpreting. Towards Reliable Admission Testing*, Lessius University College (28–29 May 2009).

Salaets, H. and M. Vermeerbergen, 'Community Interpreting: Training and Research at University Level', *CIUTI Symposium*. Graz (17–19 Sept. 2009).

Sawyer, D. B., *Fundamental Aspects of Interpreter Education* (Benjamins, 2004).

Schaeffner, Christina, 'Running before Walking? Designing a Translation Programme at Undergraduate Level', in Christina Schäffner and Beverly Adab, eds, *Developing translation competence* (Amsterdam & Philadelphia: John Benjamins, 2000), xvi + 244.

Schjoldager, A., 'Assessment of Simultaneous Interpreting', in C. Dollerup and V. Appel, eds, *Teaching Translation and Interpreting 3: New Horizons* (Amsterdam/Philadelphia: John Benjamins 1996), 187–195.

Taylor, W. L., 'Cloze procedure: a new tool for measuring readability', *Journalism Quarterly* 30 (1953), 415–433.

Ulrych, M., 'Training Translators: Programme, curricula, practices', in Martha Tennent, ed., *Training for the New Millennium* (Amsterdam: Benjamins, 2005).

MARÍA LUISA PÉREZ-CAÑADO

2 The Use of ICT in the European Higher Education Area: Acting upon the Evidence

1. Introduction

For well over half a decade, many language studies degrees across Europe have been involved in pilot schemes for the adaptation to the European Higher Education Area (EHEA) and its new credit system (the ECTS). In pushing forward the so-called Bologna Process, language curricula have been reoriented, language departments have been reconfigured, and study plans have been revamped, all with the ultimate aim of bringing about a much yearned-for revitalisation of language teaching at tertiary level (Yu 2008). We are living what Mehisto (2008) terms a period of disjuncture, characterised by the tension between the previous order and a new approach which changes the *status quo*. Indeed, this intense period of reform in Higher Education (HE) necessitates a change of perspective in both stakeholders involved – teachers and students – as the transition needs to be made from learning by instruction to learning by construction, and teachers need to pull back from being donors of knowledge in a passive learning context to become facilitators in a student-led scenario.

Didactic materials and resources – with ICT figuring prominently among them – are pivotal in bringing about this reconfiguration of teacher and student roles and in operating the shift to a learner-centered pedagogy of autonomy (Pérez Gómez et al. 2009c). In addition to being one the core generic competencies which most European universities have worked into all their Bologna-adapted degrees, the potential of technological or digital competence for enhancing the student-centred learning process has been underscored in the official EHEA literature. According to Benito and Cruz (2007: 104), ICT is not a new fad, but a crucial tool which, in combination with the EHEA, will foster pedagogical innovation and allow all the agents involved in the teaching-learning process to expedite knowledge-building and competency development. Much the same is claimed by Pennock-Speck (2008: 70): 'ICT in the field of education is an exciting opportunity for teachers and students. With more and more teachers being expected to apply more student-centred teaching, even if they do not particularly want to (Bailey 2008), practically all teachers will end up using ICT to teach or at least to communicate with or evaluate students to a greater or lesser extent'.

The CIDUA Report (2005) already foregrounds the effectiveness of new technologies and virtual learning environments in boosting student motivation, in fostering their active involvement in the learning process, and in answering to their needs, interests, and expectations. This is also underscored by the Report by the *Red Interuniversitaria de Innovación Docente de las Universidades Andaluzas* (2008: 15–16), which views ICT as a fruitful means to foster cooperative learning, stimulate the students' problem-solving capacity, promote interaction between both agents in the teaching-learning process, accentuate the link to real-world situations, and cater for diverse learning styles. According to Pennock-Speck (2009, 2011), it favors learner autonomy and interaction, facilitates the move away from ex-cathedra lecturing, and helps teachers step down from being the center of the learning process to take on a more peripheral role. It is also a powerful means to wedge in innovation in HE, with which it is seen as almost synonymous (Pennock-Speck 2011). All in all, it enhances teaching, improves the learning of discipline-specific content, favors the acquisition of competencies, and promotes English language development, a particularly significant remit in our context, as Pennock-Speck (2011) aptly notes: 'In the context of a degree in English in a non-English-speaking country like Spain, alongside providing opportunities for students to acquire content and competencies, we must make sure that they also acquire the most important of the specific competences, that is, the ability to communicate in English'.

It is thus not surprising that the use of ICT in ECTS pilot programs at Spanish university has been found to heighten students' motivation

(Pennock-Speck 2009) and to generate positive attitudes towards the learning process (Pennock-Speck 2008). The official EHEA documents therefore propound promoting ICT in all its manifestations and possibilities (Pérez Gómez et al. 2009a, 2009b).

However, are these theoretically propounded tenets actually trickling down to on-the-ground classroom praxis within language teaching degrees across Europe? This is precisely the question which the present chapter seeks to address by providing empirical evidence from the European Project *ADELEEES*.[1] The latter has sought to carry out an in-depth analysis of the changes being operated by the current application of a competency-based model of language education in all those European universities piloting the European Credit Transfer System. To this end, it has designed, validated, and applied four sets of questionnaires which have allowed a detailed diagnosis of the way in which the new model is being implemented and which has involved both agents in the teaching-learning process.

After outlining the objectives, procedure, participants, and methodology employed in the study, this chapter will expound on its results regarding the incorporation of ICT, among other materials and resources, in Bologna-adapted language degrees across Europe. It will then outline the ways in which we have redressed the main lacunae identified in this area by presenting three pedagogical innovation projects developed at the University of Jaén and their accompanying quantitative and qualitative studies. We will conclude with some reflections ensuing from our results on the role of ICT within the new HE landscape and which largely suggest that these technological options should have an increasingly significant role in institutionalised teaching at tertiary level.

1 Project *ADELEEES: 'Adaptación de la enseñanza de lenguas al EEES: Análisis del estado actual, establecimiento de redes europeas y aplicación de los nuevos títulos de Grado'*, financed by the *Ministerio de Ciencia e Innovación* ('Subvenciones de acciones destinadas a la mejora de la calidad de la Enseñanza Superior y de la actividad del profesorado universitario en el año 2008', Programa Estudios y Análisis, Ref. EA2008–0173).

2. The evidence: The ADELEEES study

2.1 *Objective*

In order to determine the role of ICT in Bologna-adapted language degrees, the part of the broader study on which this chapter reports has sought to attain the following objectives:

1. To identify which materials and resources associated to the EHEA are being applied in language studies degrees piloting the ECTS across Europe.
2. To determine if there are statistically significant differences between students' and teachers' perceptions regarding materials and resources in Bologna-adapted language studies degrees across Europe.

2.2 *Procedure and instruments*

In order to achieve the afore-mentioned objectives, a questionnaire has been designed, validated, and applied to determine which methodologies, types of groupings, materials and resources, and evaluation procedures are being employed in language degrees piloting the ECTS across Europe. This questionnaire – with different versions for students and teachers and in both English and Spanish – along with three additional ones on competencies, workload, and satisfaction, has constituted the instrument of the present investigation.[2]

The questionnaire on methodological and evaluation aspects comprises a total of fifty-one items, subdivided into five main sections: *types of groupings* (five items), *learning modalities* (six items), *teaching methods* (nine items), *materials and resources* (eighteen items), and *evaluation* (thirteen

2 The English and Spanish versions of all four questionnaires can be found in Pérez Cañado (coord.) (2010).

items). At the end of each block of questions, the interviewee can include up to two (in the case of the first three headings) or three (in the final two sections) options not contemplated in the closed questions.

Once designed, the questionnaire was validated via a twofold process. In order to guarantee its validity and reliability, it was initially submitted to the scrutiny of six external experts and, subsequently, to a pilot study. After introducing the modifications suggested by the experts, the survey was administered to a representative sample made up of 10 teachers and 54 students in the degree of English Philology at the University of Jaén, in December 2008 and January 2009. The feedback received from both agents of the teaching-learning process led us to reformulate the phrasing of certain items, add information and new questions, specify data, break down questions, and reduce the length of certain questionnaire.

The data obtained in the pilot study was used to analyse the reliability or internal consistency of the questionnaire (February 2009). It was determined using Cronbach's α, and the extremely high values obtained for this coefficient amply guaranteed the reliability of the survey (see Table 3).

Questionnaire	Number of subjects	Number of items	Cronbach's α
Methodology students	54	51	.858
Methodology teachers	10	51	.817

Table 3 Reliability of the questionnaire

The administration of the questionnaire followed its design and validation. In order to increase return rates, a series of strategies were deployed, in line with Brown's recommendations (2001: 85–89). In order to reach as wide an audience as possible across Europe, an online system of application was chosen for the questionnaire, through the use of *SurveyMonkey* (<http://www.surveymonkey.com>; see Figure 2).

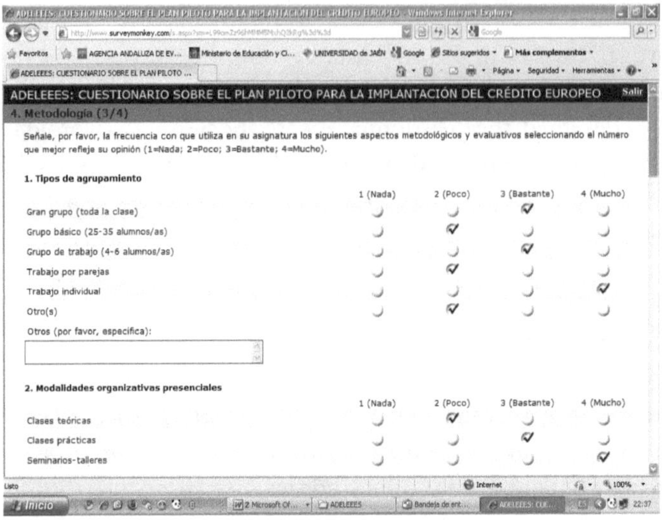

Figure 2 Screenshot of the methodology questionnaire

A *cover letter* (in Spanish and English) was sent out introducing the Project, its objectives, and the affiliation of the researchers, together with the links from which to access the survey. Following Brown's guidelines (2001: 86), it was brief and thanked potential participants in advance. The questionnaire itself was also kept as *short* as possible, with a predominance of closed questions which could be answered simply by clicking on the desired option. An *incentive* (two laptops and five 4 GB pendrives) was offered to the participants. *Follow-up phone calls* were made to ECTS coordinators at two different moments: before mailing the questionnaire and after its reception, in order to supervise the process and solve possible problems which had arisen. Finally, the questionnaire was also administered 'to a large group of people at one time' (Brown 2001: 89) at the University of Jaén, by taking *large groups of students* to the computer lab in order to monitor their completion of the surveys and thereby ensure their participation.

2.3 *Participants*

The sample which participated in the investigation is detailed in this next heading. The global figures are initially presented, followed by a more detailed rendering of the teachers and students who answered the questionnaire, glossed in terms of the variables of gender, nationality, university, and degree.

The total number of participants has been 469 – 69.1% of which have been students (324) and 30.9%, teachers (145; see Figure 3).

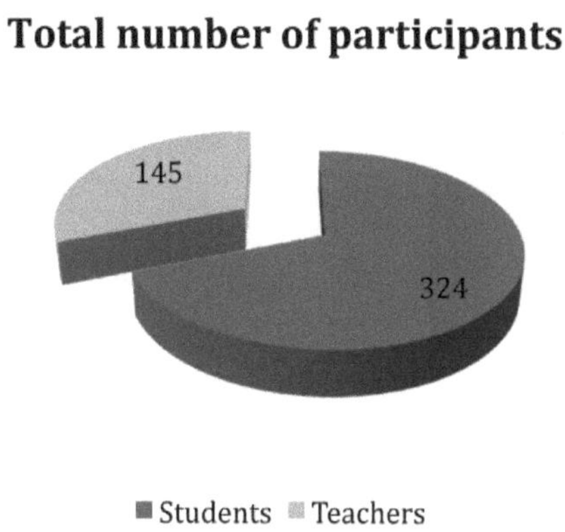

Figure 3 Total number of participants

Almost three fourths of the participating students have been women: 71.3% (231), vs. only 28.7% of men (93). In terms of nationality, there is a clear predominance of Spanish students (87% – 282 of the 324 participants). France, Rumania, England, Italy, Lithuania, and Poland follow suit in terms of interviewees. In line with the foregoing, Spanish universities have again been the most participative, with 301 students (92.9% of the total). Central and Northern European universities have contributed with 16 and 4 students, respectively. Finally, taking degree into consideration, there is a majority of students from English Studies (56.2%). The other four degrees whose students have mainly participated in the study are Translation and Interpretation (15.1%), Teacher Training: English as a Foreign Language (5.9%), Tourism (4%), and Spanish Philology (3.4%).

Of the 145 participating teachers, 59.31% (86) have been women and 40.69% (59), men. The same tendency observed for the students is thus once more discerned in this second group, albeit in a slightly more balanced proportion.Nationality-wise, an almost identical percentage of Spanish teachers and students have taken part in the investigation: 86.21% (i.e., 125 of the 145 participants). The remaining 13.79% includes teachers from Cuba, Georgia, England, and Macedonia. A very similar tendency is perceived in terms of universities: 88.3% of the teachers are from Spanish ones, followed by Northern and Eastern Europe, with 5 and 4 participants, respectively.

Finally, more than half of the professors teach in English Studies degrees (57.24%). The remainder develop their teaching activity in exactly the same degrees as the students interviewed (with the exception of Tourism), that is, Teacher Training and Pedagogy (11.03%), Spanish Philology (8.28%), and Translation and Interpretation (6.9%).

2.4 *Statistical methodology*

Employing the SPSS program in its 16.0 version, the following statistical operations have been performed:

1. To determine the reliability of the questionnaires, *Cronbach α* has been used.
2. To attain objective 1, the following descriptive statistics have been employed:
   2.1 Central tendency measures:
      2.1.1 Mean
      2.1.2 Median
      2.1.3 Mode

2.2 Dispersion measures:
 2.2.1 Range
 2.2.2 Standard deviation
3. To achieve the second objective, analysis of variance (ANOVA) and the *t* test have been used.

2.5 *Results and discussion*

The outcomes of the study are now presented and discussed. Both students' and teachers' perceptions are considered and subsequently compared to determine if statistically significant differences can be discerned between them.

Interestingly, our results seem to point to divergence between theory and practice in the incorporation of ICT within the ECTS. A limited use of ICT for language teaching is clearly confirmed in this heading, as there is little or no incorporation (with the mode coinciding with this last option) of webquests, wikis, blogs, *Second Life*, videogames, digital storytelling, or teaching software. Authentic materials or *realia* are also sparsely employed in the classroom. Educational web portals are used to a greater extent, as well as audio and video materials, although they are still seldom used. It is interesting to ascertain that the textbook is also scantily employed. These findings are surprising, particularly considering the extremely beneficial effects which ICT is exerting on language learning and competency development, as has been revealed by a notable number of recent studies (Brígido Corachán 2008; Gregori-Signes 2008; Jordano de la Torre 2008; O'Dowd 2008; Pennock-Speck 2008, 2009; Zaragoza Ninet and Clavel Arroitia 2008), which propound the incorporation of these resources into the language classroom (CIDUA 2005).

The most frequently used materials are those compiled by the teacher, created by him/her, and downloaded from the Internet. Online and printed dictionaries are also quite regularly employed, together with *PowerPoint* presentations and, paradoxically, the OHP (see Figure 4).

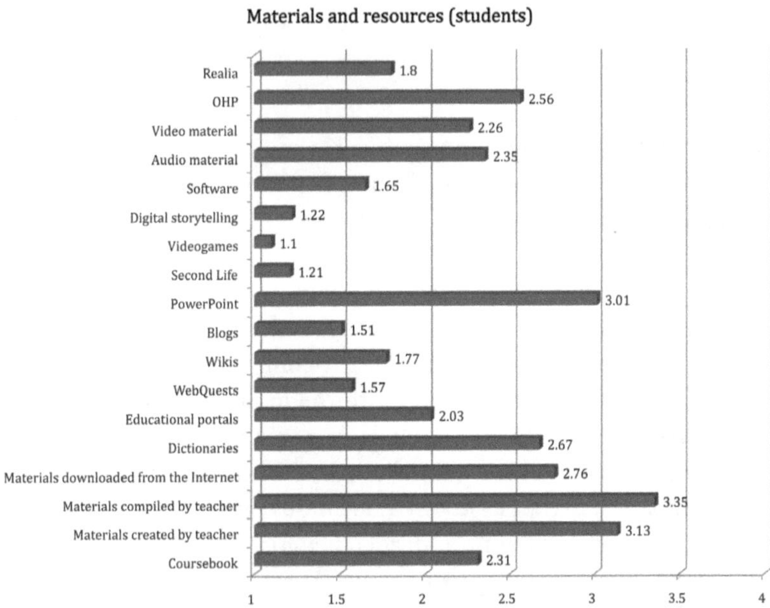

Figure 4 Materials and resources (students)

This tendency is confirmed by the second cohort – that of teachers – who, while harboring a much more positive view of the way the ECTS is playing itself out in other methodological aspects, largely coincide with the studentship on the scant use of technological options for language teaching. Those resources related to ICT are once again very sparsely employed (*Second Life*, videogames, digital storytelling, wikis, blogs, webquests, teaching software), something which reinforces the outcomes obtained in the previous heading. The textbook, educational web portals, *realia*, audio and video material, and online and print dictionaries are not very frequently employed, albeit more assiduously than those materials related to new technologies. On the opposite side of the cline are materials compiled or created by the teacher, *PowerPoint* presentations, and Internet downloads, which come across as the most frequently employed resources by teachers. However, the OHP is scarcely used, something which contrasts with the students' opinion (see Figure 5).

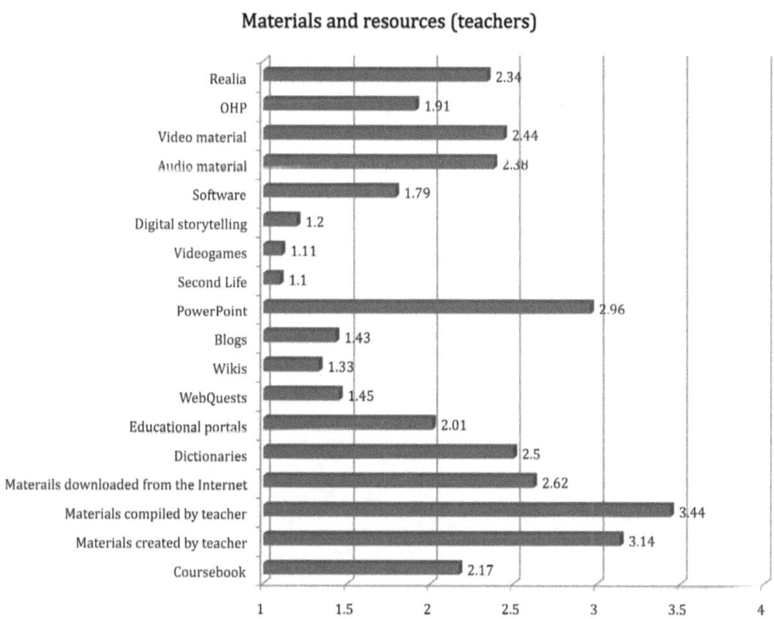

Figure 5 Materials and resources (teachers)

The ANOVA and *t* test have allowed us to confirm statistically that both sets of perceptions are essentially parallel. The only significant differences detected affect wikis (p = .000) and the OHP (p = .000), which the students consider are more frequently employed, and the use of *realia* (p = .000), where exactly the opposite holds true (see Table 4).

Materials and resources	gl	*F*	*p*
Coursebook	1	1.625	.203
Materials created by the teacher	1	0.004	.952
Materials compiled by the teacher	1	2.063	.152
Materials downloaded from the Internet	1	2.290	.131
Online and print dictionaries	1	2.350	.126
Educational web portals	1	0.037	.848
WebQuests	1	1.747	.187
Wikis	1	22.657	.000
Blogs	1	1.061	.304
PowerPoint presentations	1	0.235	.628
SecondLife	1	3.492	.062
Video games	1	0.124	.725
Digital storytelling	1	0.134	.714
Teaching software	1	1.894	.170
Audio material	1	0.109	.742
Video material	1	3.376	.067
OHP	1	32.543	.000
Realia	1	23.135	.000

Table 4 Differences between students and teachers in materials and resources

2.6 *Conclusions*

Thus, our outcomes evince that the practical incorporation of ICT in language studies degrees piloting the ECTS across Europe runs counter to the theoretical accounts which extol on its many virtues in official EHEA documents. We are clearly not reaping the benefits which ICT has to offer in the language teaching arena. Indeed, both teacher and student perceptions on the scarce use of ICT options have concurred in this European study and have furthermore been statistically confirmed via the extremely reduced number of significant differences detected among them. It would therefore be recommendable to analyse in greater depth which aspects of ICT are being employed to develop and evaluate competencies, the main hurdles being faced in their incorporation into language teaching, and which measures can be adopted to overcome them and thus ensure a heightened presence of technology-enhanced teaching options in Bologna-adapted language degrees. This is precisely what we have been doing at the University of Jaén via three different pedagogical innovation projects on whose rationale, procedure, and results we now report.

3. Acting upon the evidence: English Studies at the University of Jaén

In order to pre-empt the absence of ICT in language teaching and thereby act upon the lacunae diagnosed in this area through our study, we have set up, developed, and evaluated three different pedagogical innovation projects[3] within the degree of English Philology at the University of Jaén. The latter have incorporated computer-assisted language learning (CALL), data-driven learning (DDL), computer-mediated communication (CMC), telecollaboration (TC), podcasting, virtual learning environments (VLE), or blended learning to work on different linguistic skills and components, as well as cultural aspects. Through them, we have attempted to anchor ICT within our language teaching and use it to maximise good practice, in compliance with the parameters of the EHEA. We have always viewed it

3 These different projects and their respective studies have been carried out by the ESECS research team (*English Studies in the European Credit System*): <http://www.esecs.eu>.

as a complement to in-class tuition, and not as a substitute for traditional teaching (Pennock-Speck 2011), and have followed the recommendations set forth by this same author (Pennock-Speck 2009) for the integration of ICT in the language classroom: it should only be used if it substantially adds to teaching with more traditional resources, if it is not too expensive, and if it does not involve inordinate amounts of work for the teacher and students.

3.1 CALL and DDL

Our first project sought to determine whether awareness-raising through a brief, explicit intervention using CALL understood in the inclusive sense (Levy and Hubbard 2001: 148) and DDL could significantly improve the performance on seven aspects previously identified as problematic for writing at Spanish University level – punctuation, spelling, articles, verb tenses, verbal complementation, prepositions, and vocabulary – in English Philology freshmen at the University of Jaén. A worksheet was especially designed for the study, based on data provided by a previous investigation on the problematic areas of first-year students' interlanguage at the University of Jaén. It comprised seven headings, with ten sentences included in each one, five of which contained mistakes and five of which were correct. Both the correct and incorrect sentences were taken directly from the writing of English Philology freshmen two academic years before, to ensure that we were troubleshooting problem areas for the sample and, thereby, to ensure the content validity of this instrument.

The learners were initially asked to spot and correct the mistakes they detected in each of the seven sections using a specific colour. They were given thirty minutes to do this. A further half-hour session was then provided to the students on the use of web-based resources as a means to raise consciousness of, identify, and solve writing mistakes. The students were mainly familiarised with tools in *Word*, the exploitation of search engines such as *Google* (for the consciousness-raising of spelling), the existence of dictionaries on-line (for colligations), and the *BNC online service* for spelling and lexical collocations and colligations. Subsequently, they were given sixty minutes to use web-based resources (each learner had access to a computer with the necessary software) to contrast their initial error identification. They were asked to correct these mistakes on the same worksheet, but with a different colour to that employed in the first round. Finally, the explicit correction of the mistakes in each category was carried out in a fifteen- to twenty-minute session in the next class for further awareness-raising.

The intervention was found to significantly impact English Philology freshmen's writing skills on five of the seven aspects – spelling, articles, verbal complementation, prepositions, and vocabulary – while promoting discovery-learning, boosting motivation, and enhancing learner autonomy (cf. Pérez Cañado and Díez Bedmar 2006).

3.2 CMC and telecollaboration

In turn, the second project was a language-based e-tutoring experience, whereby each Jaén freshman studying English Philology was assigned a Dallas tutor with whom s/he communicated on a weekly basis to accomplish a set of ELT tasks via the Blackboard platform. The project was an instance of 'feedback-focused telecollaboration for pedagogical purposes' (Ware and Pérez Cañado 2007: 113), since the Dallas tutors were pre-service language instructors who provide language-related feedback to the Spanish foreign language learners. The exchange was thus conducted exclusively in English. It comprised eleven highly structured tasks which were carried out asynchronously and which primarily focused on the writing genres the Spanish students were expected to master by the end of the academic year (see Table 5 for the full set of tasks).

Activity	Description
Video presentations and message exchange	Watch the short video presentations which your partner has prepared and exchange 4 messages with him/her in order to introduce yourself and to get to know him/her better.
Writing: Description	Elicit feedback/correction from your partner on the description you have been assigned. Use this feedback to correct your writing and to prepare the final draft you have to hand in. Ask him/her one question you have on an aspect related to the English you are seeing in class (grammar, style, usage, idioms, vocabulary, etc.).
Grammar: Oral presentation	Prepare the oral presentation on the grammatical aspect(s) you have to explain to the class with the help of your partner.
Listening	Listen to a song which both you and your partner like. Justify why you have chosen this particular song. Ask him/her about the questions/problems you have and talk about your tastes in music. Identify a minimum of 3 idiomatic expressions and 3 grammatical constructions which are new or interesting for you, and discuss them with your partner. Write a summary of both your discussion and the lexical and grammatical information you have learnt in the song.
Writing: Article	Elicit feedback/correction from your partner on the article you have been assigned. Use this feedback to correct your writing and to prepare the final draft you have to hand in. Ask him/her one question you have on an aspect related to the English you are seeing in class (grammar, style, usage, idioms, vocabulary, etc.).
Short article: Reading and discussion	Choose an online article from www.breakingnewsenglish.com with your partner based on your common interests, and decide what part of the lesson and discussion you want to do together.

Writing: Report	Elicit feedback/correction from your partner on the report you have been assigned. Use this feedback to correct your writing and to prepare the final draft you have to hand in. Ask him/her one question you have on an aspect related to the English you are seeing in class (grammar, style, usage, idioms, vocabulary, etc.).
Writing: Discussion	Elicit feedback/correction from your partner on the discussion you have been assigned. Use this feedback to correct your writing and to prepare the final draft you have to hand in. Ask him/her one question you have on an aspect related to the English you are seeing in class (grammar, style, usage, idioms, vocabulary, etc.).
Sitcom and idiomatic expressions	Watch a sitcom which both you and your partner enjoy and ask him/her about (at least) five idiomatic expressions you have heard in it and whose meaning you would like to know. Initiate a discussion on the topic of the episode you have watched.
Writing: Narrative	Elicit feedback/correction from your partner on the narrative you have been assigned. Use this feedback to correct your writing and to prepare the final draft you have to hand in. Ask him/her one question you have on an aspect related to the English you are seeing in class (grammar, style, usage, idioms, vocabulary, etc.).
Oral interaction	Talk with your partner for at least twenty minutes on Skype *or* send your partner at least five minutes of a voice recording.

Table 5 Tasks in the Jaén-Dallas telecollaboration project

After an initial theoretical lockstep session where the experience was contextualised and explained, two hours of independent work were ascribed to the completion of each TC task in a virtual learning environment. An additional hour per activity was then assigned for the students to fill and hand in an Activity Feedback Form aimed at encouraging reflection on the procedural aspects of the experience and on its most outstanding outcomes. Finally, an hour per task of contact sessions with the Jaén teaching staff was devoted to monitoring, evaluating, and following up on the TC exchange.

In this project, telecollaboration was evinced to make a unique contribution to the development of professional, disciplinary, and academic subject-specific competencies, and to cross-curricular generic ones of the interpersonal, systemic, and instrumental type. It also transpired that the main principles of TC satisfy the underlying philosophy of the EHEA and how, from a more practical perspective, it fully accommodates the methodological diversity, gamut of learning modalities, and more diversified evaluation system inherent in the ECTS system. It was also observed that the use of TC impinged on the participating students' attitudes towards language learning and improved their English language skills (especially grammar and vocabulary), gave them insight into American culture, and increased their confidence, motivation, learner autonomy, and cooperation in the EFL class. Overall, it paved the way towards a new teaching style on the part of the lecturers involved, one where ICT is incorporated in language teaching, and coordination and cooperation among the teaching staff are increasingly present (cf. Pérez Cañado and Ware 2009).

3.3 Podcasts, VLE, and blended learning

Finally, podcasts and virtual learning environments, in conjunction with blended learning, were all employed to work on vocabulary, motivated by the extremely low lexical achievement evinced by pre-service English teachers at the University of Jaén from the academic year 2004–2005 onwards. Of all the linguistic areas involved in the purely instrumental subjects of the degree in English Philology – grammar, vocabulary, the four skills, and phonetics –, lexical competence was the one which yielded the poorest outcomes, to the extent that a significant worsening in the students' lexical performance was ascertained from the February to June exams (Pérez Cañado 2010). Thus, in line with the foregoing, the main aim of the project was to determine whether the use of podcasts, VLE, and blended learning within the ECTS with English Philology freshmen (experimental group) could develop superior lexical competence to that promoted by the traditional system of credits in English Philology + Tourism freshmen (control group). We also sought to complement this quantitative data with a questionnaire which probed the participants' opinions, attitudes, and motivation as regards the use of these technological options within an ECTS methodology to develop their lexical competence.

The project involved the creation of an original bank of material on diverse lexical aspects central to the development of lexical competence in pre-service English teachers in Spain. To enhance the students' motivation, the activities were designed on the basis of popular and extremely recent podcasts and sitcoms which the students themselves selected. Each episode focused on a specific semantic field covered in the syllabus of the subject within which the project was developed (e.g., health, food, family, new technologies, or turning points in life). The activities then exploited using blended learning (Thorne 2003; O'Dowd 2007), that is, a combination of traditional face-to-face interaction and online activity.

In this sense, a whole-class, lockstep theoretical session was initially employed to introduce the vocabulary pertaining to each of the general topics covered. Each of the episodes was then presented and watched in a practical class, at the end of which a global listening comprehension activity was completed and handed in. After this, they were encouraged to devote an average of two hours of independent study time to carrying out the activities on the ILIAS platform (cf. Fig. 13). Finally, a seminar was devoted to commenting on the episode and the outcomes of its exploitation from a lexical viewpoint. Awareness-raising of diverse metacognitive vocabulary learning strategies was also encouraged in the latter. Thus, face-to-face and on-line activity mutually reinforced each other in the project, following what Vaughan (2007: 82) terms a 'hybrid model', as a significant amount of learning activities were moved online and time traditionally spent in the classroom was reduced, albeit not eliminated.

The initiative was found to enhance the vocabulary acquisition of English Philology undergraduates within the ECTS scheme. While the experimental group significantly improved its performance on the vast majority of lexical aspects sampled, the control group significantly worsened on practically all of them, and what is more, at extremely high confidence levels. Hence, it seems that the use of podcasts and blended learning to teach vocabulary for a single semester was sufficient to counter the worrying decline in lexical performance of pre-service English teachers at the University of Jaén which had been ascertained in previous years and which was once more confirmed in the control group.

These outcomes were further reinforced by the extremely positive responses of the trainees on the qualitative questionnaire which was administered at the end of the project to complement the quantitative data. The experience was embraced with enthusiasm and positive attitudes, as the students highly valued the initiative for its organisational aspects, motivational capacity, and learning potential (cf. Torralbo Jover 2008; Pérez Cañado 2010).

4. Conclusion

This chapter has explored how ICT is being incorporated into the EHEA language teaching arena. Although in the official literature ICT has been heralded as an unrivalled opportunity to foster innovation in language teaching (Michavila 2009) and has been found to be fully in keeping with the theoretical underpinnings of the EHEA, we have ascertained that empirical evidence from the European study ADELEEES unequivocally indicates that it is not being practically worked into Bologna-adapted language studies degrees.

In order to redress this lacuna, we have then expounded on how we have acted upon it at the University of Jaén, where technological options such as, inter alia, CALL, CMC, or VLE have acquired a particularly sharp relief within our ECTS pilot scheme in English Philology. Three pedagogical innovation projects have been described and their overwhelmingly positive outcomes have been outlined.

The latter seem to make a compelling case for the incorporation of ICT into the new language learning scenario provided by the implementation of the ECTS. In the light of these findings, the use of technology should not be seen, as Kessler and Ware (2011: in press) put it, 'as a separate competency, but rather as a vehicle for accomplishing other tasks'. Whether we like it or not, ICT is here to stay, and its role is becoming increasingly significant in our HE system: 'If our university and state universities in general are to remain at the forefront in teaching and research in the future, we have to make sure that we implement ICT as effectively as possible in the new degree and postgraduate degree structure' (Pennock-Speck 2009: 183–184). According to our experience, it certainly appears to be providing a unique opportunity to revise and update HE methodology and to reinvigorate English language teaching.

5. References

Benito, Águeda, and Ana Cruz, *Nuevas Claves Para La Docencia Universitaria en el Espacio Europeo de Educación Superior* (Madrid: Narcea, 2007).

Brígido Corachán, Anna, 'Collaborative e-learning in the European Higher Education Area (EHEA): Towards a peer-assisted construction of knowledge', *GRETA Journal* 16/1–2 (2008), 14–18.

Brown, James Dean, *Using Surveys in Language Programs* (Cambridge: Cambridge University Press, 2001).

CIDUA, *Informe sobre la Innovación de la Docencia en las Universidades Andaluzas* (Sevilla: Consejería de Ecuación, Junta de Andalucía) <http://www.uca.es/web/estudios/innovacion/ficheros/informeinnovacinjuntaabril2005.doc> accessed 29 June 2010.

Gregori-Signes, Carmen, 'Integrating the old and the new: Digital storytelling in the EFL language classroom', *GRETA Journal* 16/1–2 (2008), 43–49.

Jordano de la Torre, María, 'Propuesta para la práctica y evaluación de la competencia oral en los estudios de Turismo a distancia de acuerdo con el EEES', *GRETA Journal* 16/1–2 (2008), 50–57.

Kessler, Greg, and Paige D. Ware, 'Addressing the Language Classroom Competencies of the European Higher Education Area through the Use of Technology', in María Luisa Pérez Cañado, ed., Competency-based Language Teaching in Higher Education (Amsterdam: John Benjamins, 2011), in press.

Levy, Mike and Philip Hubbard, 'Why call CALL "CALL"?', Computer Assisted Language Learning 1/3 (2001), 143–149.

Mehisto, Peeter. 'CLIL counterweights: Recognising and decreasing disjuncture in CLIL', International CLIL Research Journal 1/1 (2008), 93–119.

Michavila, Francisco, 'Preface', in María Luisa Pérez Cañado, ed., *English Language Teaching in the European Credit Transfer System: Facing the Challenge* (Frankfurt am Main: Peter Lang, 2009), 9–16.

O'Dowd, Robert, 'Foreign language education and the rise of on-line communication: A review of promises and realties', in Robert O'Dowd, ed., *Online intercultural exchange* (Exeter: Multilingual Matters, 2007), 17–40.

——, 'Assessing online language learning in the European Higher Education Area', *GRETA Journal* 16/1–2 (2008), 58–64.

Pennock-Speck, Barry, 'The implementation of ICT in the second-cycle History of the English Language module at the Universitat de València', *GRETA Journal* 16/1–2 (2008), 65–70.

——, 'European Convergence and the Role of ICT in English Studies at the Universitat de València: Lessons Learned and Prospects for the Future', in María Luisa Pérez Cañado, ed., *English Language Teaching in the European Credit Transfer System: Facing the Challenge* (Frankfurt am Main: Peter Lang, 2009), 169–185.

——, 'Teaching competences through ICTs in an English degree programme in a Spanish setting', in María Luisa Pérez Cañado, ed., *Competency-based Language Teaching in Higher Education* (Amsterdam: John Benjamins, 2011), in press.

Pérez Cañado, María Luisa, 'Using VLE and CMC to Enhance the Lexical Competence of Pre-service English Teachers: A Quantitative and Qualitative Study', *Computer Assisted Language Learning* 23/2 (2010), 129–152.

——, coord., *Claves para la Adaptación de la Enseñanza de Lenguas al EEES: Un Estudio Europeo* (Madrid: Síntesis, 2010).

——, and María Belén Díez Bedmar, 'Data-Driven Learning and Awareness-Raising: An Effective Tandem to Improve Grammar in Written Composition?', *iJET: International Journal of Emerging Technologies in Learning* 1/3 (2006), 1–11.

——, and Paige D. Ware, 'Why CMC and VLE are Especially Suited to the ECTS: The case of Telecollaboration in English Studies', in María Luisa Pérez Cañado, ed., *English Language Teaching in the European Credit Transfer System: Facing the Challenge* (Frankfurt am Main: Peter Lang, 2009), 111–150.

Pérez Gómez, Ángel, Encarnación Soto Gómez, Miguel Sola Fernández, and María José Serván Núñez, *Aprender en la universidad. El sentido del cambio en el EEES* (Madrid: Ediciones Akal, S. A., 2009a).

——, *Orientar el desarrollo de competencias y enseñar cómo aprender. La tarea del docente* (Madrid: Ediciones Akal, S. A., 2009b).

——, *Contextos y recursos para el aprendizaje relevante en la universidad* (Madrid: Ediciones Akal, S. A., 2009c).

Thorne, Steve, 'Artefacts and cultures-of-use in intercultural communication', *Language Learning and Technology* 7/2 (2003), 38–67.

Torralbo Jover, Marina, 'Las Nuevas Tecnologías en el ECTS: El Desarrollo de la Competencia Léxica en Inglés a través de los Podcasts', *GRETA Journal* 16/1–2 (2008), 71–77.

Vaughan, N., 'Perspectives on blended learning in higher education', *International Journal on E-learning* 6/1 (2007), 81–94.

Ware, Paige D., and María Luisa Pérez Cañado, 'Grammar and Feedback: Turning to Language Form in Telecollaboration', in Robert O'Dowd, ed., *Online Intercultural Exchange* (Exeter: Multilingual Matters, 2007), 107–126.

Yu, Yueming, 'Restructuring Foreign Language Curricula to Meet the New Challenge', *The Modern Language Journal* 92/2 (2008), 301–303.

Zaragoza Ninet, María Goretti and Begoña Clavel Arroitia, 'ICT implementation in English Language and English Dialectology', *GRETA Journal* 16/1–2 (2008), 78–84.

CHELO VARGAS-SIERRA

3 Translation-oriented Terminology Management and ICTs: Present and Future

1. Introduction

The need that specialized translators have for knowing terminology, solving terminological problems and managing term-related information within the translation process is nowadays in no doubt. Translators were the first group to be aware of the importance that term-related issues and terminology management had in their everyday tasks (Antia et al. 2005). Concerning term-related tasks, translators should be able to (a) identify and interpret the terminology in the source text (ST) adequately; (b) find and use proper documentation and information resources both for acquiring various kinds of information about terms (conceptual, pragmatic, and linguistic), and for applying their correct equivalents; and (c) retrieve and store terminological data.

The development of ICTs designed for the translator's workbench has been phenomenal over the past decade. Ramirez-Polo and Hang-Ferrer (2010: 24) suggest as possible reasons, firstly, the rapid evolution of the Internet and other innovations in hardware and software, and the increase of texts to be translated as a result of the globalization of the market, products and services. Another reason could be the pressure put on translators to produce target texts quickly and efficiently. Finally, translation in general, and translation-oriented terminology in particular, have become increasingly computerized over the past twenty years.

This chapter addresses different aspects of terminology management and its computerized workbench, all with regard to translation-oriented terminology tasks and ICTs. It begins with a brief description of the improvements carried out in terminology management over time, followed by some key definitions of terminology management highlighting the process carried out within the context of translation. It then goes on to describe and classify the types of translation practices related to terminology management, including the software that can be used in a particular task. Finally, future prospects with regards to the translators' workstation in its relation to terminology work will be briefly examined.

2. Qualitative improvements in terminology management

The 1980s witnessed the first electronic dictionaries and terminology management systems TMS which were designed to be used in personal computers and, consequently, available for a great number of users. Translators have been able to use these tools to create, maintain, manage and disseminate their own term bases to include terminological units and their related information gathered during the documentation or translation process (Bowker 2003: 51). Nevertheless, this first generation had its limits, such as the following (Bowker 2002: 78):

1. It was not possible to share terminological repositories in local networks;
2. They were unidirectional in nature, i.e., work could be carried out from English to Spanish, but this linguistic direction could not be reversed;
3. The number and type of data fields; and
4. The storage capacity.

Two of the most powerful and best-selling terminology management tools integrated in Translation Memory Systems are *MultiTerm* and *TermStar*. The first *MultiTerm* version was launched for DOS in 1990 and two years later for Windows. *TermStar* was launched for the first time in 1991 (DOS), and it adapted for the Windows (3.1) platform with *Transit/TermStar* 2.0 in 1994. Since then, a lot of new tools have been marketed and updated to conform to the recent improvements made by computing and linguistic engineering. The implementation of state-of-the-art translation technologies, such as the above mentioned translation-oriented terminology management systems has proved to be very useful both in supporting, facilitating and speeding up translators' work, as well as in providing resources that can be reused in the future.

In a previous paper (Vargas 2007: 47), the qualitative improvements that terminology management in general achieved were mentioned and classified into four main benefits. The first was concerned with quick and easy access to existing multilingual terminology and documentation via the Internet, which also facilitates the second, i.e., the compilation of a collection of electronic texts to build up a domain-specific representative corpus to be processed for terminology purposes. It is necessary to highlight the fact that terminology is a corpus-based activity. From a corpus that is gathered, the third benefit is gained; that is the possibility to extract specialized knowledge with the help of semi-automatic term extractors. The final improvement that will be presented refers to terminology management systems. Thus, the information taken from the text material can be organized in the form of electronic registers, each one having all the information related to each and every term, distributed in different fields (term, definition, context, part of speech, etc.). In summary, in the last twenty years or so, four technological concepts have played a leading role in terminography: the Internet, electronic corpora, term extractors (using linguistic, statistical or hybrid approaches) and TMS, also know as terminological databases.

3. Translation-oriented terminology management – Some definitions

Terminology management is defined by Galinski and Budin (2005) in the following way:

> Terminology management is primarily concerned with manipulating terminological resources for specific purposes, e.g., establishing repertories of terminological resources for publishing dictionaries, maintaining terminology databases, or ad hoc problem solving in finding multilingual equivalences in translation work or creating new terms in technical writing.[1]

From this definition, we can distinguish two different axes: one concerned with systematic terminology projects, and the other related to ad hoc ones. On one hand, systematic terminology aims to develop wide-coverage terminology resources (vocabularies, databases, dictionaries, etc.) to meet the needs of a specific kind of user; while the second focuses on handling precise terminology problems or working on a small group of terms. Both systematic and ad hoc terminography can be carried out by translators, but not necessarily. In fact, within a translation context, translation will be more frequently exposed to ad hoc terminology work. Candel-Mora (2006) points out that the main difference between systematic and translation-oriented terminology work is that the latter is characterized by the limitations inherent to the peculiarities of the work environment, and more specifically, to translation deadlines and planning, which leads translators to conduct ad hoc terminology work or work addressed to solving the terminological problems encountered during the initial phase of ST analysis. Wright and Wright (1997:148) illustrate these differences in terms of methodology:

> In scope the methodology, the systematic model is *subject-field-driven*. [...] In contrast, ad hoc terminology management is *text-driven*: terminologists and translators creating their own terminology resources are presented with random extractions from a domain.

Both systematic and ad hoc terminology management is a computer-assisted activity. In translation, it means that the human translator, in any of the roles s/he may play (terminologist, localizer, translator, reviewer, etc.), uses computer software that has been designed to support and facilitate

1 Taken from <http://cslu.cse.ogi.edu/HLTsurvey/ch12node7.html> accessed 18 October 2010.

all translation, textual and terminological tasks, i.e., from those aiming at acquiring knowledge through documentation, to translating and generating the target text with the same format and visual aspect as the ST. Then, a current definition for translation-oriented terminology management would refer to the computer-assisted creation, maintenance, management and dissemination of term databases useful for translation. In this article, by translation-oriented terminology management we will refer to that performed by translators and integrated into a translator's workbench.

The software generally used within this context is a Translation Memory (TM) – which falls into the broad category named 'computer-aided translation (CAT) systems'. A TM is made up of different components, the most important being two data bases: the translation memory, a computer file that contains translation units (aligned pairs of source and target language segments); and the terminology database, a computer file designed to store terminological information. It is important to note that TMs can read and work with more than one translation memory and term base at the same time.

Next I will describe and classify the types of practices related to terminology management that translators go into during the process, the purpose of which is to provide an account of the technologies these professionals use or can use for a specific task. This description will be provided from a user's point of view without going very deeply into technical details.

4. Practices in translation-oriented terminology management

All fields of knowledge or professional activity are characterized by a significant amount of terminology that is used in oral or written texts circulating in the field. Terminology in specialized texts is considered to be a 'translation problem', i.e., an obstacle that any translator has to overcome when the source text is decoded and/or the target text is reformulated. In fact, it is estimated that over 40% of the time invested in a technical or scientific translation is devoted to solving terminological problems inherent to each text (Arntz 1993; Walker 1993). Working out term-related issues, like research in neologisms, in linguistic or conceptual equivalence, in denominative variation (concurrence of synonyms), etc., are all time-consuming tasks. Once the specific problem has been handled, translators do not want to spend more time with research already undertaken in the past. Here terminology management becomes a crucial activity, since it enables translators to do the following:

1. search for a given term more efficiently when compared to searching in printed dictionaries and other sources;
2. ensure the reliability of information retrieval, since terminological records are added and edited by translators on the basis of sources they trust and on consultation with experts;
3. check how to use a term in context;
4. deal more efficiently with several languages;
5. store the solutions found for terminological problems to avoid duplicate research and unnecessary rework;
6. record multilingual domain-specific or in-house terms;
7. enlarge the database and then increase productivity during the ongoing translation or in a later translation;
8. systematize terminology;
9. use terminology consistently over the same or similar projects;
10. prevent mistakes, or unsuitable usage of terms in a particular situation;
11. exchange terminological resources with colleagues, institutions, companies, etc.

In summary, the aim in translation-oriented terminology management is to deal quickly and efficiently with terms in two or more languages. Terminology management will help to achieve this, and, in fact, translators have always recorded terminological information for later use. A basic method of storing terminology used to be, or is in some cases still, in a dual or multi-column word list, using text editors and spreadsheets; the first column containing the SL terms and the others with the equivalent terms in one or several target languages (TL). However, this solution is not structured properly to manage terms, not is it scalable for more terms to be added of for multiple users to share access. A more sophisticated method for managing terminological data has been adopted since the 1980s, as we already mentioned and involves the use of TMSs. Broadly speaking, a TMS is a computer-based information management system for collecting, storing, manipulating, importing, exporting and managing terminological data, which is structured according to particular criteria andusers, and for the purpose of term compilation. It should be designed to allow extensive documentation of the entry. From the translation perspective, this software is not only used with compiled terminology, but also for the import and export of terms, the creation of new entries, and for recording additional terminological information in the entry (contexts, definitions, cross-references, domain, images, etc.).

It should also be pointed out that computer-assisted translation is a complex process consisting of several stages. Managing large translation projects involves a number of phases, and tasks can be grouped into translation and non-translation or, according to the POINTER report,[2] the phases are: pre-translation editing, translation process itself, and post-translation edit phase. This survey indicates the global aim in each of these phases:

> [...] terminological information is required throughout the translation process: during pre-translation editing to *clarify the source language terms*; in the translation process itself to *identify and use target language terms*; and during the post-translation edit phase for *checking the accuracy of target language terms*. [The italics are mine]

Terminology management, like many other tasks in the translation workflow (proofreading, desktop publishing, text processing, project management, etc.), is considered to be a non-translation task, but it cannot be taken for granted by any translator. Next, I will deal with the description of these translation phases focusing on terminology and ICT issues.

2 POINTER, Proposals for an Operational Infrastructure for Terminology in Europe, a project carried out by terminology specialists in 1995–1996. <http://www.computing.surrey.ac.uk/ai/pointer/ptsurvey.html> accessed 18 October 2010.

4.1 Phase 1: Pre-translation editing

To clarify SL terms, several tasks can be performed in the first phase, but they can be grouped into one, i.e., documentation, used here in a broad sense. This allows translators to acquire knowledge about the different issues of a particular topic, or about lexicographical or terminographical material already published and available in any format. In translation-oriented terminology work, documentation provides sources that will be useful to check the terms in particular communication contexts, and permits verification or contrasting data. At this initial stage, translators need to focus on the text topic and delimit conceptually the area before creating a reference corpus[3] (RC) made up of relevant terminological resources of different kinds that may be useful during translation. For this purpose, as is widely known, the technology that translators use more extensively is the Internet, which has ushered in a new era, and become the primary information resource for professionals in need of information of any kind. Web pages frequently provide direct access to online dictionaries and glossaries, some of them downloadable for local storage and offline viewing.

Compiling an ad hoc corpus may be also useful at this point. However, the compilation can introduce time-consuming tasks into the translation process, so it is necessary to balance the time and effort required to build up a quality ad hoc corpus against the benefits that can be gained by processing and consulting it (Bowker and Pearson 2002).

For this purpose, a concordancer, such as *WordSmith Tools*, *AntConc*, *ConcApp*, and the like, can provide clues to the key words or terms in the ST by creating a monolexical or polilexical wordlist that can be ordered by frequency. Stopword lists will avoid the noise – or irrelevant data – in the list and may help to determine the topic of the texts (*cf.* Vargas 2006).

3 Note that 'reference corpus' is not used here with the same meaning Corpus Linguistics applied to the term. In Terminology, this kind of corpus contains lexicographical and terminological resources (dictionaries, databases, data banks, vocabularies, and so on) that are already available and may help terminologists to get mono- multilingual, conceptual, linguistic and pragmatic information about terms or to verify them (Cabré 1993).

It can also give translators useful information about the lexical problems they will encounter: unknown terms, terms not compiled in the term base, neonyms, synonyms, abbreviations, etc. The first terms in the list can also serve as seeds – words or word clusters that identify the domain being investigated – not only to compile glossaries already available about the topic on the Web, but also to try to find parallel corpora in the form of memories (in Translation Memory eXchange format, TMX), or as a collection of texts in language A and their translations to one or several languages. Another kind of corpus used in translation is called 'comparable corpora', which consists of 'texts in the languages involved, which share similar criteria of composition, genre, and topic' (Zanettin 1998: 2). The usefulness of both kinds of corpora in translation was expressed by Laviosa (2002: 104) in the following way:

> Parallel corpora are invaluable resources of information for discovering typical and well established translation equivalents of given terms and expressions, while comparable corpora are particularly useful for discovering the typical co-text of assumed equivalent terms and expressions in the source and target language.

As previously mentioned, parallel corpus may already be available in TMX, an open standard for the exchange of translation memories, so this file type can be imported quickly and easily into a translation memory, whereas parallel texts need a process of alignment, which converts them into what is known as a 'bitext'; then, it will be possible to import this bilingual document into the translation memory to feed it. Provided that the quality of these existing memories and parallel corpora can be positively assessed, this material will undoubtedly be useful for terminology purposes, as the extract of a GPS device translation memory shows (see Table 6).

Entering Coordinates	Introducción de coordenadas
Lane Assist Page	Página Indicación de carriles
Routes Page	Página Rutas
Trip Computer Page	Página Procesador de trayecto
Compass	Brújula
Enabling Fuel Tracking	Activación del seguimiento de combustible
Using Hands-free Calling	Uso de las funciones de manos libres
Pairing Your Devices	Vinculación de dispositivos
Receiving a Call	Recepción de llamadas
Severity Color Code	Código de colores de gravedad
Traffic on Your Route	Tráfico en la ruta
Viewing the Traffic Map	Visualización del mapa de tráfico
Using the Media Players	Uso de reproductores multimedia ...
Using a Wireless Headset	Uso de auriculares inalámbricos

Table 6 A fragment of a GPS translation memory (English-Spanish)

Therefore, compilation of parallel corpora can be a viable solution with regards to terminology detection and extraction.[4] Automatic web file downloaders may be useful tools for this task, and can be defined as online or offline computer software for bootstrapping specialized corpora from the web. To illustrate the way this software works, we can take as an example the user-friendly and freely-available software named *BootCat front end*. It uses as input a set of seed terms, combines these seeds in random tuples – sequences of *n* seeds – queries a search engine to find web pages that

4 There are some parallel corpora already available on the Web. Some examples are: OPUS: Search Word Alignment Database (<http://urd.let.rug.nl/tiedeman/OPUS/lex.php>), European Parliament Proceedings Parallel Corpus 1996–2009 (<http://www.statmt.org/europarl/>), and JRC-Acquis Multilingual Parallel Corpus (<http://langtech.jrc.it/JRC-Acquis.html>), accessed 18 October 2010.

contain the generated tuples and downloads the relevant pages that the search engine hits page points to; then it cleans up the HTML code and converts all compiled texts into one TXT file, thus creating the corpus (*cf.* Baroni et al 2006). It is obvious that this software offers a great number of advantages, although for translation or terminology purposes, this kind of software should probably incorporate some additional features in order to provide both:

1. a preview of the texts found, in order to determine their adequacy for inclusion in the corpus and not only the URLs, since the latter are not always descriptive enough;
2. a keyword extractor that provides the translators with an idea of the content of each document so they have more parameters to decide if a given text should be incorporated into the corpus.

Other tasks to be performed in this pre-translation process have to do with terminology leverage (or term base match scores), and glossaries import. TMs leverage the memory to match and retrieve segments that were previously translated, but term leverage is unfortunately not always included in these systems. The ideal process would involve scanning the terms encountered in the ST and matching them with the ones recorded in the term base, resulting in a new list with all unknown terms. Thus, it would be able to know the terms that may need a more in-depth investigation in advance. With respect to the collection of available machine-readable glossaries, vocabularies, or other terminology applications, the tasks are concerned with the collection and processing to be imported into the term base set up in the translation project. There are clients who provide a list or a database of multilingual in-house terms, but this is not always the case and, as has been previously mentioned, some time should be devoted to search for and find relevant terminological resources. Budin and Wright (1997: 845) called this process *term mining*, which is 'grounded in the efficient use of search engines'. The tasks involved are listed in two groups: online, related to the use of search engines and assessment of results given, and offline, associated with data processing for local storage. On one hand, the online tasks may require:

1. use of an appropriate query syntax to filter results, avoid noise, and consistently yield the most relevant results possible;
2. identification of the relevant pages in order to consult only the best results;
3. consultation of each page which is considered relevant to see the resource offered;
4. assessment of the quality, accuracy and credibility of the resource;
5. study of the structure of the entries to establish their field sequence and to set a pattern;
6. exploration of the technical possibilities of downloading or copying the resource, including legal barriers; and
7. retrieval of the task for local storage.

On the other hand, the offline tasks may involve processing the resource to ready it for the import process by using a word processor or a spreadsheet, and converting it into an importable format in accordance with the TMS being used, unless the resource is already available in a Term Base eXchange (TBX) format, an open, XML-based standard for the exchange of terminological databases. TMs have integrated this format into the import and export features, so the transfer of information from one term base to another among different TMSs has become much easier.

Terminology extraction for translation purposes needs to be mentioned. The integration of term extraction methods into current ICT should be considered as very helpful and, in fact, terminology extraction from a bilingual corpus is probably the most desired function of a term extraction tool, particularly at a time when translation memories and texts with their translation to one or several languages are only a keyboard and a screen away, or can be created by the users themselves through alignment. The ideal software for this purpose would automatically perform a mono- or bilingual terminology candidate identification and extraction from the source text(s) or the parallel corpus, compiled as TMX or converted to a bitext. This functionality does not usually come with TMs and, when available, needs to be purchased separately.

Once the documentation and import processes are completed and translation memory database and term base ready, they should be selected when setting up the project in TMs. The access to a term base (and to memory databases too) can be local or remote. A local term base is located on your computer or on a local network. However, it is possible to simply publish the database over a server to be accessible in real time by any Internet browser with an established IP address, then it can be used by anyone who has the necessary network (or Internet) and term base access rights. The main differences between both, local and remote, have to do with term base creation, login and access rights, which are controlled by the system administrator. Remote ICTs are becoming very common nowadays, due to the stability and reliability of the Internet, as well as higher speed rates. A server-based term base offers several advantages, as it allows geographically distributed translators to have access to it or other shared applications from any computer connected to the Internet in the world.

TMs can perform several tasks that are run individually or as a sequence.[5] The aim of the initial one is to prepare the source text(s) and involves converting, analyzing and pre-translating the file(s). Pre-translation refers to the automatic translation of segments in the source file(s) by applying translations found and taken from translation memories and term bases. Then, the translation process itself may begin.

4.2 *Phase 2: Translation process*

During the second phase, the main task is concerned with identification and proper usage of target terms. Here, TMs automatically look up terminology from the associated local or server-based term base(s), compare the current source sentence with the data contained in it/them, and suggest terms as documents are being translated. Translators can manually perform a search in the term base and insert the equivalent into the active segment.

5 In this paper, the computer-assisted translation procedure will be illustrated according to some of the most widely-used commercial and powerful TMS, i.e., SDL Trados Studio 2009 and Transit NXT.

Concerning the usability of a terminology management system, the search function is of key importance. Multiple types of searching functions are nowadays available in TMS. Apart from simple searches to locate specific terms, it is generally possible to perform a wildcard search, i.e., by using placeholders (such as * or ?) for unspecified characters in the search, fuzzy searches – the term base will find terms that are similar to the search value, so it is possible to find a term even if the translator is unsure of its correct spelling. Full text search may also be possible, that is, the search value is located in all text fields of each database entry in any language.

Creating filters is another way to perform searches, especially when the terminology collections are very extensive, and the search is not term-oriented but field- or condition-oriented (e.g. when the translator wishes to retrieve all terms that have images or synonyms). A system in which filter criteria can be combined using operators goes one step further.

Searching for term equivalents on the Web is a new feature integrated within the editor of Transit NXT. This option has several advantages bearing in mind the time translators devote to searching in different dictionaries and resources on the web during translation itself. As a built-in module (called 'Web search window'), the searches are performed with no requirement to leave the TM editor and by means of only one action, like a meta-search engine, since it searches for a term (in source or target language) throughout several web-based multilingual resources that are preset by default. The results for the respective web-based resource are shown in the right-hand portion of the Web search window. This new feature enables translators to save time and effort, so it should be included in all TMs.

Throughout the translation process, new terms can be added to the term base, either by selecting both the original term and its equivalent and automatically send the pair to the term base or by manual data entry. When the translator wishes to study a term record in more detail, it is possible to switch between the editor module and the terminology management module.

Finally, proper usage of a term may be checked by way of a concordance search in the translation memory, provided it is fed with previous translation units that contain the term or expression that has been searched for. This feature searches the translation memory for a particular word,

word sequence or phrase. If the TM finds translation units containing the searched for word or phrase, the translator will be able to see the way they were previously translated. This can be done by selecting some text in a source language segment and/or some text in a target language segment.

4.3 Phase 3: Post-translation edit phase

Once the previous process is finished, reviewing and spell checking are standard quality assurance (QA) tasks performed on the target texts internally. The target text will then be edited and proofread by the translators themselves; or externally, by a third party commissioned by the client.

Concerning terminology-related issues, this last phase aims to check the accuracy of target terms. TMs also have features for terminology verification and translators can specify what checks should be run as part of this process. These systems run some testing procedure to ensure that the target terms in the term base have been used in the translation and to detect if target terms, marked by the users as forbidden, have been employed.

Spell-checking can also be run automatically. This is a very important terminology task as well, since misspellings may result in a term retrieval problem; the software will not be able to automatically identify and match automatically the term in the active segment with the wrongly spelled one contained in the term base. Needless to say that every correction, change, additional information or improvement should be registered in the TMS to avoid reproducing a mistake or error when using the term base for a future translation.

5. Some future prospects for translation-oriented terminology

Even at the risk of making some mistakes, especially bearing in mind that the ICT industry is quite unpredictable, due to the fact that social demands may determine the course of technological developments, I will try to examine some paths through which, in my opinion, translation-oriented terminology software could progress.

Concerning a terminological workstation, in 1989 Auger was already able to foresee what software developments were going to take place and be implemented for the benefit of terminologists (quoted in Cabré 1998: 160):

> In a futuristic scenario, terminologists will have access to huge data (or knowledge) banks; (...) they will classify, choose, merge and edit data bases reducing their intervention to a minimum. Their work station (...) equipped with advanced and intelligent office tools, will allow them to control, by themselves and throughout the whole process, the elaboration of their product and carry it under the best conditions.

More than twenty years later, we can see that the introduction of computer tools in translators' and terminologists' workstations has changed the methodology of translation and terminology production completely. As foretold by Cabré (2007: 105), integral workstations were going to have a leading role in terminology work scenario. This is a fact nowadays, and we can find some examples[6] of management systems which include modules for carrying out all the tasks involved in terminology work: corpus compilation and processing, term extraction and elaboration and editing of glossaries. The next thing that should be implemented in these terminology workstations is the integration of a Translation Memory in the system, and other features suited to the terminology work carried out within a translation project.

6 See, for example, *Terminus Station*, by IULA, Pompeu Fabra University (<http://melot.upf.edu/Terminus2009/>), and *Corpógrafo*, by Linguateca (<http://www.linguateca.pt/corpografo/>).

During the last decade, the ICT industry has experienced a continuous surge together with the worldwide web, which has gone a step further to become what is known as the Social Web (or Web 2.0), a more dynamic web that has greatly contributed to collaboration between people and to the appearance of new forms of knowledge exchange and social interaction. Other web concepts are the Semantic Web (or Web 3.0), and the Ubiquitous Web (Web 4.0), which pays particular attention to 'technologies to enable Web access for anyone, anywhere, anytime, using any device'.[7] From this last web concept, some new ones have developed, such as cloud computing and collaborative software. The first one refers to 'both the applications delivered as services over the Internet and the hardware and systems software in the data centers that provide those services' (Armbrust et al. 2010). Collaborative software can be defined as software which enables concurrent users who may be geographically distributed to work on a common project Therefore, it is possible for almost any task to be done via the computer and over the web. Cloud-based SaaS (software as a service) translation environments and collaborative workstations for translation have recently been made available on the market, such as *Lingotek's Collaborative Translation Platform* and *XMT Cloud*. The collaborative translation platforms allow multiple translators and others to work on a single document at the same time while keeping track of the whole process.

Within this context, the term 'collaborative terminology' may be used in a similar way to that of 'collaborative translation'. In this type of translation, two or more people work together on the translation of the same ST; both the construction of meaning and the production of the target texts emerge as a result of an individual translator's cognitive process, but supported by the constructive interaction among the team members, which results in a case of optimized synergy. In collaborative terminology, two or more people would be involved in the elaboration or editing of the same term record, which will also result from an individual terminologist's cognitive process, but supported by cooperative interaction among colleagues, domain specialists, multilingual experts, and so on. Actually, the interaction and cooperation with other colleagues, experts, translators, linguists, etc.,

7 Taken from <http://www.w3.org/UbiWeb/> accessed 18 October 2010.

is not new in terminology work. What is new is both the incorporation of collaborative software in workstations and volunteers, staff, bilinguals, professional reviewers pooling their special skills or knowledge built up from experience, training, or study, to create content more dynamically. The possibility to submit content by volunteers is already being offered by online dictionaries, like MacMillan, which has an application for adding new words.[8] Moreover, a validation or quality assurance process is not difficult to implement on a web-based system.

The development of a greater collaborative consciousness and the use of collaborative translation platforms could one day contribute to all of the following:

- globalization and internationalization of translation memories and term bases;
- simultaneous publication of bi- or multilingual content;
- development of new forms of work organization and of simpler procedures;
- real integration of multidisciplinary groups (experts, linguists, translators, reviewers, terminologists, etc.) working at the same time on/within a translation or terminology project;
- more active collaboration with clients and colleagues;
- tasks traditionally done individually will be shared;
- increase of visibility of translators and terminologists on the web;
- discovery of new needs that IT will have to satisfy;
- appearance of new systems that integrate all the tools needed in only one environment;
- less time and effort required for carrying out certain tasks;
- increase of productivity;
- achievement of synergistic solutions and shared benefits for all those involved in a group.

8 See <http://www.macmillandictionary.com/open-dictionary/submit.html> accessed 20 January 2011.

Next-generation CAT tools will deal with online workflows and collaborative translation and terminology. According to what is currently hinted at in translation technology webpages and tweets, the near future scenario will be characterized by two key elements: collaborative work and the Web. We will witness an increase and consolidation of web-based applications, browser-based CAT tools and terminology management systems, interfaces between translators' tools and authoring systems and ways for collaborative translation and terminology work.

6. References

Antia, Bassey E., Budin, Gerhard, Picht, Heribert, Rogers, Margaret, Schmitz, Klaus-Dirk, Wright, Sue Ellen, 'Shaping Translation: A View from Terminology Research', in *For a Proactive Translatology, Meta 50/4, 50th anniversary colloquium of Meta: Translators journal* (Montreal: University of Montreal, 7–9 April 2005), <http://www.erudit.org/revue/meta/2005/v50/n4/index.html> accessed 18 October 2010.

Armbrust, Michael, Fox, Armando, Griffith, Rean Joseph, Anthony D., Katz, Randy Konwinski, Andy Lee, Gunho, Patterson, David Rabkin, Ariel, Stoica, Ion and Zaharia, Matei 'A view of Cloud Computing', in *Communications of the ACM* 4, vol 53 (2010), 50–58. <http://cacm.acm.org/magazines/2010/4/81493-a-view-of-cloud-computing/fulltext> accessed 18 October 2010.

Arntz, Rainer, 'Terminological Equivalence and Translation', in Sonneveld, B. and Loening, K. L., eds, *Terminology: Applications in Interdisciplinary Communication* (Amsterdam/Filadelfia: John Benjamins, 2003), 5–19.

Baroni, Marco, Kilgarrif, Adam, Pomikálek, Jan, and Rychlý, Jan, 'WebBootCaT: instant domain-specific corpora to support human translators', in *Proceedings of EAMT 2006 – 11th Annual Conference of the European Association for Machine Translation* (Oslo, 2006), 247–252.

Bowker, Lynne, 'Terminology tools for translators', in Somers, Harold, ed., *Computers and Translation* (Philadelphia: John Benjamins, 2003), 49–65.

Bowker, Lynne, *Computer-Aided Translation Technology. A Practical Introduction* (Ottawa: University of Ottawa Press, 2002).

Bowker, Lynne, and Pearson, Jennifer, *Working with Specialized Language. A practical guide to using corpora* (London/New York: Routledge, 2002).

Budin, Gerhard andWright, Sue Ellen, 'Terminology Resources on the Internet', in Wright, Sue Ellen, and Budin, Gerhard, eds, *Handbook of Terminology Management* (Philadelphia: John Benjamins, 1997), 845–858.

Cabré Castellví, María Teresa, *La terminología. Teoría, metodología, aplicaciones* (Barcelona: Editorial Antártida/Empúries, 1993).

Cabré Castellví, María Teresa, 'La terminologie, une discipline en évolution: le passé, le présent et quelques elements prospectifs', in L'Homme, Marie-Claude and Vandaele, Sylvie (dir.), *Lexicographie et terminologie: comptabilité des modèles et des méthodes* (Ottawa: Les Presses de l'Université d'Ottawa, 2007).

Candel Mora, Miguel Ángel, *Propuesta de metodología para la gestión terminológica aplicada a la traducción profesional* (Valencia: Editorial Universidad Politécnica de Valencia, 2006).

Laviosa, Sara, *Corpus-based Translation Studies. Theory, Findings, Applications* (Amsterdam: Rodopi, 2002).

Ramirez Polo, Laura and Ferrer Mora, Hang, 'Aplicación de las TIC en Traducción e Interpretación en la Universidad de Valencia: experiencias y reflexiones', in *Redit* 4 (2010), 23–41.

Vargas-Sierra, Chelo, 'El léxico especializado y las ontologías', in Alcaraz Varó, Enrique, Mateo Martínez, José, and Yus Ramos, Francisco, eds, *Las Lenguas Profesionales y Académicas* (Barcelona: Editorial Ariel, 2007), 41–52.

Vargas-Sierra, Chelo, 'El proceso terminográfico multilingüe con *WordSmith Tools*', in *CONFLUENCIAS – Revista de Tradução Científica e Técnica* (2006), 84–107. <http://hdl.handle.net/10045/8513> accessed 18 October 2010.

Walker, D. G., 'Translation Problems as They Occur in Everyday Practice', in Schmitz, Klaus-Dirk, ed., *TKE'93, Proceedings Third International Congress on Terminology and Knowledge Engineering* (Cologne, 1993), 221–224.

Wright, Sue Ellen, and Wright, Leland D., 'Terminology Management for Technical Translation', in Wright, Sue Ellen, and Budin, Gerhard, eds, *Handbook of Terminology Management* (Philadelphia: John Benjamins, 1997), 147–159.

Zanettin, Federico, 'Bilingual Comparable Corpora and the Training of Translators', in *Meta* XLIII 4 (1998), 1–14.

FRANCISCO YUS

4 Relevance Equations of Effective Internet Communication

1. Human cognition, effects, effort and relevance

Human beings are geared to the maximisation of relevance; we tend to pay attention to inputs to our cognitive system that might yield benefits, and that applies to all the inferential activity of the human mind, not only to communication-centred cognitive reasoning. In short, human attention and processing resources are aimed at information that seems potentially relevant (of course, the fact that it eventually turns out to be relevant is a different issue). Our relevance-oriented mind, together with an evolved mind-reading ability, lie at the heart of successful human evolution. In Wilson & Sperber's (2002: 254) words,

> as a result of constant selection pressure towards increasing efficiency, the human cognitive system has developed in such a way that our perceptual mechanisms tend automatically to pick out potentially relevant stimuli, our memory retrieval mechanisms tend automatically to activate potentially relevant assumptions, and our inferential mechanisms tend spontaneously to process them in the most productive way.

Among the different inputs for our relevance-centred cognition, we can list the following:

1. Information from the physical environment, filled with visual information that is processed through the perceptual module. Most of this information is processed at a sub-attentive level (for example visual input from most of the people that pass by us in the street),

but other inputs, the potentially relevant ones, stand out and reach a more conscious level (for example, the visual input of smoke coming out of one of the windows of one's house).

2. Other people's nonverbal behaviour, which may either be exuded non-intentionally or directed at the interlocutor with specific underlying intentions, as in many instances of irony, whose meaning is often foregrounded by an ironic tone of voice and by gestures (i.e., smiles). In these cases, paying attention to this nonverbal behaviour is potentially relevant,
3. One's thoughts, some of which are more likely to be entertained in a specific context.
4. Finally, and crucially, people' utterances that they intentionally (i.e. ostensively) direct at their addressees with the intention of generating a certain interpretation. This is the source of cognitive activity that relevance theory (Sperber & Wilson, 1986, 1995) and cyberpragmatics (Yus, 2001, 2010) have mainly focused on.

One of the most interesting cognitive procedures that humans apply to potentially relevant inputs is the combination of the input with contextual information[1] to yield interesting conclusions that can only be derived from the combination of input and context, and not from these taken separately. And this cognitive operation is performed regardless of the source of the input. In Yus (2008: 632) the example (1) is offered, in which the input is visual and there is no underlying communicative intention, and in which conclusion (3) can only be obtained by combining the visual input in (1) and the contextual (*manifest*) information in (2):

1 Specifically, with *manifest* information. What is 'manifest' is what one is capable of inferring or capable of perceiving, even if one hasn't done so yet. The sum of all the manifest information is the person's *cognitive environment*. Information which is manifest to several individuals constitutes their *shared cognitive environment*. When it is manifest to all the people sharing a cognitive environment that they share it, then, this is a *mutual cognitive environment*, made up of mutually manifest information.

1. New information (visual input):
   A yellow Mercedes is parked near our department.
2. Information already available (from encyclopaedic knowledge):
   a. Professor Smith, who supervises my thesis, owns a yellow Mercedes.
   b. Professor Smith usually takes the bus to university.
   c. Only when he intends to stay at university till late in the evening does he drive his car to university (since there are no late buses returning to where he lives).
3. (Relevant) conclusion (inferred by combining (1) and (2)):
   This evening I will be able to discuss with him at length how my thesis is progressing.

Similarly, verbal communication with underlying communicative intentions also fits this schema of combination of input plus context to yield conclusions. Needless to say, linguistic communication is more complex, since it involves a unique mental (pragmatic) module in charge of obtaining interesting conclusions from (schematic) linguistic inputs (Sperber & Wilson 2002). However, intentionally communicated utterances also demand combinations of (verbal) inputs and manifest information, as in Tom's understanding of Ann's utterance in the following example, in which the conclusion (6) can only be obtained from combining the information from Ann's utterance in (4) and manifest information in (5):

4. New information (verbal input):
   Tom: There's a huge party next Saturday. Are you coming?
   Ann: My parents are away on a trip this weekend.
5. Manifest information (from encyclopaedic knowledge):
   a. Ann lives with her parents and her old, disabled grandmother.
   b. It's usually her parents that look after her grandmother.
   c. When her parents are away, she has to take care of her grandmother.
6. (Relevant) conclusion (inferred by combining (4) and (5)):
   Ann will be unable to go to the party on Saturday (since she has to look after her grandmother).

Making this kind of conclusion and, in general, interpreting utterances (and other types of inputs for processing) involves working out the balance between the interest that interpreting the utterance produces (called *positive cognitive effects* in relevance-theoretic terminology) and the mental effort that obtaining this interpretation entails. To do so, hearers will consider interpretive hypotheses in order of accessibility (following a path of least effort) and stop when they arrive at an interpretation which satisfies the expectations of relevance raised by the stimulus itself. The two conditions of relevance are defined as follows (Sperber & Wilson 1995, slightly adapted):

> Condition (a): An assumption (i.e., a piece of information) is relevant to an individual to the extent that the contextual effects (i.e. the interest) achieved when it is optimally processed are large.
>
> Condition (b): An assumption (i.e., a piece of information) is relevant to an individual to the extent that the effort required to process it optimally is small.

This definition of relevance as a combination of effects and effort does not imply that hearers do not pay attention to stimuli that are too effort-demanding or that the most effort-relieving interpretation is invariably the most relevant one[2] but, rather, that if obtaining the cognitive effects is more effort-demanding, an increased quality of these effects necessarily has to offset the effort. Consider the dialogue in (7):

7. [*Ann and Tom enter a pub. It is filled with people singing and dancing*].
   Ann: There is nothing like a lively pub!
   Tom: Indeed! Shall we go to another pub?
   Ann: Please!

2 As Diderichsen (2006) seems to imply: 'the most relevant interpretation of some stimulus is also the most cognitively accessible one, so that the most relevant interpretation will automatically come to mind first'.

In this dialogue, Ann could have spared Tom a lot of effort if she had simply said 'I don't like this pub; it's too overcrowded and noisy'. Instead, she chooses an ironic utterance that demands from Tom the retrieval of information from context about Ann's likes and dislikes (e.g. Ann hates overcrowded places; she prefers a quiet atmosphere where she can talk quietly) to yield the conclusion that she does not mean what she is saying. But for Tom the reward is also higher: the joy of 'mutual manifestness' of that information about Ann (the foregrounding of information shared by both interlocutors) and also the joyful entertainment of irony. In short, higher processing effort must be offset with higher or better cognitive effects in exchange. Later in this chapter this claim will be essential to understand several sample relevance equations of internet communication.

2. Relevance in (user to user) internet communication: Cognitive rewards vs environmental constraints

Several theories have underlined the specificity of internet-mediated communication due to the fact that the internet is typically a cues-filtered medium that suppresses attributes of contextual information (user's non-verbal communication, physical environment ...) that play an important part in face-to-face interactions. On the contrary, within cyberpragmatics (Yus 2001, 2010) it is claimed that communication on the internet does not differ from any other type of communication, oral, written, or typed; and all means of communication involve interpretation as an inferential gap-filling activity between what the sender has coded (i.e. spoken, written, typed ...) and what the sender intends to communicate[3] (related in

3 This is the *underdeterminacy thesis*, according to which the intended meaning is typically – if not always – more informative than the literal meaning and hearers have to undergo inferential procedures to turn the schematic meaning of the utterance into meaningful and relevant interpretations. Among these, we can list disambiguation, reference assignment, conceptual adjustment, free enrichment, etc. See Carston (2002).

terms of greater or lesser resemblance) and between what has been coded and what is finally interpreted by the addressee (related, again, by resemblance), the latter constrained by the general relevance-seeking quality of human cognition.

Besides, there are multiple ways in which communication, interactions and information transmission on the internet may turn out to be relevant to the user, beyond the relevance arising from productive combinations of new information and the user's manifest information (e.g. to yield relevant conclusions). Indeed, there is myriad of forms of cognitive satisfaction that may offset the effort involved in processing the information and that have often been dismissed, including a whole range of feelings, emotions, empathy, phatic connotations, community membership, socialisation, mutual awareness of one's and other people's presence in a group or network, etc.[4] I will group all of these 'alternative' sources of user satisfaction under the generic label of *cognitive rewards*. It adds to the normal sources of cognitive satisfaction centred upon combinations of information and context (i.e. manifest information) to yield relevant conclusions.

Additionally, the eventual relevance is influenced by the type of cognitive task that the user is currently engaged in while surfing the Net, which also affects the user's willingness to devote mental effort to the task at hand. In this sense, Amichai-Hamburger et al. (2007) applied Cacioppo & Petty's (1982) notion of *Need for Cognition* to internet communication. It refers to the individual's tendency to engage in and enjoy effortful cognitive endeavours, and it ranges from those users who have a 'low need for cognition' (i.e., those who do not enjoy cognitive efforts and acquire information by using simple cues offered by the environment) to users who have a 'high need for cognition' (i.e. have motivation to seek knowledge and will devote whatever effort it takes to get the information they need).

The combinations of cognitive effects and mental effort, as predicted by relevance theory, are also influenced by the kind of internet navigation.

4 In a way, the theory of *Uses & Gratifications* predicts this kind of 'alternative' reward for people using the medium. It focuses on the use of media in terms of the gratification of social or psychological needs of the individual rather than in purely informational terms (Blumler & Katz, 1974).

Indeed, the search for relevance, the expectation of cognitive effects, and the willingness to devote mental effort to the surfing activity will vary enormously depending on whether the user is simply browsing[5] the Net without a specific purpose[6] (e.g. to kill time) or is engaged in a focused search for specific information. In the former case, the users will expect to devote few mental resources, while in the latter the users will be willing to spend as much effort as necessary to obtain the information that they are looking for.

Besides, relevance outcomes depend on the current position in which the medium used for internet communication can be placed, specifically in the scales of oral-written, visual-verbal, and synchronous-asynchronous, a position that is in a non-stop process of transformation through advances in the interfaces and in the growing integration of sound, voice and visual information in everyday interactions on the Net. If we draw up a general scale ranging from contextually rich face-to-face interactions to cues-filtered plain-text mediated communication, we can place on it all the forms of internet-mediated communication, but the place that an interface occupies on the scale changes constantly. Initially, for instance, chat rooms were plain-text-mediated (unlike today's availability of voice-mediated chat rooms), and this is why a whole range of techniques for oralizing typed text were created in order to make it more realistic (i.e., closer to speech). The outcome was what was labelled *oralized written text* in Yus (2001, 2010) and *text deformation* in Yus (2005), a hybrid of the stability and rigidness of typed text and the dynamic and ephemeral quality of oral conversations. And this oralisation generates supplementary informational gaps that might play a part in the eventual relevance of the typed utterances being processed (Yus 2008: 635):

5 Bodoff (2006: 70) defines browsing as 'actively looking through information (active) or keeping one's eyes open for information (passive), without a particular problem to solve or question to answer (unfocused need)'.

6 This is what Marchionini (1995, quoted in Choo et al. 2000) calls *undirected browsing* (no real goal and very little focus), opposed to *directed browsing* (systematic, focused and directed by a specific object or target) and *semidirected browsing* (predictive or generally purposeful).

What the internet 'addresser user' intends to communicate with his/her utterance ...
[resembles]
What the internet 'addresser user' would have said (in a face-to-face situation) ...
[resembles]
What the internet 'addresser user' actually encodes (i.e., types on the keyboard).
[resembles]
What the internet 'addressee user' would have listened to (in a face-to-face situation) ...
[resembles]
What the internet 'addressee user' actually reads (on the computer screen) ...
[resembles]
What the internet 'addressee user' interprets (selects as the intended interpretation).

Therefore, the design of the interface and its qualities in the aforementioned scales play an important part in the amount of cognitive effects obtained by the user and the mental effort involved in obtaining relevant conclusions. In this sense, Hasan & Ahmed (2007) applied Davis' (1989) *Technology Acceptance Model* to internet communication. The model predicts that perceptions of ease of use and usefulness are directly determined by external variables, and these authors concluded that the interface style affected the user's willingness to accept and use this interface.

In this sense, the designers of interfaces who aim at usability face the challenge of making designs that suit different users with different cognitive environments, different surfing styles and different informational needs. Indeed, some users like to be offered total freedom of navigation, for example, to see on the web page a number of tags or options on a side-frame with no hierarchical organisation, whereas other users prefer to be guided in their navigation, to have a clear picture of the map of the site, etc. If the user accesses a web page whose interface does not suit his/her personal surfing style, the eventual relevance of the web content will probably decrease.

Needless to say, the user's familiarity with the interface, even if it is not user-friendly, and also the user's intuitive ability to interact with the interface also affect the balance of cognitive effects and mental effort involved in processing information from the interface, generating multiple outcomes of (in)efficient interpretations. And frequency of use is a parallel variable affecting relevance.[7]

From now on, all of these non-propositional aspects of internet communication that may influence negatively the balance of cognitive effects and mental effort, as predicted by relevance theory, will be generically labelled *environmental constraints*. Among these are the user's need for cognition (high/low), the type of surfing (browsing vs. focused search), the position of the interface in the different scales (oral/written, visual/verbal, synchronous/asynchronous), the user's familiarity with the interface, frequency of use, the suitability of the interface to the user's navigational pattern, and the quality of the interface design.

3. Sample relevance equations of successful internet communication

Communication is effective when the reward that the information accessed provides (cognitive effects) offsets the effort needed to obtaining it. In general, information (a set of assumptions in relevance-theory terms) that interacts fruitfully with the person's cognitive environment without excessive effort in exchange will generate relevant outcomes.

Internet communication does not differ from this conceptualisation of relevance, but in this chapter I have added two variables for internet-mediated communication that may affect the eventual balance of effects and effort, one on the positive side (adding to the cognitive effects that information provides) and the other on the negative side (constraining and possibly increasing mental effort and hence relevance assessment). The former has been labelled *cognitive rewards* (feelings, emotions, empathy, phatic connotation, feelings of community membership, of socialisation,

7 Small wonder, Johnson (2008) concluded that frequent Internet users cognitively outperform infrequent Internet users.

mutual awareness of one's and other people's presence in a group or network, etc.). The latter has been labelled *environmental constraints* (the kind of internet navigation, need for cognition, browsing vs. focused search, interface design, user's familiarity with software, user's ability to interact with the interface, etc.).[8] If relevance is a balance between effects and effort, a sort of equation in which one of the variables (effects) necessarily has to offset the other variable (mental effort involved), this equation has to include the supplementary aspects mentioned: *cognitive rewards* and *environmental constraints*, both of which may alter or influence the outcome of interpretation. To illustrate this claim, nine sample relevance equations of effective internet communication will be commented upon below.

Sample relevance equation 1

THE COGNITIVE EFFECTS FROM A DIFFICULT TEXT TO PROCESS
[+]
COGNITIVE REWARDS
[EXCEEDS ...]
THE MENTAL EFFORT NEEDED TO PROCESS IT
[+]
ENVIRONMENTAL CONSTRAINTS

Sometimes the user faces the processing of a text that is dense, difficult to read, but whose information combines fruitfully with the user's cognitive environment producing relevant outcomes. Even though mental effort is high (and some *environmental constraints* may also be involved, such as lack of familiarity with reading texts on the screen, etc.), the user's reward in terms of cognitive effects offsets the effort. An example would be someone who thinks that he has all the symptoms of an illness and reads a dense

8 In this chapter I will be considering only those *environmental constraints* that are detrimental to the user's relevance assessment. But it is obvious that these constraints may also aid the user and make interpretations easier (i.e., users who are very familiar with software, who are accessing information from a well-designed interface, etc.).

academic article on the internet in order to check whether he/she has contracted it. In this case, the informational reward will make the outcome of processing relevant to the user despite the high mental effort.

Sample relevance equation 2

THE COGNITIVE EFFECTS FROM AN 'ORALIZED WRITTEN TEXT' FILLED WITH UNUSUAL ORTHOGRAPHY AND CREATIVE USE OF SPELLING

[+]

COGNITIVE REWARDS

[EXCEEDS ...]

THE MENTAL EFFORT NEEDED TO PROCESS IT

[+]

ENVIRONMENTAL CONSTRAINTS

One of the objectives of cyberpragmatics (Yus 2001, 2010) is to analyse the way in which users deform the text typed on the keyboard to create a hybrid of written and oral communication, especially in chat rooms and instant messaging. This text deformation, basically a creative use of punctuation marks, repetition of letters and word shortenings, together with the use of emoticons, may pose a challenge for interpretation if the user is a neophyte in this kind of communication, does not know how to use the software for synchronous text-based interactions, or gets annoyed at how fast the threads of conversations disappear from the top of the screen (the so-called *scroll factor*), all of which are covered by the label *environmental constraints*. Even if the information in the conversations is the same, the innovative way of coding it may increase processing effort enormously.

For these neophytes, innovative text-mediated conversations will require additional *cognitive rewards* that compensate for the increased effort demanded, so that the interaction proves to be effective, for example, in terms of feelings of empathy, sociability, community membership, or what Thompson (2008) called *ambient awareness*, the feeling of being physically near the interlocutor and picking up on his mood through the typically useless words he types in the virtual conversation. On the contrary, users who are experts in typing this kind of *oralized written text*, are familiar with the chat room software and even know which techniques of oralisation have become conventionalised in this kind of interaction, will reduce the impact of these *environmental constraints* and obtain a more effective relevance equation.

Sample relevance equation 3

THE COGNITIVE EFFECTS FROM AN INTERACTION WITHIN A VIRTUAL WORLD USING A 3D AVATAR

[+]

COGNITIVE REWARDS

[EXCEEDS …]

THE MENTAL EFFORT NEEDED TO PROCESS UTTERANCES IN VIRTUAL WORLDS

[+]

ENVIRONMENTAL CONSTRAINTS

Interactions in virtual worlds (e.g. *Second Life*) using a 3D avatar are interesting for pragmatics because they offer the possibility of mixing verbal and nonverbal communication (of both intentional and exuded quality) in the interaction. The users can find many kinds of *cognitive reward* from these 3D interactions, for instance reward from the satisfaction of being able to sustain text-based and nonverbal communication simultaneously, or from the attention-drawing potential of the avatar designed by the user. However, these interactions also pose a challenge for effective interactions through a number of *environmental constraints*, among them the different options for verbal communication (in *Second Life* there are three: chat room, messenger and real voice) that intertwine with the avatar's intentional nonverbal behaviour (as intended by the user) and the avatar's exuded nonverbal behaviour (as generated by the software beyond the user's control). Suler (2007) explains his frustration at being unable to master all of these sources of information from the avatar:

> It took me several minutes just to figure out how to move my avatar, and then I was literally walking into walls and trees. I spent most of the first day learning how to move about without looking like a complete idiot, how to visually survey and interact with the environment ... Even after several hours, when I thought I was doing reasonably well, a more experienced user who I met in the Second Life version of Amsterdam commented on me being a newbie. When I asked how she knew, she replied, 'By how you walk'.

For this relevance equation to be effective, the user needs to find *cognitive rewards* that make up for the *environmental constraints* of the 3D scenario that increase mental effort. For example, the user might find a reward when succeeding in engaging in profitable verbal-nonverbal interactions, plus feelings of empathy, the possibility of having multiple identities with parallel discursive manifestations, etc.

Sample relevance equation 4

THE COGNITIVE EFFECTS FROM MULTIPLE MESSENGER WINDOWS OPENED SIMULTANEOUSLY AND SEVERAL CONVERSATIONAL THREADS FOLLOWED SIMULTANEOUSLY

[+]

COGNITIVE REWARDS

[EXCEEDS ...]

THE MENTAL EFFORT NEEDED TO PROCESS IT

[+]

ENVIRONMENTAL CONSTRAINTS

Today's adolescents, typically 'digital natives', follow multiple messenger conversations opened in different windows on the computer screen (typically while engaging in multi-tasking with other activities such as writing a paper, downloading files or updating their *Facebook* profile). Following multiple threads of conversation is demanding, an *environmental constraint* that adds to other limitations such as mastering techniques of text deformation, frequency of internet use and familiarity with software (most of these are not a problem for adolescents, though). Increased effort in managing these multiple interactions must be compensated for with additional *cognitive rewards* that make the equation relevant. In Yus (2010: 217–218) several of them are proposed, among them the users' need of mutuality of information, the need to feel the co-presence with friends in cyberspace, the need to show other users that one is 'connected' to the network of friends and is able to follow any conversation, and the aforementioned *ambient awareness* that prevents users from leaving the messenger session while forcing them, at the same time, to answer multiple users in multiple windows while doing another activity.

The equation, hence, will be effective especially for adolescents, who are used to multi-tasking and having multiple windows opened simultaneously, who are familiarised with the interface for messenger interactions and surf the internet on a daily basis. Older people who are 'digital immigrants' will face an increase in the *environmental constraints* that might even lead to a negative relevance equation and hence to unsatisfactory internet communication.

Sample relevance equation 5

THE COGNITIVE EFFECTS FROM QUANTITATIVE RELEVANCE OF WEB PAGE USABILITY

[+]

COGNITIVE REWARDS

[UTTERLY EXCEEDS ...]

THE MENTAL EFFORT NEEDED TO PROCESS IT

[+]

ENVIRONMENTAL CONSTRAINTS

Relevance is a balance between cognitive effects (i.e., interest, reward) and mental effort. One of the discussions within relevance theory concerns whether this balance can be computed quantitatively or it can only be assessed qualitatively. Several authors claim that there should be some way to compute numerical values of relevance, based perhaps on neuro-chemical mental steps taken during interpretation. But it is really difficult for analysts to assess relevance in purely quantitative terms and also for people in general when they are selecting the most interesting inputs. As Wilson &

Sperber (2002: 253) stress, it is highly unlikely that individuals compute numerical values for effort and effect when assessing relevance 'from the inside'. Computation of this kind would itself be effort-consuming and therefore detract from relevance. Moreover, even when individuals are clearly capable of computing numerical values (for weight or distance, for example), they generally have access to more intuitive methods of assessment which are comparative rather than quantitative, and which are in some sense more basic.

However, for the interpretation of user-to-user information on web pages, a link-based proposal of quantitative relevance was proposed in Yus (2008: 638):

> Condition (a): An assumption is relevant to an individual to the extent that the contextual effects achieved when it is optimally processed are large.
>
> Condition (b): An assumption is relevant to an individual to the extent that the number of clicks that the user has to make in order to obtain these effects is small.

If the interface of the web page is well-designed for usability (e.g. with tags or frames that indicate sections clearly), with links that effortlessly lead to the information that the user is looking for (added to the *cognitive reward* of the user's satisfaction at finding the information), then the effort demanded for processing and the number of *environmental constraints* will be reduced to the minimum, hence producing the prototypical notion of relevance, namely a high number of cognitive effects in exchange for little processing effort.[9]

9 Pirolli & Card (1999, cited in Murphy et al. 2006) suggest the analogy of a user who is exploring a web page to an animal foraging for food. For animals, the calories spent foraging for food must be less than the calories that the food provides. Similarly, the wording of a hyperlink promises a potential benefit to a site visitor while the time that the visitor spends reading and choosing a link, and also finding an adequate inter-link interpretation, represent a cost.

Sample relevance equation 6

THE COGNITIVE EFFECTS FROM QUALITATIVE RELEVANCE OF WEB PAGE USABILITY

[+]

COGNITIVE REWARDS

[UTTERLY EXCEEDS ...]

THE MENTAL EFFORT NEEDED TO PROCESS IT

[+]

ENVIRONMENTAL CONSTRAINTS

In Yus (2008) a qualitative version of relevance in link-mediated web pages was also suggested, this time related to the coherence that the user expects to find in-between the chunks of text related by hyperlinks:

> Condition (a): An assumption is relevant to an individual to the extent that the contextual effects achieved when it is optimally processed are large.
>
> Condition (b): An assumption is relevant to an individual to the extent that the level of coherence obtained from linking different bits of information is optimal despite the non-linear arrangement of the linked texts.

With link-mediated texts, the reading strategy becomes less fixed (and less author-supported), it is also more open to personal interpretations and the danger of increased effort (through useless clicks or incoherent reading paths) increases accordingly.[10] Again, a good and coherent design of linked texts will reduce the effort devoted to obtaining effects and will make this equation effective, basically through the *cognitive reward* of the user's satisfaction at finding the information easily and coherently.

10 Diderichsen (2006) states that 'the sender of a non-linear text dispenses with the ability to assume a particular order of reception of the material. This results in fewer assumptions being mutually manifest, and the sender should therefore preferably make each node in a hypertext equally meaningful in all the contexts it might occur in. For instance, it is not very meaningful to use abbreviations which have been introduced in another node if the sender cannot be sure of the reading order of the nodes'.

Sample relevance equation 7

THE COGNITIVE EFFECTS FROM AN EMAIL MESSAGE THAT PROVIDES INTERESTING INFORMATION TO THE USER AND IN WHICH THE SENDER HAS TYPED HIS WORDS INSERTED IN THE INITIAL SENDER'S MESSAGE

[+]

COGNITIVE REWARDS

[UTTERLY EXCEEDS ...]

THE MENTAL EFFORT NEEDED TO PROCESS IT

[+]

ENVIRONMENTAL CONSTRAINTS

The main aim of communication, according to relevance theory, is to obtain a mutuality of information (i.e. a 'mutually manifest' set of assumptions). Face-to-face interactions (in which speakers ostensively call the attention of their interlocutors towards potentially relevant information that can be extracted from the speaker's utterance) are very efficient ways of foregrounding the mutuality of information. Traditionally, many forms of media communication have been ineffective at obtaining a mutuality of assumptions. Unidirectional flow of information makes information manifest, but not *mutually* manifest. E-mail is an example of asynchronous communication which poses a challenge for mutuality, and it also exhibits a number of *environmental constraints* (rigid format, typically plain text-mediated, unable to express feelings and emotions faithfully, etc.).

However, the technique of answering an e-mail by inserting our words inside the initial message to which we are replying generates a sudden and unexpected level of mutuality of information (both the initial sender and the addressee-turned-sender are aware of the text of the e-mail) and provides a compensating *cognitive reward* that may offset the typical *environmental constraints* of e-mail (for example, the burden of spam) and make the equation effective in relevance-theory terms.

Sample relevance equation 8

THE COGNITIVE EFFECTS FROM A LIST OF TWITTER MESSAGES
[+]
COGNITIVE REWARDS
[EXCEEDS ...]
THE MENTAL EFFORT NEEDED TO PROCESS THEM
[+]
ENVIRONMENTAL CONSTRAINTS

Twitter messages are intended to answer the question 'what are you doing?'. As such, these messages (*tweets*) tend to be uninformative, dealing with 'interesting' activities such as making a sandwich, watching TV or taking the dog for a walk. Besides, Twitter messages exhibit an *environmental constraint* of being typed in no more than 140 characters, so very often these *tweets* are coded in sub-sentential utterances that underdetermine the user's intended meaning (the reader has to turn these schematic messages into meaningful and relevant interpretations). Another constraint is the fact that when one tries to follow a Twitter conversation on the profile page of a user, we only have access to half of the conversation, and this feature makes comprehension very difficult.

In theory, all of these constraints should outweigh the small interest that these 'everyday life messages' provide. But the practice of Twitter communication shows that a number of *cognitive rewards* make the equation relevant and effective. Among them, the knowledge of the user's everyday activities, which can turn into valuable background encyclopaedic knowledge upon which new conversations can be constructed. Secondly, Twitter interactions can provide additional *cognitive rewards* such as feelings of empathy, ambient awareness, feelings of mutual manifestness, a preliminary context of routine behaviour that can be used later as a preliminary context on which to build future interactions, etc.

Sample relevance equation 9

THE COGNITIVE EFFECTS FROM AN UTTERLY TEDIOUS, UNINFORMATIVE WEB PAGE

[+]

COGNITIVE REWARDS

[EXCEEDS ...]

THE MENTAL EFFORT NEEDED TO PROCESS IT

[+]

(NEGATIVE) ENVIRONMENTAL CONSTRAINTS (POSITIVE ONES ARE ALSO POSSIBLE BUT ARE NOT ADDRESSED IN THIS CHAPTER)

A type of web page is becoming popular: the ones with an utterly uninformative content but which, at the same time, demand little or no mental effort in return. In Yus (2010) some of them are cited, for instance, a page that displays web-cam images of a cheddar cheese rotting (at <http://cheddarvision.tv/>) or a page that shows images of hens walking around in a henhouse (at <http://www.hencam.co.uk>). These are clearly non-informative pages but their effectiveness does not lie in how much information they provide, but in the *cognitive reward* that they encourage, pages that one can watch without any mental effort, and therefore the *cognitive reward* is, paradoxically, a lack of cognitive activity, 'cognitive relaxation' that produces a relevant outcome.[11]

11 It may be, as Burkeman (2007) argues metaphorically, that we suffer a lag in which the slow horse of human comprehension is unable to keep up with the fast horse of the information that is available on the Net, and maybe dull websites are popular because they are a rebellion against information overload, a space for our slow horses to graze.

4. Concluding remarks

Relevance is a balance between the interest (cognitive effects) that information provides, basically through effective interactions of new information and contextual (manifest) information, and the mental effort that obtaining this interest demands. On paper, internet content and users' utterances that generate a high number of cognitive effects in exchange for little mental effort are bound to be highly relevant, thus the relevance equation for content on the Net should be clear-cut.

However, a number of elements can influence relevance outcomes (and, in parallel, relevance equations) affecting both variables: effects and effort. The former refers to what in this chapter has been labelled *cognitive rewards*, and comprises non-propositional effects such as empathy, ambient awareness, group membership, identity shaping, etc. The latter has to do with what has been given the label of (negative) *environmental constraints* (positive ones are also possible but are not addressed in this chapter), for instance familiarity with the software, position of the interface in different scales (oral/written, verbal/visual, etc.), frequency of use, etc.

The main conclusion is that any relevance equation that we apply to internet communication (and, to a greater or lesser extent, to any type of communication) should include an analysis of these aspects that generate alterations in the eventual validity of the relevance equation. In this chapter nine sample equations have been analysed. These are not exhaustive, nor are the range of *cognitive rewards* and *environmental constraints* that we can find in today's and tomorrow's internet communication.

5. References

Amichai-Hamburger, Yair, Or Kaynar, and Adi Fine, 'The effects of need for cognition on internet use', *Computers in Human Behavior* 23 (2007), 880–891.

Blumler, Jay G. and Elihu Katz, *The Uses of Mass Communication* (Newbury Park, CA: Sage, 1974).

Bodoff, David, 'Relevance for browsing, relevance for searching', *Journal of the American Society for Information Science and Technology* 57/1 (2006), 69–86.
Burkeman, Oliver, 'Brilliantly Boring'. *The Guardian* (3 April 2007, G2, 4–7).
Cacioppo, John T., and Richard E. Petty, 'The need for cognition', *Journal of Personality and Social Psychology* 42 (1982), 116–131.
Carston, Robyn, *Thoughts and Utterances* (Oxford: Blackwell, 2002).
Choo, Chun Wei, Brian Detlor, and Don Turnbull, 'Information seeking on the web: An integrated model of browsing and searching', *First Monday* 5/2 (2000).
Davis, Fred D., 'Perceived usefulness, perceived ease of use, and user acceptance of information technology', *MIS Quarterly* 13/3 (1989), 319–340.
Diderichsen, Philip, 'Augmented communication: The communicative potential of the internet', *Lund University Cognitive Studies* 132 (2006).
Hasan, Bassam, and Mesbah U. Ahmed, 'Effects of interface style on user perceptions and behavioral intention to use computer systems', *Computers in Human Behavior* 23 (2007), 3025–3037.
Johnson, G. M., 'Cognitive processing differences between frequent and infrequent internet users', *Computers in Human Behavior* 24 (2008), 2094–2106.
Murphy, Jamie, Charles Hofacker, and Richard Mizerski, 'Primacy and recency effects on clicking behavior', *Journal of Computer-Mediated Communication* 11 (2006), 522–535.
Sperber, Dan, and Deirdre Wilson, *Relevance: Communication and Cognition* (Oxford: Blackwell, 1986).
Sperber, Dan, and Deirdre Wilson, *Relevance: Communication and Cognition*, 2nd edition (Oxford: Blackwell, 1995).
Suler, John, 'Second life, second chance', in *The Psychology of Cyberspace.*
Sperber, Dan, and Deirdre Wilson, 'Pragmatics, modularity and mind-reading', *Mind and Language*, 17/1–2 (2002), 3–23.
Thompson, Clive, 'Brave new world of digital intimacy', *The New York Times Magazine* (5 September 2008).
Wilson, Deirdre, and Dan Sperber, 'Relevance theory', *UCL Working Papers in Linguistics* 14 (2002), 249–290.
Yus, Francisco, *Ciberpragmática. El uso del lenguaje en internet* (Barcelona: Ariel, 2001).
Yus, Francisco, 'Attitudes and emotions through written text: The case of textual deformation in internet chat rooms', *Pragmalingüística* 13 (2005), 147–174.
Yus, Francisco, 'Alterations of relevance in cyber-media', *Universitas Psychologica* 7/3 (2008), 623–636.
Yus, Francisco, *Ciberpragmática 2.0. Nuevos usos del lenguaje en internet* (Barcelona: Ariel, 2010).

BEATRIZ GALLARDO-PAÚLS AND VERÓNICA MORENO-CAMPOS

5 Linguistic Models in Learning Innovation Theories: Linear Approaches versus Interactive Practices

1. Introduction

In his 'Seven Complex Lessons in Education for the Future', Edgar Morin (1999: 39) mentioned two key elements of innovation: its inevitability and the need to integrate it into a given context in a sort of dynamic adaptation:

> L'inattendu nous surprend. C'est que nous nous sommes installés en trop grande sécurité dans nos théories et nos idées, et que celles-ci n'ont aucune structure d'accueil pour le nouveau. Or le nouveau jaillit sans cesse. On ne peut jamais le prévoir tel qu'il se présentera, mais on doit s'attendre à sa venue, c'est-à-dire s'attendre à l'inattendu. Et une fois l'inattendu survenu, il faudrait être capable de réviser nos théories et idées, plutôt que de faire entrer au forceps le fait nouveau dans la théorie incapable de vraiment l'accueillir.

Assuming this general approach, we will dedicate the chapter to revising the teaching and learning dimension that university educational innovation based on Information and Communication Technology (ICT) has to offer, with special focus on the linguistic model associated with it and the need to choose a model compatible with truly interactive teaching practices.

2. Educational innovation

A closer look at the concept of innovation from the business or the research and educational point of view allows us to identify three necessary elements:

- An element is needed that introduces *novelty* in a certain given process (moreover, intentional novelty).
- Such an element should imply some kind of progress or *improvement* (which results in greater usefulness).
- And such an improvement must bring *added value* to the process involved (for example higher profitability).

In the educational sphere, this progress and added value obviously aim at improving the students' learning. Fidalgo (2007) describes the innovative initiatives and their effect:

> At present, from the social point of view, the success of an educational process for students (and their parents) is passing the subject and the higher the grade, greater the success. Therefore, innovation must allow the student to get the same grade as he/she would without the innovation but with less effort, or to get a higher grade with the same effort. From the teacher's point of view, the grade reflects a student's acquisition of knowledge, abilities and capacities. Thus, innovation for a teacher would consist in the student's acquisition of knowledge, abilities and capacities related to the subject given. In doing that, if the student is also led to believe that it is something useful, that would be the greatest success imaginable. [our translation]

In the most widely used version of educational innovation, the novelty introduced in the teaching/learning processes usually consists of changes supported by ICT, although it is worth remembering that:

1. Innovation doesn't always involve ICT, and
2. ICT doesn't always involve innovation.

From a historiographic point of view it seems coherent to think that the appearance of information and communication technology might mean a turning point similar to the one signalled by Ong (1982) with the consecutive appearance of the printing press and audiovisual electronic technology. One can identify precedents in the medieval systematisation of knowledge, whose identification of the seven liberal arts (*Trivium* and *Quadrivium*) was linked, according to Casiodoro, to those that needed the technology of the *Liber* for their development. As in these situations (the book, the printing press, the media), we are at a crossroads where once again technology may lay the grounds for the new literacy, which, however, drags on cognitive factors:

> Digital literacy has a lot in common with its logical and linguistic colleague: the critical literacy. It consists of a set of tools, abilities and capacities that allow the manipulation of the design and not only to be manipulated by it. It is more than a simple defence; moreover it is a way to project our own intentions towards the world. It's not a matter of being taught by the world but about being taught through the process of acting on it. (Downes 2010: XI)

According to these criteria we define educational innovation as creativity applied to teaching/learning processes, with the active participation of students as an essential requirement, and in most cases with the concurrence of digital technology.

Educational action is, by definition, communicative and linguistic action. It is therefore relevant to consider what the linguistic model that underlies the description, proposal and design of educational innovation initiatives is. Digital technology simultaneously constitutes a scenario of both access to knowledge and communicative and informative saturation (Gergen 1984; the 'new abundancies', Reig 2010) that changes the concept of knowledge and, therefore, the social appreciation of actors such as 'student' and 'teacher'. With these being the two participating roles that define educational interaction, it is essential to link them to a specific linguistic-communicative model.

3. The technological diglossia of digital students

In order to analyse the predominant linguistic model in teaching proposals for educational innovation it is essential to know the presuppositions those proposals include regarding teachers and learners or, to be more precise, the prototypical representation of the communicative agents that make up teaching interaction.

In the 1960s when, thanks to the spread of tape recorders, discourse analysis studies began to develop, John Sinclair's group, as it is generally known, recorded classes in British schools. But the children and teachers that helped the Birmingham group set the grounds of discourse analysis are not the same as those that fill today's classrooms. On the contrary, those children may now be teachers themselves and teach students most of whom have never used a tape recorder but are experienced users of digital telephony, audio and video mechanisms. These teachers are facing the professional obligation that C. Wright (2008) describes in these terms: 'We have a responsibility to prepare them for their future, not our past'.

In our universities, the vast majority of students already belong to this generation of 'digital natives' (Prensky 2001a, 2001b), who communicate mostly through electronic devices and the internet, and whose teachers are basically, according to the same proposal, 'digital immigrants'. On the other hand, we have to consider that the 'digital' profile of present-day university students coincides from a sociological point of view with an essential change within the university itself: its transition to mass university. Ariño (2008: 19) has analysed this process of change and the protest discourse it causes among many teachers. Teachers complain of

> a change in the student profile, of a decrease in the academic level with which students gain access to university, especially so as regards expressive competence and willingness to read. However, regardless of whether or not such assertions are true, it is unquestionable that you don't go from 150,000 students to 1,500,000 without profound quantitative and qualitative changes in the social background and profiles of those receiving a university education. And very significantly in the implicit curricula of students. [our translation]

These implicit curricula are partly subject to the use of technology. Therefore, universities have to attend to an overcrowded and digital student body, to which the discourse on educational innovation attributes characteristics well-known since Prensky's proposal:

- They multitask.
- They possess great technological prowess.
- They are defiant, impatient.
- They are used to interactiveness.
- They are used to participating in virtual communities and to sharing information (P2P).
- Their habits privilege communication over information.
- They are accustomed to a diverse and multicultural environment.
- They are at ease in an audiovisual culture. They are visual learners.

As pointed out by Cerezo (2008), the vast majority of technological changes are led and promoted by digital immigrants; and the Spanish and European universities in general have been promoting the introduction of ICT in their classrooms for over a decade, with a very satisfying response. Hence, recently the 'native/immigrant' dichotomy has become a triad where 'digital migrants' (Piscitelli and Adaime 2010: XVII) represent an equidistant point between natives and immigrants. Nevertheless, as opposed to Prensky's description, many university students seem to identify themselves more with the portrait of the Google Generation painted by Cobo and Pardo (2007); these authors in 'Planeta 2.0' give them notoriously different traits, which may be related to the protest discourse mentioned by Ariño:

- *low comprehension* of accessed contents;
- *insufficient capacity to assert* the relevance of the on-line content;
- *unsophisticated mental maps* on how information on the Internet works;
- *ignorance* of how search engines work;
- there is no evidence to prove they are better *information managers* than those who were born 25 years before them.

This double characterisation, contradictory in appearance, emphasises the dissociation between the digital abilities students show outside the academic sphere and the scant application of such abilities when studying; and this dissociation, which may be considered a *technological diglossia* (much as Ferguson 1959), is born within the education system itself.

From childhood our society promotes the separation between the communicative and the technological abilities that belong to the academic sphere, and those that belong to the social sphere. Consequently, after going through primary and secondary school, the average student gains access to higher education without having had sufficient practice in digital and oral enough. On the one hand, this is due to models that privilege writing for student development that are still in place; on the other hand, because theories on learning based on competencies have not yet developed proposals that compactly integrate these three levels of academic literacy: speech, writing and digitalisation. However this integration is essential since these are clearly interdependent abilities. We recover here an interesting appreciation by Jenkins at al. (2006: 19) on the textual and linguistic abilities that digital literacy requires:

> Before students can engage with the new participatory culture, they must be able to read and write. Just as the emergence of written language changed oral traditions and the emergence of printed texts changed our relationships with written language, the emergence of new digital modes of expression changes our relationship to printed text. In some ways ... the new digital cultures provide support systems to help youth improve their core competences as readers and writers.

As we will see, the psychoeducational models governing certain academic spheres, based in turn on linear communicative (monologic) models and on modular neuropsychological models, facilitate the consolidation of this functional separation, a separation that notably hinders the new alphabetisations.

4. Linear elements in educational theories

By 'linear elements' we mean that an essential part of the psychoeducational discourse assumes communicative models which are not compatible with the interactive nature of the educational act. Although approaches centred on teaching staff and on a unidirectional transmission of the information being taught are criticised, the theory does not abandon certain elements which are inherent to this linear approach. To illustrate this, three elements are worth noting which contradict the interactive nature of teaching-learning processes:

- The technological conditioning of SCORM platforms.
- Instructional, prescriptive approaches of some theories on education.
- The theoretical ambiguity which characterises key ideas such as 'student centrality' or 'autonomous learning'.

One of the usual *clichés* when reflecting on educational technology refers to stances which seem to defend technology *per se*, accepting the use of technology as the new panacea against academic failure; as if merely adopting wikis, blogs and virtual platforms would bring on real educational change. On other occasions, it is the Information Technology which seems to determine the pedagogical approaches, with the imposition of engineering techniques and/or standardisation processes; thus, technology becomes a constrictive corset instead of a support tool for teaching. Adell, Bellver & Bellver (2008: 285) summarise this as 'a kind of terrible IT hegemony in an essentially pedagogical task'.

The technology behind Web 2.0 is a tool for the transmission/sharing of contents of an informative, competential, or procedural nature, in the absence of which the academic interaction is meaningless. As we all know, in the 2.0 model such contents can be contributed by any member of the process: the teacher who gives a lecture; the student who summarises an article from the bibliography; the group who does a presentation on a subject which has already been seen in class; the students who create a Wiki for the subject; their entries in the blog; the group who explains a lab practice session, etc. Therefore, the pragmatic notions of interaction, participation, and co-operation are essential and are not always taken into account in the design of digital educational platforms. As communication theorists emphasise, this interactivity is specific of the Web 2.0 and its applications, and it defines a series of prototypical activities which characterise the model.

In pragmatic terms, we may consider that Web 1.0 reproduced monologic, static models (speech act, intervention), while Web 2.0 suggests the praxis of an essentially conversational dialogue (exchange). However, this apparent emergence of interactive and dialogic models is hindered by the technological/pedagogical reality which constitutes the general framework. The SCORM model (Sharable Content Object Reference Model) which produced a great part of the theory on computer-aided education, originated as a military pedagogy (McGee & Green 2008; Adell, Bellver & Bellver 2008; Witthaus 2009; Adell 2009) which was designed based on the model of an isolated student, away from educational institutions. Such a model which, as denounced by Friesen in 2004, does not respond to the interactive and cooperative reality of secondary and university education, but to military logic: SCORM was financed by the White House and the US Department of Defense. We all know the statement made by Kraan, one of its creators (Whitthaus 2009):

> SCORM is not for everyone (...) SCORM is essentially about a single-learner, self-paced and self-directed. It has a limited pedagogical model unsuited for some environments. SCORM has nothing in it about collaboration. This makes it inappropriate for use in Higher Education and K-12.

Having the known characteristics of *accessibility, adaptability, affordability, durability, interoperability* and *reusability* does not guarantee the interactive, dynamic or relational nature of a technological model; quite the opposite, it can help to reinforce passive, static and linear teaching-learning paradigms. The teaching model underlying the SCORM technology is unidirectional, and describes a semiotic system of information exchange/

transmission, and not one of real communication. This model defines the virtual environment platforms which are generally used by universities (Virtual Learning Environment, VLE), but it does not allow the creation of real Personal Learning Environments (PLE). Witthaus (2009: 186) links this learning concept to behaviourist models:

> It should perhaps come as no surprise then, that many of SCORM's proponents promote a decidedly behaviourist view of learning. McGee and Green (2008) locate this approach within a Fordist view of the world, pointing to the emphasis on administrative control and the use of standardised, mass-produced courses. They note that this approach is clearly suited to the military, and possibly also to large corporate training departments in organisations that have 'command and control' style leadership.

The second characteristic of unidirectionality in pedagogical theories about university teaching is what Knight & Trowler (2000) identify as *prescription*. Beyond criticism from Radical Pedagogy (Giroux 1996), which insists on how new technology contributes to destabilise and redefine power relations in teaching, we can observe that, indeed, a part of the theoretical discourse on constructivist-based teaching innovation tends to be instructional (Ramsdem 1998): it gives teachers prescriptions without paying attention to the possible reactions and responses when trying to put them into practice. On the other hand, teachers in their daily teaching practice experience the need of contextual adaptation for any kind of innovation (Biggs & Tang 2003).

These are attempts to improve teaching by coercion, often oblivious of the operational reality of university and problems in their application: they merely state 'what teachers should do for their lesson to be successful' without really considering the restrictions of the specific context where the methods are implemented. This (hierarchical) prescriptive approach addresses the student, usually ignoring the fact that such a student is, in fact, another teacher (that is, a colleague): a frequently overlooked recursion which causes rejection in some teachers who, voluntarily, enrol in pedagogic training courses and workshops (Benedito & Imbernón 2006). Friesen's (2003) well known complaint regarding ineffectual technological proposals can also be applied to these discourses:

> Innovations are introduced into educational contexts and practices clearly bearing the stamp of their technical origin. Instead of being presented in terms familiar and meaningful to educators, they bear connotations that appear unclear or even negative in these practical contexts (...) It is not that the innovation should not come from outside of education, or that it can only come from within. It is simply that innovations must be presented in terms that are meaningful for teaching practice.

This discursive attitude may be due to the institutional origin (Top Down) of many of these training initiatives. Observe a typical example of what any well-meaning university teacher looking to improve their teaching techniques might find when resorting to the bibliography:

> Average university teachers (if we may call them that), have an extensive knowledge of their subject, but they are unable to effectively communicate it to their students, thus causing them not to receive significant learning experiences, since such teachers do not act as mediators in the educational act. It has been proven that the teaching-learning process is carried out effectively when a mediation is established by the teacher between the learning subject and the knowledge object. But, what happens if the teacher is incapable of accomplishing the mediator role? We don't mean to be negative, nor give biased opinions, but all one has to do is review the academic results of first-year students' in science degrees and one will know what to expect. (Ocaña, Quijano, Pérez & Vida, 2005)

This, unfortunately frequent, normative and instructive discourse also explains the current success of mentor programmes in university teacher training, which encourage a more horizontal and contextualised training relationship.

Thirdly, the monologic communicative model underlying a lot of pedagogical thinking is also conveyed in theories about the student's centrality and the importance of autonomous learning. Paraphrasing the motto of enlightened despotism, it could be stated that many texts seem to uphold the stance of 'everything for the student but without the student'. Obviously, nothing can be said against the student's centrality or to the shift from a teaching/teacher-centred model to a learning/student-centred one (Samuelowicz & Bain 1992, 2001). Nevertheless, and although it is stated that students are at the centre of the training process and it is assumed that they must be motivated and should obtain feedback during their learning activity (Biggs 2001; Alonso Tapia 2001; De Miguel 2004; Lucas 2007), nobody talks about the students' response to each attempt by the teacher at motivational and active involvement. The theoretical discourse lacks a real interactive approach. In pragmatic terms, we could say that the necessary steps from an enunciative pragmatic (speech act-centred) approach to an interactive pragmatic one (intervention and exchange-centred) aren't being taken. This may well be the most negative fallacy of the institutional pedagogical discourse on teaching innovation: while attempting to put students at the centre of the process, the theory is based solely on teachers' attitudes and behaviours, while also blaming and making them responsible (and blamed) for efficient learning. Similarly to Friesen (2003) who wondered, 'where is the learning in learning objects?' we wonder where the Learner is in some Learning theories.

We often witness how bibliography (or courses) on teaching innovation in Spanish universities present a student who is likened to a clean slate: with no past, since we know nothing of the *specific competencies* with which students gain access to higher education; and with no future, as employment observatories or even master's degrees are structurally dissociated from the degree itself. And almost with no present either, because the student is shown as a mere addressee of what teachers and the university may offer. See, for example, how students in the European Tuning Project appear as passive subjects (González & Wagenaar 2003: 59):

> The fundamental reason to undertake a project such as Tuning and, without a doubt, the great impulse which supports the Bologna-Prague process, is the conviction that young Europeans must be equipped culturally and intellectually in an innovative way, so that they can individually and collectively build their lives in a satisfactory and significant manner.

The aforementioned prescriptive discourse is finally completed with the concept of a passive student: with no individuality and no capacity for response, a simple recipient of the curricular design exuded from the Institutions. Some analyses have linked this student-type model to the differences between the European and the North American higher education systems:

> The student is to rise to a level of competence equal to the researcher who is 'leader,' 'guide,' but never 'teacher.' This tradition can be seen as a form of research apprenticeship, but with a freer relationship between professor and student than in the traditional master-apprentice relationship. (...). The student was considered to be an adult, and learned only by dint of self-education. In opposition to this tradition stands the American one, which in some respects may be seen as the blueprint of the Bologna-process, not only in its use of the Anglo-Saxon vocabulary 'bachelor,' 'master' and 'PhD' but also in its educational rationale. The American residential college has traditionally had a much stricter educational function, in loco parentis, than its European counterpart. (Eckhardt 2006: 309)

All the characteristics we mentioned: the disconnected concept of academic abilities (orality, writing, digital literacy), the linearity of the SCORM model, the prescriptive approaches of pedagogical thinking, and the consideration of the student as a mere passive recipient all contribute to create what we may describe as a static, unidirectional linguistic model. This model refers to the classical theories, both structuralist and generativist, which focus on the features of language assuming the perceptive polarity of signifier, speaker, and emission (vs. signified, hearer and reception), and also ignoring feedback.

As with many pre-pragmatic theoretical linguistic models, these teaching approaches maintain a linear and unidirectional view of human communication, which, at best, shows interaction as fixed stimulus-response patterns (Bloomfield, Skinner). These are stances which more or less explicitly accept the famous Saussurean description of the communicative fact (1916: 76–77), compatible with processes of successive transmission of information. This view of the communicative process is equally linear in Bloomfield's physico-mechanistic approaches, as well as in Chomsky's subsequent psycho-mentalistic approach, and Shanon and Weaver's classical model adapted by Jakobson: there is a source-transmitter (teachers), a message which is transmitted (contents), and an addressee-recipient (students), and these three basic functors have a sequential relationship; this model is implicit within educational theories about transfer of skills or competencies, but not contents. In other words, according to this model, the academic process is conceived of as information, not as communication; as a result, not as a process.

This monologic linguistic model, be it of structuralist or generativist origin, underlies some atomistic and modular approaches of learning and is often endorsed by psychological models of the cognitive-radical kind, that is, led by a predominant equally linear and encapsulated modularism (Minsky, Pinker, Hebb). Nonetheless, this radical interpretation of Fodorian modularism, assumed by Chomsky's Linguistics and by cognitive neuropsychology, is refuted by current research on neuronal functioning, which favours relations of reticular interconnection and simultaneity. Similarly, in communicative processing pragmatic models linked to the contextualised use of language prevail – as suggested by the different cognitive linguistics schools.

5. Interactive models of academic processes

Several proposals analyse teaching/learning processes from approaches compatible with the linguistic interaction and the communicative dynamism characteristic of natural languages. The theoretical paradigm which, in our opinion, best allows this task is Connectivism, developed mainly by George Siemens and Stephen Downes. These authors have developed Connectivism Theory when considering the effects of ICT on our way of life, on how we communicate and learn:

> At its heart, connectivism is the thesis that knowledge is distributed across a network of connections, and therefore that learning consists of the ability to construct and traverse those networks. (Downes 2007)

> Connectivism is the view that knowledge and cognition are distributed across networks of people and technology and learning is the process of connecting, growing, and navigating those networks. (Siemens & Tittenberger 2009: 11)

In keeping with the pedagogical theories which suggest shifting the emphasis from teaching to learning, connectivism involves a review of the traditional roles in the academic process (Downes 2007), a review which actually describes a model of an active student, parallel to that of the teacher: 'To teach is to "model" and to "demonstrate". To learn is to "practice" and "reflect"' (Downes 2008). 'Teachers are nodes, students are nodes. Both teaching and learning consists of sending and receiving communications to other nodes' (Downes 2009).

The teachers' function is inserted in a communicative, interactive context, with two basic aims:

- To guide students in their own process of searching for information and knowledge.
- To demonstrate, namely, to connect the learner with the community at work.

Moreover, the description of the student's role (what Ariño called 'the craft of studying') is emphasised from that same interactive viewpoint. Its objectives are collaborative learning and critical thinking; it suggests an emphasis on pattern recognition and experiential learning as opposed to an emphasis on rules and contents. With this approach, the requirements on students are greater first, their active implication, instead of passive observation/memorisation; secondly, critical thinking regarding contents; and thirdly, their responsibility to freely design their own learning itineraries (to individually decide, as when you follow the links on a web page). This approach truly describes 'student-centred learning'; thus, the issue of digital literacy is conceived as part of academic literacy. As we mentioned before, new information and communication technology outlines the list of competencies of new alphabetisations, which are necessarily linked to information processing (searching, accessing, reutilisation, interpretation, assessment, organisation, integration, analysis, synthesis and dissemination; Padilla & Douglas 2010).

A recurrent idea in these approaches to digital literacy is that digital technology is not the end, but the means. The purpose of compulsory education is to train students in the skills of the twenty-first century which, although partly justified by the emergence of digital technology, have social and cognitive dimensions that go beyond the purely technological sphere. The usual lists include Communication, Innovation, Creativity, Problem

Solving, Interactivity, Collaboration and Critical Thinking. For Siemens & Tittenberger (2009: 28) these required skills suggest multiple literacy which points in turn to information management skills (anchoring, filtering, connecting, interacting, creating and deriving meaning, critical and creative thinking, contextualising, etc.).

The communicative model underlying the connectivist proposals and the new alphabetisations is essential insofar as it determines the possible roles of teachers and students and, in consequence, learning models. The technological resource which complements these skills is Web X.0, which Downes himself (2010b) describes as follows:

> The idea of Web X is that it combines web 2.0 (social web) and web 3.0 (semantic web) to create what I have called, in the past, the semantic social web. But it's more than just that, because it takes these and moves them off the web and into your hand. And more than just that, because it's the web of data, the geoweb, augmented media, the 3D web, and more. The eXtended web – the web, extended from the internet, into your life.

In contrast to theoretical stances that focus on a passive student, with neither initiative nor answers, Connectivism assumes explicitly interactive and conversational approaches, which culminate in the concepts of 'Web 3.0' or 'Semantic Web' and, more recently, 'Pragmatic Web' (Singh 2002; Moravec 2008; Wheeler 2010):

- Web 1.0: the Web = Syntactic Web: anything can link to anything
- Web 2.0: Social Web: user participation
- Web 3.0: Semantic Web = Data Web: 'existing data re-connected for other (smarter) users' (Wheeler 2010).
- Web X.0: Meta Web = Semantics Social Web = Pragmatic Web = xWeb: 'xWeb is the utilization of smart, structured data drawn from our physical and virtual interactions and identities to extend our capacity to be known by others and by systems.' (Siemens 2010). That means it brings Artificial Intelligence to information management.

6. Conclusion

The effective development of educational innovation proposals must be carried out from theoretical standpoints compatible with the interactive reality of the teaching/learning processes, while bearing in mind the characteristics of the current university student body: overcrowded and accustomed to the use of technology in their extracurricular activities.

Too often we encounter theoretical stances which try to describe (and prescribe) educational innovation from the point of view of static, linear approaches, compatible with the teaching practices witnessed by Behaviourism, Radical Cognitivism or Constructivism theorists. It has been adduced that the linguistic model underlying these educational psychological theories refers to unidirectional descriptions where successiveness prevails over simultaneousness, and the transmission of information over communication (Saussure, Chomsky, Pinker, Jakobson), and where there is no feedback. Three well-known elements of the institutional discourse on educational innovation have been mentioned to explain this situation: the predominance of SCORM technology, designed for computer receptive (not interactive) use; the prescriptive attitudes regarding teachers; and the apparent centrality of a student which is described as passive.

However, classrooms and students have changed. Even the teaching staff has changed and such changes have been boosted by the emergence of digital technology. One theoretical proposal among those which can actually account for teaching based on learning and on a truly interactive didactic relationship, has been highlighted: Connectivism. This theory assumes truly pragmatic-linguistic-communicative approaches, capable of adding the addressee's variables to the theoretical description, which is what in fact characterises interactive pragmatics.

In short, theories on educational innovation have to take into account pragmatic linguistic approaches that are able to integrate the interactive communicative processes, as well as the capabilities of digital communication and the variables defined by the type of student. The following quote from Siemens (2004) connects with the needed change of paradigm requested by Morin at the beginning of this essay:

Many important questions are raised when established learning theories are seen through technology. The natural attempt of theorists is to continue to revise and evolve theories as conditions change. At some point, however, the underlying conditions have altered so significantly, that further modification is no longer sensible. An entirely new approach is needed.

7. References

Adell, Jordi, 'La competencia digital, 2007', *Averroes. Red Temática Educativa de Andalucía* <http://www.juntadeandalucia.es/averroes/mochiladigital/didactica/Adell_competencia_digital.pdf> accessed 3 August 2010.

——, 'Los repositorios de Objetos Digitales: luces y sombras', *I Jornadas Interuniversitarias Valencianas sobre Acceso Abierto al Conocimiento*, 24 de marzo de 2009.

——, and Bellver, Antoni, and Bellver, Carles, 'Entornos virtuales de aprendizaje y estándares de e-learning", in César, Coll & Carles, Monereo, eds, *Psicología de la educación virtual* (Madrid: Morata, 2008), 274–298.

Alonso Tapia, Jesús, 'Motivación y estrategias de aprendizaje: Principios para su mejora en alumnos universitarios', in A. García and V. Muñoz, eds, *Didáctica Universitaria* (Madrid: La Muralla, 2001).

Ariño, Antonio, 'El compromiso flexible', in Ariño et al., *El oficio de estudiar en la universidad: compromisos flexibles* (Valencia: PUV, 2008).

Benedito, Vicente, and Imbernón, Francisco, 'La formación en docencia universitaria, asignatura pendiente', *Universitas Tarraconensis. Revista de Ciències de l'Educació* (2006), 15–24.

Biggs, John, 'The Reflective Institution: Assuring and Enhancing the Quality of Teaching and Learning', *Higher Education* 41/3 (2001), 221–238.

——, and Tang, Catherine, *Teaching for Quality Learning at University* (Buckingham: The Society for Research into Higher Education and Open University Press, 2003).

Capdet, Dolors, 'Visualización de un PLE', *I Trobades d'Innovació Educativa*, Universitat de València, 7–8 July 2010.

Cerezo, José M., 'Hacia un nuevo paradigma: la era de la información fragmentada', *TELOS 76*, 2008.

Cobo, Cristóbal and Pardo, Hugo, *Planeta 2.0. Inteligencia colectiva o medios Fast-food* (2007) <http://www.flacso.edu.mx/planeta/> accessed 24 January 2011.

De Miguel, Mario, 'La calidad y la docencia universitaria', *III Jornades sobre Convergència Europea: Promoure la docència i l'aprenentatge per transformar la Universitat, 2004.*

Downes, Stephen, 'New tools for personal learning' (2009) <http://www.downes.ca/cgi-bin/page.cgi?presentation=234> accessed 24 January 2011.

——, 'Personal Learning' (2008) <http://www.downes.ca/presentation/179> accessed 24 January 2011.

——, 'Prólogo', in Alejandro, Piscitelli, Adaime, Iván, and Inés, Binder, eds, *El proyecto Facebook y la posuniversidad. Sistemas operativos sociales y entornos abiertos de aprendizaje* (Barcelona: Ariel /Telefónica, 2010a), I–XIII.

——, 'Web 3.0: The Way forward?' (2010b) <http://www.downes.ca/cgi-bin/page.cgi?post=52864> accessed 24 January 2011.

——, 'What Connectivism Is' (2007), <http://halfanhour.blogspot.com/2007/02/what-connectivism-is.html> accessed 24 January 2011.

Eckhardt, Larsen, Jesper, 'The Role of Humanities in the Bologna Idea of a University: Learning from the American Model?', *Revista Española de Educación Comparada*, 12 (2006), 309–327.

Ferguson, Charles, 'Diglossia', *Word*, 15 (1959), 324–40.

Fidalgo, Ángel, 'Qué es la innovación educativa' (2007) <http://innovacioneducativa.wordpress.com/2007/01/09/¿que-es-innovacion-educativa/> accessed 24 January 2011.

Friesen, Norm, 'Three Objections to Learning Objects and E-learning Standards' (2003), <http://www.learningspaces.org/n/papers/objections.html> accessed 24 January 2011.

——, 'Three Objections to Learning Objects and E-learning Standards', in R. McGreal, ed., *Online Education Using Learning Objects* (London: Routledge, 2004).

Gallardo-Paúls, Beatriz, 'Docencia y libre acceso: el Open Course Ware de la Universitat de València', *@tic.revista d'innovació educativa*, 1(2008), 16–25. <http://ojs.uv.es/index.php/attic/article/view/45/39> accessed 24 January 2011.

Gargallo, Bernardo, 'Estilos de docencia y evaluación de los profesores universitarios y su influencia sobre los modos de aprender de sus estudiantes', *Revista española de pedagogía*, 66/241 (2008), 425–446.

Gergen, Keneth, *El yo saturado. Dilemas de identidad en el mundo contemporáneo* (Barcelona: Paidós, 1996).

Giroux, Henry A., *Cultural Studies and Critical Pedagogies in Postmodern Spaces* (Nueva York: Routledge, 1996).

González, Julia, and Wagenaar, Robert, *Tuning Educational Structures in Europe, Informe Final, Fase I.* Univ. de Deusto, 2003.

Jenkins, Henry, Purushotma, Ravi, Clinton, Katherine, Weigel, Margaret, and Robinson, Alice J., *Confronting the Challenges of Participatory Culture: Media Education for the 21st Century* (Chicago: MacArthur Foundation, 2006) <http://digitallearning.macfound.org/atf/cf/{7E45C7E0-A3E0-4B89-AC9C-E807E1B0AE4E}/JENKINS_WHITE_PAPER.PDF> accessed 24 January 2011.

Knight, Peter, and Trowler, Paul, 'Department-level cultures and the improvement of learning and teaching', *Studies in Higher Education* 25/1 (2000), 69–83.

Lucas, Susana, 'Desarrollo de las competencias "preocupación por la calidad" y "motivación del logro" desde la docencia universitaria', *Red U. Revista de Docencia Universitaria*, 2 (2007) <http://www.um.es/ead/Red_U/2/lucas.pdf> accessed 24 January 2011.

McGee, Patricia, and Green, Marybeth, 'Lifelong learning and systems: A post-Fordist analysis', *MERLOT Journal of Online Learning and Teaching*, 4/2 (2008), 146–157.

Moravec, John, 'Moving beyond Education 2.0' (2008)<http://www.educationfutures.com/2008/02/15/moving-beyond-education-20/>.

Morin, Edgar, *Les sept savoirs nécessaires à l'éducation du futur* (Unesco, 2009).

Ocaña Moral, Mª. T., Quijano López, R., Pérez Ferra, M., and Vida Sagrista, L. C., 'El docente en la universidad: ¿cómo enseñar cuando no te han enseñado a hacerlo?'. *Educaweb.com* 108, junio de 2005. <http://www.educaweb.com/esp/servicios/monografico/docencia/> accessed 24 January 2011.

Ong, Walter J., (1982). *Oralidad y escritura. Tecnologías de la palabra* (México: Siglo XXI, 1997).

Padilla, Constanza; Douglas, Silvina and López, Esther, 'Argumentative Skills in Academic Literacy', @tic. revista d'innovació educativa, 2010 <http://ojs.uv.es/index.php/attic/article/view/177/208> accessed 5 August 2010.

Piscitelli, Alejandro, Adaime, Iván, and Binder, Inés, eds, *El proyecto Facebook y la posuniversidad. Sistemas operativos sociales y entornos abiertos de aprendizaje* (Barcelona: Ariel /Telefónica, 2010).

Prensky, Marc, 'Digital natives, digital immigrants', *On the Horizon*, 9/5 (2001a), 1–6.

——, 'Digital natives, digital immigrants part II: Do they really think differently?', *On the Horizon*, 9/5 (2001b), 7–9.

Ramsden, Paul, *Learning to Lead in Higher Education* (London: Routledge, 1998).

Reig, Dolors, 'Abundancia y educación en la sociedad en red', 2010 <http://www.slideshare.net/dreig/abundancia-y-educacin-en-la-sociedad-red> accessed 29 January 2011.

Samuelowicz, K., and Bain, J. D., 'Conceptions of teaching held by academic teachers'. *Higher Education*, 22 (1992), 229–249.

——, 'Revisiting academics' beliefs about teaching and learning'. *Higher Education*, 41 (2001), 299–325.

Saussure, Ferdinand de, *Curso de lingüística general*, Trans. Amado Alonso (Madrid: Alianza, 1983 [1916]).

Siemens, George, 'Connectivism: a Learning Theory for the Digital Age', 2004 <http://www.elearnspace.org/Articles/connectivism.htm> accessed 29 July 2010.

——, 'Education: An Ecology of Connections', 2008 <http://www.slideshare.net/courosa/george-siemens-at-tlt> accessed 28 January 2011.

——, 'xWeb', 2010, <http://www.connectivism.ca/?p=264>.

——, and Tittenberger, Peter, *Handbook of Emerging Technologies for Learning*, 2009, <http://umanitoba.ca/learning_technologies/cetl/HETL.pdf> accessed 28 January 2011.

Singh, Munidar, 'The Pragmatic Web: Preliminary Thoughts', *Proceedings of the NSF – OntoWeb Workshop on Database and Information Systems Research for Semantic Web and Enterprises* (2002), 82–90.

Trigwell, K., 'Judging university teaching', *The International Journal for Academic Development* 6/1 (2001), 65–73.

Weinberger, David, 'Small pieces loosely joined. A unified theory of the web', 2005 <http://www.smallpieces.com/> accessed 27 July 2010.

Wheeler, Stephen, 'Web 3.0: The way forward?', 2010 <http://www.slideshare.net/timbuckteeth/web-30-the-way-forward> accessed 28 January 2011.

Witthaus, Gabrielle, 'The Implications of SCORM Conformance for Workplace e-Learning', *Electronic Journal of e-Learning*, 7/2 (2009), 183–190.

Wright, Cindy, 'Changing Education with Web 2.0 Tools', 2008 <http://www.slideshare.net/lwright3768/changing-education-with-web-20-tools> accessed 28 January 2011.

FRANÇOISE SALAGER-MEYER

6 Interdisciplinarity and Languages for Specific Purposes in Latin America

1. Introduction

Latin America is a huge continent with very heterogeneous countries, each having its own very specific problems. Given the extension of the continent and of the subject I was asked to write about – interdisciplinarity and Languages for Specific Purposes (LSP) in Latin America – it would be very pretentious for me to say that this paper will present a state of the art of the LSP situation in the region. Nevertheless, the issues that I will address hereafter certainly reflect the problems that have been and still are of concern to most Latin American LSP practitioners throughout the region. In the first part of this chapter, I will refer to the genesis of the ESP movement in Latin America. I shall then specifically deal with LSP teaching and with LSP research that has recently been and is currently being carried out in different Latin American countries. I will end this chapter by referring to a project that is presently going on between the Latin American and Caribbean countries on the one hand, and the European Union, on the other.

2. The ESP movement: Its genesis and development

A question is in order here. Can we really refer to *Languages* for Specific Purposes in Latin America when, in the immense majority of the cases, the *only* language that is taught as a foreign language – and, much more so when the language is taught for 'specific purposes' – is English? Indeed, English has a long tradition in the curricula of the different Latin American countries and, in spite of the fact that, according to current education policies and official documents, schools are free to choose at least one among several foreign languages to be part of their curricula – a language which will, in turn, be a compulsory subject in the elementary and secondary school curricula – English is the chosen one.

At the tertiary level, the situation changes slightly. English may be a compulsory or an optional subject depending on the field of specialism (for example, in disciplines such as hotel industry, tourism and computing, English is generally a compulsory subject matter) or in the institutions themselves that may choose to have or not to have a foreign language at all in their curricula.

In Latin America, ESP appeared in the late 1970s as a reaction to the needs of specialised courses for various university departments (cf. Holmes 1985; Celani et al 1988; Celani et al. 2005; Holmes and Celani 2006; Ramos 2008; Balsemao et al. 2008; among others). Indeed, the demands from some pure and applied science departments at Latin American universities for specialised English courses started putting pressure on English departments that then felt obliged to show interest in ESP. In Brazil, as Ramos (2008) reports, these factors, together with the number of request for advice on the design and implementation of ESP courses from universities throughout the national territory, made Professor María Antonieta Alba Celani (then the Coordinator of the Applied Linguistics Program at the Catholic University of Sao Paulo) design a project at national level. A bid was then put in to the Brazilian Ministry of Education for financial support in 1977.

A wide range of need analyses studies were then carried out throughout the continent, the results of which showed the necessity for teacher development, materials production, the teaching of reading skills of paramount importance for students and researchers who had to read academic literature, and the setting of a Brazilian resource center. The methodology used in these courses emphasised the use of authentic texts and the teaching and learning of reading strategies. The Brazilian ESP Project provided conditions to optimise the teaching and learning of reading in a foreign language for students who needed to develop such a skill not only in English but also in Portuguese, as was found afterwards. After almost thirty years, this is still the preferred reading course throughout the country and the one that has been adopted in other Latin American countries (cf. Celani 2008).

But an examination of the academic world reveals several changes that have been going on since the implementation of these ESP courses that mainly focused on general reading comprehension. Indeed, today students need to not only read but also to *write* a much wider range of different *genres*, such as academic and research articles, academic textbooks, dissertations, theses, review articles, abstracts. And they also need to develop skills to search for support materials on the Internet, to present papers orally, to attend lectures and deliver oral presentations in English, etc. In other words, students now need new kinds of courses. Let us examine, then, the teaching situation.

3. LSP and interdisciplinarity: The teaching situation

Most major universities in Latin America offer ESP courses in various schools (social sciences, hard sciences, engineering, law, medicine, etc). In *Central America*, for example, ESP *teaching* is, due to lack of research funds, the main ESP activity. What is more, most ESP practitioners in public universities[1] write their own materials. In Nicaragua, for instance, the UNAN offers English in all engineering disciplines, in computer science and in architecture. In San Salvador, ESP per se is only taught at the business school and in tourism, whereas in Guatemala, there are a few language courses in engineering, agronomy, medicine, dentistry and political sciences. At the University of Costa Rica, ESP is taught in engineering and computer sciences. In all these cases –except tourism – courses are scientific English *reading* comprehension courses.

1 The situation of *private* universities is quite different. In some instances indeed, courses are entirely taught in English, for example in business schools.

In the particular field of EMP (English for Medical Purposes), Venezuela and Cuba are quite strong. EMP is indeed taught at various medical schools in Venezuela (at the pre- and postgraduate levels). In Cuba, the Ministry of Public Health takes complete responsibility for all medical education, including English language training for its undergraduates and doctors (Maclean et al. 2000). The English language teachers in every medical school are employed by the Ministry of Public Health, and it is the Ministry of Public Health – not the Ministry of Education – that is responsible for their professional development. An oral approach is instituted for all five years of the medical undergraduate curriculum.

It is important to remark here that a major step in EMP teaching in Cuba was the establishment in 1989 of a link with a professional and academic institution abroad: the Institute for Applied Language Studies (IALS) of the University of Edinburgh, Scotland, which has specific experience in the field of medical English as well as a wide teacher education expertise. IALS used to provide two scholarships every summer for Cuban teachers to attend a range of short teacher education courses in Edinburgh on general communicative methodology, principles of ESP and EMP. Additionally it was agreed that IALS staff would visit Cuba, if possible every year, to run workshops. A similar project is now running with the University of Westminster (UK), London providing Master's degrees and summer courses to Cuban Medical English teachers working at the Havana Medical Science University, and some of the University of Westminster staff has visited Cuba to run workshops since the year 2000.

The first two scholars attended courses in the summer of 1990, and, on their return to Cuba, immediately gave workshops to colleagues, presenting their own blends of materials collected at the Edinburgh courses. No specific funding was granted for carrying out these workshops in different parts of the country. As Maclean et al (2000) remark, this method of disseminating information has been used in Cuba since the 1960s, notably in the 1961 literacy campaign, where everyone over the age of fifteen who knew how to read and write taught those who did not. Since then, the technique has been used in Cuba for all kinds of professional training (Maclean et al. 2000). The La Havana Medical Science University has closed ties too with the University of Valencia (Spain): together they recently ran a project to develop ESP teaching at the University of León (Nicaragua).

Like their colleagues in Nicaragua or El Salvador, most Cuban ESP practitioners – especially those in the field of medicine, nursing, dentistry and health technologies – produce their own materials, including CDs and videos. Moreover, the ESP Cuban community has its own journal, called *Approach. A Journal of Foreign Language Teaching in Cuba*, published by the Linguists Cuban Association (ALC-GELI which stands for *Asociación de Linguistas de Cuba, Grupo de Especialistas en Lengua Inglesa*).

In the *online* context, some courses have been emerging, especially in Brazil: an ESP course for the reading of academic texts and digital journal abstracts for medicine professionals has recently started being offered at the Catholic University of São Paulo as extra-mural studies courses. More recently the ESP research group that belongs to the Post Graduate Applied Linguistics Program at Catholic University of São Paulo developed an ESP Teacher Development Project. This project was funded by Vitae, an international agency operating in Brazil, and the Catholic University of São Paulo. The local British Council also took part and offered a grant-in-aid for a project evaluation consultant. The project is being developed in six Brazilian Federal Technological Centers (CEFETs) located in the various regions of Brazil and aims at providing technological knowledge, digital literacy and knowledge of the ESP approach for the local English teams that will then be able to offer consultancy in ESP and online ESP teacher development courses for other centers in their regions (Ramos et al. 2006, 2008).

Regarding *scientific writing courses*, they are sometimes taught especially in science faculties, but these are still isolated cases. I personally believe that their frequency should be much greater in order to allow Latin American researchers to participate in the worldwide dialogue of science. Iliana Martínez (2002) for example, reports her experience in EAP in a course on academic writing for researchers and doctoral candidates of the experimental sciences, taught at the National University of Río Cuarto (Argentina), and other universities in the country since 1996. The course, described in detail in Martínez (2002) and updated yearly, aims at developing genre awareness, leading to writing research for publication in English-medium indexed journals. In the course, awareness is raised at three levels: cultural, rhetorical, and linguistic. The cultural level is informed by the contributions of New Rhetoric (e.g. Bazerman 1988; Berkenkotter &

Huckin 1995; Miller 1994; Myers 1996); the rhetorical level is based on the contributions of the school of English for Specific Purposes (ESP) (e.g. Brett 1994; Dudley-Evans 1994; Swales 1990; 1996; 2004) and the linguistic level draws on contributions of different schools, such as Systemic Functional Linguistics, ESP, and corpus linguistics (e.g. Halliday 1993; Hyland 2000, 2005; Martínez 2001, 2002, 2003, 2005, 2008; Martínez et al. 2009; Salager-Meyer 1994; Thompson & Ye 1991).

Unfortunately, as Vasconcelos (2007a, 2007b, 2008) argues, developing competence for writing research papers is not part of the academic tradition of most Latin American universities, and funding to provide writing support for Latin American scientists is scarce. Vasconcelo's data indicate that language matters in Brazilian science matters, and they point to a linguistic handicap that has been – and still is – largely overlooked. This is why that Brazilian author believes – as many others do – that improving the number of researchers who are fully proficient in English might help to enhance international awareness of the Latin American region's scientific contributions.

4. LSP and interdisciplinarity: The research situation

Most major universities in Latin America conduct research in *English-* and, to a lesser extent (in the case of Brazil), *Spanish for specific purposes.* Since there is no room here to mention every single investigator, I shall mention only the most relevant research that has been conducted in the last five years or so.

Let us start with the course design-oriented research. In the *occupational/professional* context, several rather recent investigations have been conducted in the areas of tourism (Sprenger 1997; Belmonte 2003), hotel tourism (Cardoso 2003; Gomes 2003), bilingual executive secretary courses (Araújo 1999; Pinto 2002), international commerce (Gomes 1998); technology (Vaccari 2004) and publicity (Quaresma 2005). The main focus of these investigations is *needs analysis* involving graduate students taking these courses, teachers, coordinators, heads of departments, as well as the market to map the target and learning needs of these different target groups and situations so that the results might serve as guidelines for the design and implementation of ESP courses.

In relation to the *business* context, some relevant studies conducted in Brazil must be mentioned. These either focus on the design of courses for major Brazilian banks focusing on the students' communicative needs based on genre or on the design of online business course tackling the issue of an ongoing negotiated syllabus (Weyersbach 2002).

Other research (e.g., Acosta 2000; Costa 2002) investigates representations that professionals have in their workplace about the role of English and the teaching and learning of English as a foreign language. Other studies deal with business discourse per se (Ramos 1994a, 1994b, 1997; Santos 1996, 2002). The topics investigated are related to the construction and projection of the image of international companies, culture-related issues, and the identification of electronic and printed documents that are circulated in different companies.

This kind of research provides empirical data that have been, and still are, of great assistance for ESP practitioners to design courses that mirror the kind of tasks required of students in their future professional contexts. Its findings also provide knowledge about different target situations and authentic documents that may be used to produce appropriate materials and more realistic activities to be performed in the classroom.

The other kind of LSP research that is being conducted in the continent focuses on genre/scientific/academic discourse analysis. One of the most productive groups regarding *Spanish* for Specific Purposes is that of Adriana Bolívar from the Venezuelan Central University who has published quite extensively in the field of reading and writing at the university level (<http://www.catedraunescoucv.blogspot.com>), linking this to the teaching of reading and writing at the secondary school level. Bolívar also worked a lot in the field of political discourse and in academic discourse analysis in general (Bolívar 2004, 2006, 2008, 2009; Beke and Bolívar 2009; Bolívar et al. 2010 to name just a few of the group's most recent publications).

Another productive group in Spanish for Specific Purposes is that coordinated by Guiomar Elena Ciapuscio from Buenos Aires University (cf. Ciapuscio 2003a, 2003b, 2003c, 2007, 2009; Ciapuscio et al. 2002, 2005). She and her group also conduct research into French and German Scientific/academic discourse (cf. <http://www.dissoc.org/dissoc/comite>). Ciapuscio has published quite extensively too in the field of scientific popularisation, the use of metaphors in oral and written scientific discourse and scientific terminology, the purpose of this latter field being the production of specialised dictionaries and glossaries to assist translators and interpreters.

Academic and scientific discourse is also one of the main foci of Anamaría Harvey from the University of Santiago de Chile (cf. <http://www.dissoc.org/dissoc/comite>) and of Alma Ortiz from the National Autonomous University of Mexico (UNAM) whose research objective is more precisely to evaluate reading comprehension in different academic disciplines (cf. <http://dla.cele.unam.mx/evaluacion/contenido/EVAproyectos2.html>).

In the field of *medicine* per se, we could start by citing several Brazilian studies (e.g., Carvalho 2003), the objective of which is either to investigate the Portuguese-speaking audience's listening comprehension of research articles being presented at congresses (the aim of that research is to develop courses and materials in listening and writing in this area) or to describe the rhetorical organisation of oral (medical) presentations delivered in English by Spanish-and Portuguese-speaking scientists. Some research is also concerned with needs analysis of postgraduate medical students to help them to find the genres they need most in their areas of specialism in order to design more appropriate academic reading courses (Ramos, Lima-Lopes and Gazotti-Vallim 2004).

Venezuela is also strong in medical discourse analysis. As a matter of fact, the activities of the Scientific Discourse Analysis Research Group of the University of the Andes (Mérida) are entirely devoted to the diachronic (nineteenth, twentieth and twenty-first centuries), cross-linguistics (mostly Spanish, French and English) and cross-generic (research and review articles, editorials and case reports) analysis of medical discourse. Some of the most recent research results can be found in Salager-Meyer (2008, 2009) and Salager-Meyer et al. (2003, 2009). The Group is currently working – together with the University of Catamarca (Argentina, see Horsella and Llopis de Segura 2005 and Llopis 2008) – on the analysis of acknowledgments – seen from the various abovementioned perspectives – in written medical discourse. No research, though, has been conducted on *oral* medical discourse, very likely because that kind of research requires more sophisticated equipment than research conducted into written materials.

Research into *political* discourse is thriving as well, especially that conducted at the Universidad Central de Venezuela under the direction of Adriana Bolívar (2008, 2009) and that carried out by Alejandro Raiter and Laura Pardo (<http: //www.filo.uba.ar/contenidos/carreras/letras/catedras/>) from Buenos Aires University (Argentina), by Teresa Carbo from Mexico and Leda Berardi Drudi from Chile (cf. <http://www.dissoc.org/dissoc/comite/>).

We cannot mention discourse analysis without referring to Federico Navarro's discourse-oriented blog (<http//:discurso.wordpress.com>) that provides an extremely rich array of discourse-related news (congresses to be held, on-going research projects, Spanish and Latin American research groups, recently published books, databases, Latin American researchers' interests and links, dictionaries and encyclopedias and a very useful list of discourse-related publications written in Spanish and in English). From my standpoint, this blog is a 'must' for all those who are interested in what is going on not only in Argentina but also in Latin America as far as discourse studies are concerned (see also Navarro 2006, 2008 and Vallejos Llobet 2002a, 2002b, 2006).

The previously mentioned research, experiments and efforts delineate the urgency of a certain number of steps those who work with LSP should undertake in the continent:

- conduct new surveys and implement needs analyses that would focus on ESP listening and writing skills.
- produce teaching materials, since even if there are materials available on the market for many of the areas mentioned above (Tourism or Business, for example), it is well known that they do not attend the specificities and peculiarities of certain groups.

- elaborate materials for situations that require computer-mediated communication.
- design (on-line) scientific writing courses because Latin American researchers are evaluated by the number of their citations and publications in internationally-indexed (i.e., English-medium) journals and the 'publish or perish' principle is a constant menace over their heads. We all know that writing scientific articles in English is not a simple matter: it involves not only linguistic and rhetorical aspects but also power negotiation issues (Swales 1990; Myers 1990). What is more, in certain Latin American countries national language scientific journals have switched to English. This is the case of *Ciência e Cultura* (Science and Culture), the journal of the largest Brazilian scientific association, the Brazilian Society for the Advancement of Science.[2]

I would like to close this section by mentioning that Latin America has an ESP journal of its own that was created in 1983, during the ESP 'boom' in the region. It is called '*The ESPecialist*' and is published by the Reading Research Information Center of the Pontifícia University of Sao Paulo (Brazil). It publishes articles and research notes related to questions concerned with LSP in general (practical and theoretical issues alike). Languages for contributions may be English, Portuguese, French and Spanish.

5. The European Union and the Latin American/ Caribbean region

I would like to end this chapter about LSP/ESP and interdisciplinarity in Latin America by referring to a much wider project called NECOBELAC, which stands for *Network of Collaboration Between Europe and*

2 A considerable number of Brazilian journals publish articles written in English only. Among them, we can mention the *Journal of the Brazilian Chemical Society*, the *Journal of the Brazilian Computer Society*, the *Brazilian Journal of Chemical Engineering*, etc. (cf. Menezes de Oliveira e Paiva and Pagano 2001).

Latin American-Caribbean Countries. The project started in February 2009 and will last three years. It is a European project that aims at improving the production and dissemination of scientific information in public health. It is coordinated by the *Instituto Superiore di Sanità* (*ISS*), Rome, and funded under the 7th Framework Program of the European Commission.

The project aims at establishing a network of collaboration between European countries (EU) and countries in Latin America and the Caribbean (LAC) to spread knowledge on the methods of scientific writing and publishing and on appropriate tools for the open access dissemination of information for the protection of public health (cf. de Castro et al. 2009a and 2009b, Pulido et al. 2009, among others).

NECOBELAC partners include *Istituto Superiore di Sanità* (ISS) from Italy, *Consejo Superior de Investigaciones Científicas* (CSIC) from Spain, the University of Nottingham, *SHERPA* from the UK, *BIREME* from Brazil, the *Instituto de Salud Publica* (ISP) from Colombia, the *Universidade do Minho* (UMINHO) from Portugal.

The project will benefit from European and LAC experiences and take into account different socio-cultural scenarios. The health information needs of the areas involved will contribute to stress the importance of creating awareness of document and data diffusion at different levels. A network of institutions was created to collaborate in ad hoc training programmes in information production and dissemination, including technical and ethical issues, among all stakeholders.

It is hoped that NECOBELAC will foster the coordination and effectiveness of the existing health-related information infrastructures in Europe and LAC countries to achieve a wider scale uptake of community engagement, embedding the use of open access methods within accepted working practices. The project languages are English, Italian, Portuguese, Spanish, and the European Union financial support amounts to 800,000 Euros.

6. Conclusion

The panorama sketched above clearly shows that LSP teaching and research are still alive and well in Latin America, especially in regard to occupational and academic courses. Indeed, apart from the strictly ESP reading comprehension courses that are still being taught at most major Latin American universities, LSP is mostly concerned today with scientific/academic discourse analysis to help students cope with their university requirements (Spanish and Portuguese as LSP) and to aid researchers to participate in the ongoing international dialogue of science. In the latter case, it is English as LSP because that language is the most widely taught in Latin America.

Regarding the teaching of English scientific writing per se, some sporadic efforts are in progress despite the scarcity of human and economic resources for such a demanding task. This increase, however, would be greater if there were institutional policies for the development of such courses that are still absent in most Latin American countries. The problem is that in Latin America – and even in Brazil, the most productive Latin American country – formal training in English is not part of the academic culture, and policy makers in Latin American countries appear to take English proficiency for granted in the development of science policies.

It is widely accepted that writing a publication for English language international journals is a linguistic burden that most scientists from Latin America have to bear themselves. These constraints do affect the visibility of Latin American science, an issue that calls for government attention. But this is not an issue for Latin America only: it is an issue for all non-native English speaking countries, especially those from the developing world.

I strongly believe that improving the writing competence of Latin America's scientific community should not be a minor issue in policy-making. Increasing the number of researchers who are fully proficient in English will help enhance international awareness of this region's scientific contributions, but not enough is being done in this respect in the continent. It is to be hoped that the NECOBELAC project will substantially improve the situation.

7. References

Acosta, M. A., *Reflexões sobre o processo de ensino-aprendizagem de inglês em um ambiente de trabalho.* Dissertação de Mestrado. (Pontifícia Universidade Católica de São Paulo, Brazil, 2000).

Araújo, M. G., *Análise de Necessidades para um Curso Superior como Subsídio para a posterior Elaboração de um Programa de Curso.* Dissertação de Mestrado. (Pontifícia Universidade Católica de São Paulo, Brazil, 1999).

Balsemao, Oss, Débora Izé, and Magaly Ruwer, 'ESP: from theory to practice in a Brazilian setting', in Mark Krzanowski, ed., *English for Academic and Specific Purposes in Developing, Emerging and Least Developed Countries.* (International Association of Teachers of English as a Foreign Language: Darwin College, 2008), 52–68.

Bazerman, Charles, *Shaping written knowledge* (Madison, WI: The University of Wisconsin Press, 1988).

Beke, Rebeca, and Adriana Bolívar, 'Certainty and commitment in the construction of academic knowledge in the humanities', in Eija Suomela-Salmi and Fred Dirven, eds, *Cross-linguistic and cross-cultural perspectives on academic discourse* (Amsterdam: John Benjamins, 2009), 33–47.

Belmonte, J., *Análise de Necessidades na Área de Turismo: em busca de subsídios para uma adequação da disciplina Língua Inglesa.* Dissertação de Mestrado. (Pontifícia Universidade Católica de São Paulo, Brazil, 2003).

Berkenkotter, Carol and Tom Huckin, eds, *Genre Knowledge in Disciplinary Communication – Cognition, Culture, Power.* (Hillside, NJ: Lawrence Erlbaum Associates, 1995).

Bolívar, Adriana, 'Análisis crítico del discurso de los académicos', *Revista Signos* 37 2004: 7–18.

——, 'La función de la evaluación en artículos y ensayos humanísticos', in Johan Falk, Johan Gille and Fernando Weichmesister Bermúdez, eds, *Discurso, interacción e identidad* (Estocolmo: Universidad de Estocolmo. 2006), 109–136.

——, 'El informe de arbitraje como género discursivo en la dinámica de la investigación', *Revista Latinoamericana de Estudios del discurso* 8/1 (2008): 41–68.

——, 'Los retos lingüísticos de Venezuela: desafíos internos y globales', *Diálogos Latinoamericanos* 15 (2009), 76–93.

——, Rebeca Beke, and M. Shiro (2010). 'Las marcas lingüísticas del posicionamiento en las disciplinas: estructuras, voces y perspectivas', in Giovanni Parodi, ed., *Alfabetización académica y profesional en el siglo XXI: leer y escribir desde las disciplinas* (Santiago de Chile: Planeta, 2010).

Brett, Paul, 'A genre analysis of the results section of sociology articles', *English for Specific Purposes* 13/1 (1994), 47–59.
Cardoso, Z. C., *Análise de Necessidades no Setor de Recepção de um Hotel: Primeiro Passo para uma Proposta de Curso*. Dissertação de Mestrado (Pontifícia Universidade Católica de São Paulo, Brazil, 2003).
Carvalho, K. R. R., *Apresentações Orais de trabalhos científicos na especialidade de pneumologia*. Dissertação de Mestrado (Pontifícia Universidade Católica de São Paulo, Brazil, 2003).
Celani, María Alba Antonieta, 'Introduction'. In María Alba Antonieta Celani, A. Deyes, J. Colmes and M. Scout, eds, M. *ESP in Brazil: 25 Years of Evolution and Reflection*. (Sao Paulo: EDUC e ercado das Letras. 2005), 13–26.
——, 'When myth and reality meet: Reflections on ESP in Brasil', *English for Specific Purposes* 27/4 (2008), 412–423.
——, J. L. Deyes, L. Holmes, Michael Scott, *ESP in Brazil: 25 years of evolution and reflection*. (São Paulo: Mercado das Letras & Editora Pontifícia Universidade Católica de São Paulo, Brazil, 2005).
——, John Holmes, Rosinda Guerra Ramos and Michael Scott, *The Brazilian ESP Project: an Evaluation*. (São Paulo: EDUC. 1988).
Ciapuscio, Giomar, 'Formulation and reformulation procedures in verbal interaction between experts and (semi) laypersons', *Discourse Studies*, 5/2 (2003c), 207–233.
——, 'Metáforas y ciencia', *Ciencia Hoy, Revista de Divulgación Científica y Tecnológica de la Asociación Ciencia Hoy*, 13/76 (2003b), 60–66.
——, *Textos especializados y terminología* (Publicaciones del Institut Universitari de Lingüística Aplicada (IULA) Universitat Pompeu Fabra. Sèrie Monografies, No. 6, 2003a).
——, 'Acciones de calificación en conferencias de divulgación científica'. *Revista Internacional de Lingüística Iberoamericana* (RILI), 5/1 (2007), 59–77.
——, 'Famílias de gêneros e novas formas comunicativas para a ciência', *Calidoscopio* 7/3 (2009) 243–252.
——, and Isabel Otañi, 'Las conclusiones de los artículos de investigación desde una perspectiva contrastiva alemán-español', *Revista del Instituto de Investigaciones Lingüísticas y Literarias Hispanoamericanas* (*INSIL*). 15 (2002), Tucumán, Facultad de Filosofía y Letras, 117–133.
——, Inés Kuguel and Isabel Otañi, 'El conocimiento especializado: el texto de especialidad y los criterios para su tipologización'. In María Teresa Cabré and C. Bach, eds, *Coneixement, llenguatge i discurs especialitzat* (Institut Universitari de Lingüística Aplicada, Universitat Pompeu Fabra i Documenta Universitària, 2005), 95–110.

Costa, E. A., *A Aprendizagem de Inglês em Empresas: o Aluno e suas Representações.* Dissertação de Mestrado (Pontifícia Universidade Católica de São Paulo, Brazil, 2002).

De Castro, Paola, Elizabeth Poltronieri and Daniela Marsili, 'NECOBELAC, a European project to promote the diffusion of scientific information in public health', *European Science Editing*, 35/3 (2009), 81–82.

Dudley-Evans, Tony, 'Genre analysis: An approach to text analysis for ESP', in Coulthard, M., ed., *Advances in Written Text Analysis* (London: Routledge. 1994), 219–228.

Gomes, L. F., *Inglês Instrumental para Comércio Exterior: Proposta para um Curso universitário* (Dissertação de Mestrado. Pontifícia Universidade Católica de São Paulo, Brazil, 1998).

——. 'Uso da Língua Inglesa nos Hotéis de Sorocaba e Região:um Estudo das Necessidades na Situação-Alvo'. *The ESPecialist*. 4/1 (2003). 17–34.

Halliday, Michael A. K., 'Some grammatical problems in scientific English', in Michael A. K. Halliday and J. R. Martin, eds, *Writing Science. Literacy and Discursive Power* (London: The Falmer Press, 1993), 69–85.

Holmes, John L., 'Exchanging Experience; The Role of an Active Resource Center' *The ESPecialist*. 12 (1985). 63–87.

——, and María Alba Antonieta Celani, 'Sustainability and local knowledge: The case of the Brazilian ESP Project 1980–2005', *English for Specific Purposes* 25 (2006), 109–122.

Horsella, María, and Graciela Llopis de Segura, 'ESP and the Globalized World: A Proposal to Survey the Current Situation in Latin America', in *Proceedings of the 9th Latin American ESP Colloquium* (electronic edition) (Universidad Nacional Autónoima de México (UNAM), 2005).

Hyland, Ken, 'Speaking as an insider: Promotion and credibility in abstracts', in Ken Hyland, *Disciplinary Discourses. Social Interaction in Academic Writing* (London: Pearson Education, 2000), 63–84.

——, 'Stance and engagement: A model of interaction in academic discourse'. *Written Communication* 7/2 (2005), 173–192.

Llopis, Graciela M., 'La ciencia, el conocimiento científico y el lenguaje' *Texturas Humanas. Revista de Ciencias Humanas y Sociales* 2/2 (Secretaría de Ciencia y Tecnología de la Universidad Nacional de Catamarca: Editorial Científica, 2008).

Maclean, Joan, Zeida Santos Betancourt, and Adrienne Hunter, 'The evolution of an ESP programme in Cuba', *English for Specific Purposes* 19 (2000), 17–30.

Martínez, Iliana A., 'Impersonality in the research article as revealed by the analysis of the transitivity structure'. *English for Specific Purposes*, 20 (2001), 227–247.

——, 'Developing genre awareness in nonnative-English-speaking writers of experimental research articles: A collaborative approach', in JoAnn Crandall and D. Kaufman, eds, *Content-Based Instruction in Higher Education Settings. Case Studies in TESOL Practice Series* (Virginia: Teaching English to Speakers of Other Languages, 2002), 79/92.

——, 'Aspects of theme in the method and discussion sections of biology journal articles in English'. *Journal of English for Academic Purposes* 2 (2003), 103–123.

——, 'First person use in native and non-native writers of research articles in Biology'. *Journal of Second Language Writing* 14 (2005), 174–190.

——, 'Building consensus in science: Resources for intertextual dialog in biology research articles', *Journal of English for Academic Purposes* 7 (2008), 268–276.

——, S. Beck, and C. Panza, 'Academic vocabulary in agricultural research articles: A corpus-based study', *English for Specific Purposes* 28 (2009), 183–198.

Menezes de Oliveira e Paiva, Vera Lúcia and Adriana Silvina Pagano, 'English in Brazil with an outlook on its function as a language of science', in Ulrich Ammonn, ed., *The Dominance of English as a Language of Science. Effects on Other Languages and Language Communities.* (Mouton de Gruyter. Berlin, 2008), 425–447.

Miller, C., 'Genre as Social Action', in A. Freedman and P. Medway, eds, *Genre and the New Rhetoric* (London: Taylor & Francis, 1994), 23–42.

Myers, Greg, *Writing Biology: Texts in the Social Construction of Scientific Knowledge* (Madison, WI: University of Wisconsin Press, 1990).

——, 'Strategic vagueness in academic writing', in Eija Ventola and Ana Mauranen, eds, *Academic Writing: Intercultural and textual issues* (Amsterdam: John Benjamins, 1996), 3–17.

Navarro, Francisco, 'La *reparación* en la estructura retórica de la Reseña Académica de Libros, o cómo el escritor se transforma en autor. El caso de la *Revista de Filología Hispánica*', in M. C. Pérez-Llantada Auría, R. Plo Alastrué and C. P. Neumann, eds, *Proceedings of the 5th International Conference of the European Association of Languages for Specific Purposes* (*AELFE*) (Zaragoza: Prensas Universitarias de Zaragoza, 2006), pp. 28–34.

——, 'Análisis Histórico del Discurso. Hacia un enfoque históricodiscursivo en el estudio diacrónico de la lengua', in Ana Moreno Sandoval, ed., *El valor de la diversidad [meta]lingüística. Actas del 8º Congreso de Lingüística General* (Madrid: Universidad Autónoma de Madrid, 2008).

Pinto, M. M., *O Inglês no Mercado de Trabalho do Secretário Executivo Bilíngüe: uma Análise de Necessidades*. (Dissertação de mestrado. Pontifícia Universidade Católica de São Paulo, Brazil, 2002).

Pulido, Diony, Rocío Robledo and Carlos A. Agudelo, 'Escritura, Comunicación Científica y Acceso Abierto: un Proyecto Internacional y Multidisciplinario-NECOBELAC', *Revista de Salud Pública*, 2009, 11/2, 310–314.

Quaresma, A., *Análise de Necessidades na Área de Publicidade e Propaganda para Adequação de um Curso* (Dissertação de Mestrado. LAEL, PUC-SP, 2005).

Ramos, Rosinda Guerra, *Projeção de Imagem através de Escolhas Lingüísticas: um Estudo no Contexto Empresarial.* Tese de Doutorado (Pontifícia Universidade Católica de São Paulo, Brazil, 1997).

——, 'Estratégias Enunciativas num Relatório Empresarial'. *Intercâmbio* 4 (1994a), 85–100.

——, 'Publicity Material: Company Image Building'. *The ESPecialist.* 15 1/2. (1994b), 49–58.

——, 'ESP in Brazil: History, new trends and challenges', in Mark Krzanowski, ed., *English for Academic and Specific Purposes in Developing, Emerging and Least Developed Countries.* (International Association of Teachers of English as a Foreign Language (IATEFL). Darwin College, 2008), 68–84.

——, R. E. Lima-Lopes and M. A. Gazotti-Vallim, 'Análise de necessidades: identificando gêneros acadêmicos em um curso de leitura instrumental'. *The ESPecialist,* 25/1 (2004), 1–29.

Ramos, Rosinda Guerra et al. *Relatório Técnico Final do Projeto ESPtec: Formação de Professores e Multiplicadores de Ensino-Aprendizagem de Inglês Instrumental para o Sistema de Educação Profissionalde Nível Técnico* (Convênio Vitae – Pontifícia Universidade Católica de São Paulo, Brazil. (mimeo), 2006).

Salager-Meyer, Françoise, 'Hedges and textual communicative function in medical English written discourse', *English for Specific Purposes* 13/2 (1994), 149–171.

——, 'From the gentleman's courtesy to the scientist's caution: a diachronic study of hedges in academic writing (1810–1995)', in Inma Fortanet et al, eds, *Discourse Studies in English for Academic Purposes* (Universitat Jaume I. Spain, 1998), 133–73.

——, 'Scientific publishing in developing countries: Challenges for the future', *Journal of English for Academic Purposes* 7 (2008), 121–132.

——, 'Academic equality and cooperative justice'. *Teachers of English to Speakers of Other Languages Quarterly* (TESOLQ) 43/4 (2009), 703–709.

——, María Angeles Alcaraz Ariza, and Nahirana Zambrano, 'The scimitar, the dagger and the glove: intercultural differences in the rhetoric of criticism in Spanish, French and English medical discourse (1930–1995)', *English for Specific Purposes* 22 (2003), 223–247.

——, María Angeles Alcaraz Ariza and Maryelis Pabón Berbesí, 'Backstage solidarity in Spanish- and English-written medical research papers: publication context and the acknowledgment paratext'. *JASIST* (*Journal of the American Association of Information Science and Technology*), 60/2 (2009), 307–317.

Santos, V. B. M. P, *Padrões Interpessoais no Gênero de Cartas de Negociação.* Dissertação de Mestrado.

——, *O Perfil das Comunicações Internas Escritas de uma Empresa Brasileira: um Estudo de Caso sobre o Contexto de Produção e as Realizações Discursivas em Locais de Trabalho.* Tese de Doutorado. (Pontifícia Universidade Católica de São Paulo, Brazil, 1996).

Sprenger, T. M., *Inglês para Viagens e Turismo: Repensando um Plano de Cursoe Materiais Didáticos.* Dissertação de Mestrado (Pontifícia Universidade Católica de São Paulo, Brazil, 1997).

Swales, John, *Genre Analysis: English in academic and research settings* (Glasgow: Cambridge University Press, 1990).

——, 'Occluded genres in the academy. The Case of the submission letter.' In Eija Ventola and. Ana Mauranen, eds, *Academic Writing – Intercultural and Textual Issues* (Amsterdam: John Benjamins Publishing Company. 1996), 45–58.

——, *Research genres. Exploration and applications* (Cambridge: Cambridge University Press, 2004).

Thompson, G., and Y. Ye, 'Evaluation in the reporting verbs used in academic papers', *Applied Linguistics* 12/4 (1991), 365–382.

Vaccari, D. R. P., *Análise de Necesidades de Alunos de um Curso de Tecnología em Processos de Produção.* Dissertação de Mestrado (Pontifícia Universidade Católica de São Paulo, Brazil, 2004).

Vallejos, Llobet, Patricia, 'Discurso científico y cuestión social en la Argentina de principios del siglo XX', *Revista iberoamericana de discurso y sociedad* (2002a), 81–106.

——, 'Contribución a la historia del discurso científico en la Argentina: etapas de la estandarización del artículo experimental en el campo de la Física en le primer tercio del siglo XX', *Anuario de Lingüística Hispánica.* Vol. 17/18 (2002b), 203–219.

——, 'Estilos retóricos y género científico: un caso de texto heteroglósico en la historia del discurso científico'. *Revista de Lenguaje, Ediución y Cultura Escrita* (2006), 28–50.

Vasconcelos, Sonia M., 'Writing up research in English: choice or necessity?' *Comunicaçao Científica* 34 /1 (2007a), 62–63.

——, 'Scientist-friendly policies for non-native English-speaking authors: Timely and welcome', *Brazilian Journal of Medical and Biological Research* 40 (2007b), 743–747.

——, 'Researchers' writing competente: a bottleneck in the publication of Latin American science?', *EMBO (The European Molecular Biology Organization) Reports* 9/8 (2008), 700–703.

Weyersbach, R. S., *Curso de Inglês Negociado no Contexto Digital da Internet: Relato de uma Experiência.* Dissertação de Mestrado (Pontifícia Universidade Católica de São Paulo, Brazil, 2002).

ISABEL GARCÍA-IZQUIERDO

7 Investigating Professional Languages through Genres

1. Introduction[1]

The so-called *knowledge society*, which characterises the early part of the twenty-first century, has brought with it the emergence of new paradigms and new needs. As a result, models and theories must be reconsidered in the light of these new parameters. This is the case of the two key concepts that I am addressing in this chapter: professional languages and genre theory from the applied perspective.

In this chapter, then, I will reflect on the research currently being conducted on specialised languages, with particular attention being given to the needs of interlinguistic communication. I also propose that such research be addressed by using the concept of *genre* (as redefined in recent studies carried out in the fields of linguistics, rhetoric and translation studies) as my main tool of analysis.

1 This research has been conducted thanks to funding from the Fundación Bancaja-UJI (P112008–18) and the Spanish Ministry of Science and Innovation (FFI2009–08531).

2. Professional languages

As is well known, specialised languages, which are also called 'professional and academic languages', are those used to convey specialised knowledge produced in a given field or community. Indeed, as pointed out in studies that adopt a social view:

> Use of the term 'discourse community' testifies to the increasingly common assumption that discourse operates within conventions defined by communities, be they academic or social groups. (Harzberg, 1986: 1; cited by Swales, 1990: 21)

Hence, there is an extremely close relation between the concept of specialised language and that of discourse community. As Swales puts it (1990: 24):

> ... a *discourse community* consists of a group of people who link up in order to pursue objectives that are prior to those of socialization and solidarity [...]. In a discourse community, the communicative needs of the goals tend to predominate in the development and maintenance of its discoursal characteristics.

These communities, then, are characterised by their agreeing on and sharing certain uses and, in most cases, establishing conventions that are acknowledged by all their members.

These professional languages characterising certain communities are also *academic* 'because before they were used in each professional area, they were taught and learnt at university' [our translation] (Alcaraz 2007: 7). At the same time they are also characterised by their interdisciplinary nature, since there is a wide range of different fields of knowledge that can help us to understand and systematise them better. Such areas of knowledge range from linguistics and terminology or translation to psychology, sociology or information technology.

Moreover, in the same author's opinion (2007: 7), specialised languages share six defining features: together with their vocabulary and morphosyntax one must also take into account their discourse, their sphere of communication, the professional nature of their texts ('Their own unmistakeable professional genres') and their distinct cultural framework. In short, we are dealing with formal, communicative and cognitive aspects that also characterise genres, as we shall see in the next section.[2]

Thus, the interdisciplinarity and varied characteristics that make up specialised languages force us to look for models of analysis that can satisfy the many necessities of the professional communities that use such languages. Without denying the validity of specific approaches (some of which are traditional), such as the terminological one, I defend the need for a more comprehensive analysis which responds to the multifaceted characterisation of the reality I have just referred to.

3. Genre-based approach

We have just seen that one of the characteristics of specialised texts underlined by some studies is the fact that they belong to particular genres. And, in my opinion, this category is what will enable us to undertake the analysis of specialised texts instead of identifying them only with terminology or textual knowledge. In other words, genre is not just another feature of specialised languages but instead the organisational concept that can be used as the starting point from which to conduct the analysis.

If one focuses on the field of interlinguistic communication, one can start from what has already become a classic definition within the field of applied linguistics, and which was proposed by Swales (1990: 58), for whom:

> A genre comprises a class of communicative events, the members of which share some set of communicative purposes. These purposes are recognised by the expert members of the parent discourse community, and thereby constitute the rationale of the genre. The rationale shapes the schematic structure of the discourse and influences

2 Cabré and Estopà (2005: 69) also consider genre to be essential in defining specialised languages (see García-Izquierdo, 2007).

> and constraints choice of content and style. [...] In addition to purpose, exemplars of a genre exhibit various patterns of similarity in terms of structure, style, content and intended audience. If all high probability expectations are realised, the exemplar will be viewed as prototypical by the parent discourse community ...

In the field of translation, many definitions are based on the proposals of systemic functional linguistics (Martin 1985; Halliday & Hasan 1985; Eggins 1994; etc.), audiovisual communication (Kress 1985), rhetoric (Miller 1984) or literary studies (Fowler 1982). Thus, Hatim and Mason (1990), Trosborg (1997) or Hatim and Munday (2004), for instance, define genre as a *conventionalised text form* associated with social occasions or particular communicative events, as well as with specific rhetorical goals or purposes. But what these studies do have in common is that they all consider the multifaceted, three-dimensional nature of the concept, which comprises formal (recurrence and prototypicality), communicative (particular social occasions) and cognitive aspects (interpretation and recognition by a specific discourse community). These, in turn, will be embodied in different objective categories of analysis (cohesion and coherence, register, dialect, text typology, pragmatic intentionality, intertextuality, ideology, and so forth).

Genre, as a conventionalised text form, is a category that can be applied to any specific circumstance of communication. Nevertheless, it is especially relevant in the areas of specialised communication being dealt with here. The reason for this is that the genres in these areas (García-Izquierdo 2007: 122):

a. are associated with a particular discipline
b. possess a higher degree of conceptualisation and abstraction
c. have a restricted scope of communication

Therefore, at least in principle, it is easier to define the scope of the conventional features of the genres belonging to professional communities, which means, as we have seen, that the characteristic of prototypicality also shows itself clearly and in the same way.

Following this line of thought, the studies conducted by the Gentt (Géneros Textuales para la Traducción/Textual Genres for Translation) research group go deeper into the complexity of genres, as a means of undertaking the analysis of the fields of specialised communication (legal, medical and technical) in a multidimensional manner. It can be deduced from the research carried out by Gentt that, together with the three formal, communicative and cognitive dimensions, and the prototypical and recurrent nature of some genres from the areas under study, it is also necessary to consider the versatile, hybrid nature of many others (García-Izquierdo 2005, 2009), which are equally good representatives of the specialised discourses that they convey. Hence, only a multifaceted approach will enable us to observe the problem from different angles and to describe the way each of the characteristics manifests itself in the particular genres of particular languages, depending on the specific discursive circumstances. As claimed by Borja, García-Izquierdo and Montalt (2009: 62):

> In general, the literature stresses the need for a multidimensional approach to characterising genre. And that is how the analysis is tackled from the Gentt perspective [...], because both the intrinsic complexity and the variations in genres from one culture to another sometimes make it difficult to establish the limits of a genre.

Thus, in areas of specialisation (Hurtado 2001: 492), genre acts as an abstraction and as an interface between the text and the context. It enables us to analyse the linguistic-textual, pragmatic-communicative and cognitive variables of any interlinguistic act of communication but, more especially, those that take place within specific professional discourse communities.

4. Investigating professional languages through genres

One of the aspects that has perhaps helped research into specialised languages to advance the most has been the expansion of quantitative methodologies of analysis and empirical studies. Thus, in the vast field of interlinguistic communication there is a wide variety of research groups that use such methodologies. Within the field of translation and terminology alone there is a significant number of research groups devoted to the analysis of academic languages (including the genres of creative domains) that utilise corpus-based studies. Although it is in no way meant to be an exhaustive list of cases, as examples, I could highlight, in Europe, the work carried out in Antwerp and at the Katholieke Universiteit Leuven (Belgium); at the Università di Bologna-Forlì (Professors S. Bernardini or G. Aston) or the Università degli studi di Perugia (Professor F. Zanettin) in Italy; at the Université Stendhal de Grénoble 3, in France (Professor C. Frérot); at Manchester University, in the United Kingdom (Professors M. Baker, M. Olohan), or at Dublin University, in Ireland (Professor D. Kenny), among many others. As far as the scenario in Spain is concerned, very briefly, I could draw attention to groups such as the following:

- TECTRA, Universidade de Vigo, Álvarez Lugris, Texts for comparative stylistics and translation.
- COVALT, Universitat Jaume I, J. Marco, Corpus Valencià de Literatura Traduïda (Valencian Corpus of Translated Literature).
- ECPC, Universitat Jaume I, M. Calzada, European Comparable and Parallel Corpora, European Parliament.
- ACTRES/TRACE, Universidad de León, R. Rabadán, Contrastive analysis and literary translation/Translation and censorship.
- MYOCOR, Universidade de Vigo, E. Sánchez Trigo, Scientific-technical (neuromuscular diseases).
- TURICOR, Universidad de Málaga, G. Corpas, Texts from tourism.
- IULA, Universitat Pompeu Fabra, Teresa Cabré, Technical corpus and automatic terminology extraction.
- GENTT, Text genres for translation, Isabel García-Izquierdo, Genres for the legal, technical and medical fields.

Apart from the IULA terminology extractor, which is also independent of the field and subject area, it can be seen that many of these corpora focus on literary and contrastive analysis or, at least, on a particular area of specialisation (tourism, neuromuscular diseases or parliamentary speeches).

The exception would be the proposal put forward by Gentt, in which the analysis features two characteristics that distinguish it from the others, namely:

a. The research aims to construct, as we shall see below, a comprehensive model of analysis that can be applied to different areas of specialisation and is not specific to any of them in particular.

b. The corpus that has been compiled, and which is used as a research tool, is not built of fragments of text but from whole texts, since its defining feature is its genologic nature. This may give an idea, albeit indirectly, of the fact that the corpus aims to be more than just a terminological database and hence go beyond the traditional characterisation of specialised languages.

As pointed out earlier, partial approaches to the phenomenon of specialised languages, such as that traditionally provided by terminology, cannot be neglected at all. Moreover, in Vargas' opinion (2007: 46):

> Terminology, as a discipline, is receiving a growing amount of attention from theorists and linguists because it is the field of knowledge responsible for studying the lexical elements that make up a structured system of concepts, in which the terms are the elements mainly responsible for transmitting the knowledge of a particular scientific, technical or professional community. (my translation)

And it is true that, as advocated by Cabré and Estopà (2005: 75), the lexical level is, together with the textual level, the one that draws the clearest distinction between specialised and non-specialised discourse. But it is nonetheless true, as I see it, that in light of new paradigms it is necessary to expand the perspective and incorporate elements of analysis that are related to the context of communication and cognitive interpretation. This will allow us to view the specialised genre as a whole and not just as a collection of aspects that are more or less significant but compartmentalised. And this is why there is a need to create *Management systems* (García-Izquierdo & Borja 2009) that cover not only the linguistic-textual, but also the conceptual, communicative and cognitive aspects.

If we go back to the quote from Professor Alcaraz and return to interdisciplinarity, regardless of the discipline in which the analysis has its starting point (applied languages, translation, contrastivity, stylistics, information science, etc.), the truth is that communication needs to be improved in the socio-professional domains. And the so-called 'Knowledge management systems' (Borja 2005; García-Izquierdo & Borja 2009) can go a long way to helping to improve this communication. This is especially true in the current context in which there is a proliferation of computer tools that favour immediacy and therefore satisfy the needs of the new society.

In relation to this, the Gentt team has been researching for over a decade into the creation of an expert management system of this kind, based on the concept of genre. The main feature of the Gentt management system (the latest version of which is presently undergoing final testing before being released as v.3.0) is that it is intended to be a flexible tool, following the participative philosophy underlying Web 2.0. This system allows users to gain access to information about specialised genres that may be formal (a 'real' image of the texts, their macrostructure, linguistic-textual aspects, etc.), communicative-contextual (communicative situation, users, specific uses, etc.) and cognitive (construction of the information, value or interpretation by the specific discourse community, etc.). As a source of input, it draws on the texts compiled in the corpus and on the findings from qualitative research conducted in parallel in order to find out the opinions of the professionals (teachers, translators, lawyers, doctors, etc.) working in the fields involved, that is to say, their perceptions concerning the genres that they work with and the documentary needs they have so as to be able to write and translate them (García-Izquierdo, forthcoming).

The management tool will allow outside users different degrees of access to the material for reference and analysis purposes. In this case, I will briefly define the tool from the perspective of an administrator, that is, a person who has the right to access all the features of the corpus. Thus, first, the tool welcomes us as users, and in the top right-hand corner we can see that the user interface can be viewed in three languages, namely, English, Spanish and Catalan (see Figure 6).

Figure 6 Gentt Corpus

After accepting the conditions of use (which is exclusively for educational and research purposes), we then have to register. In this case, and as can be seen in Figure 7, we register as administrators, which will grant us access to the three tabs that are shown, that is to say, Search Corpus, Gentt Management and My profile.[3]

3 Users who are not classified as administrators are not allowed access to the Gentt Management tab.

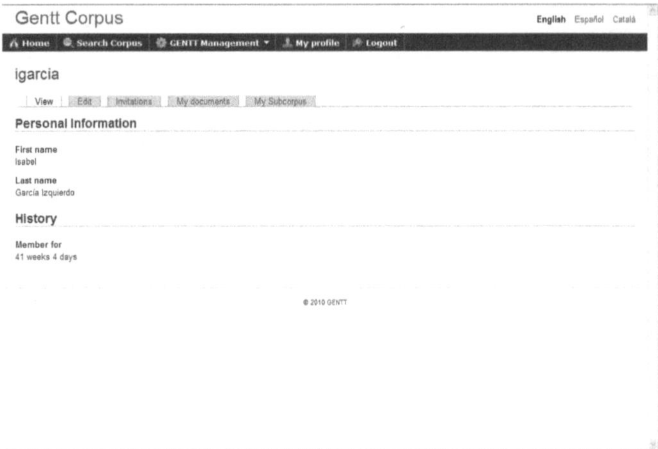

Figure 7 Personal Information. Profile

In the Search Corpus option we will be able to carry out searches using either a single word or a group of words. The results of the search will appear in the form of a table, which will include different columns of information according to the filters that we defined beforehand. In other words, the table, in its broadest sense, could show all the characteristics under each of the headings (title, author, source, subject area, etc.), plus keyword frequency and concordances. But, as can be seen in Figure 8, we can also configure the table so that only some of those categories appear, depending on the aims of our search.

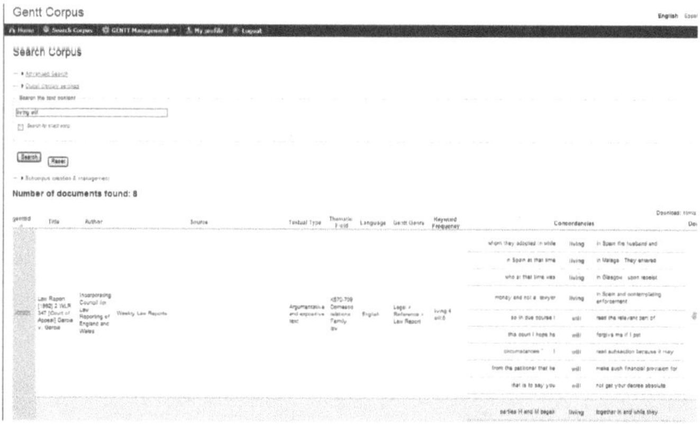

Figure 8 Search Corpus

Furthermore, we can also carry out an advanced search based on any of the categories indicated by the headings (code, author, title, source, country, text type, subject area, genre or – only in the case of legal texts – legal system), as shown in the screenshot in Figure 9.

Figure 9 Advanced Search

Once the application has presented the results of our search, we are able to open superimposed panels showing us a record with the data about each of the texts (in order to see the contextual information) and the actual texts themselves. Texts may be opened either in txt format or in image format to enable the user to determine what the real genre is like in the working language[4] and also to test whether there are differences between the different languages as regards, for example, the format or macrostructure (see Figure 10).

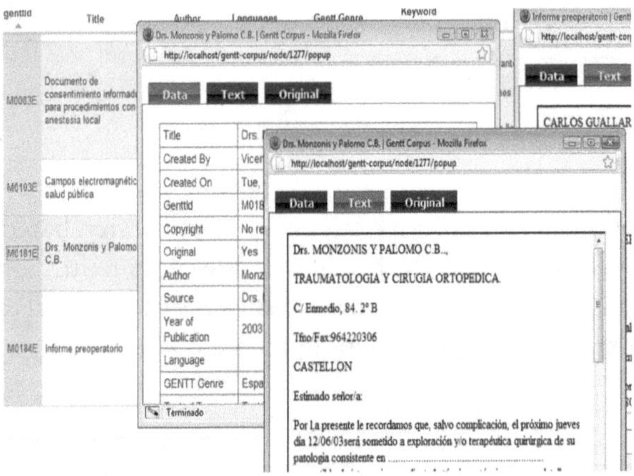

Figure 10 Superimposed panels

In addition, the results of any search can be used to create specific subcorpora, which we can either consider as being private or share with other users. So, after the Search Corpus option the next one will be that of Subcorpus Creation & Management, in which we can name it, describe it and designate it as being either a private or a shared corpus, whichever suits our search best (see Figure 11).

4 The translator might not be familiar with the conventions as regards the format of the text to be translated in either the source or the target language, and visualisation would help him or her to become acquainted with those conventions.

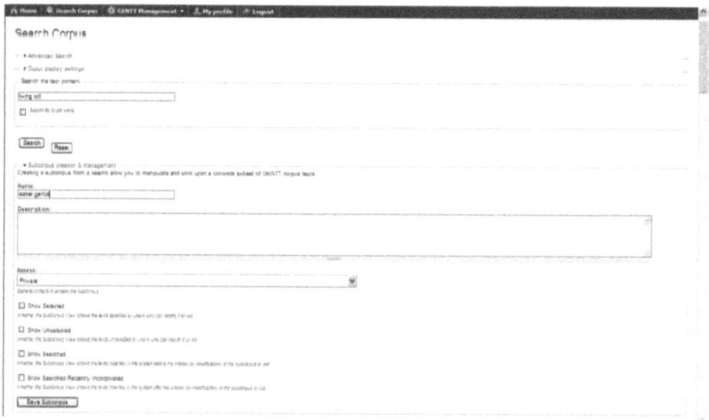

Figure 11 Subcorpus creation

With the results obtained we will also be able to filter the information using the tools on the right of the screen (Operations), which we can employ to accept or refuse the texts found in the search, according to their relevance for our purposes. We can also invite someone to share them with us. Once these operations have been carried out, we can save our subcorpus with the assigned characteristics and retrieve it whenever necessary (see Figure 12).

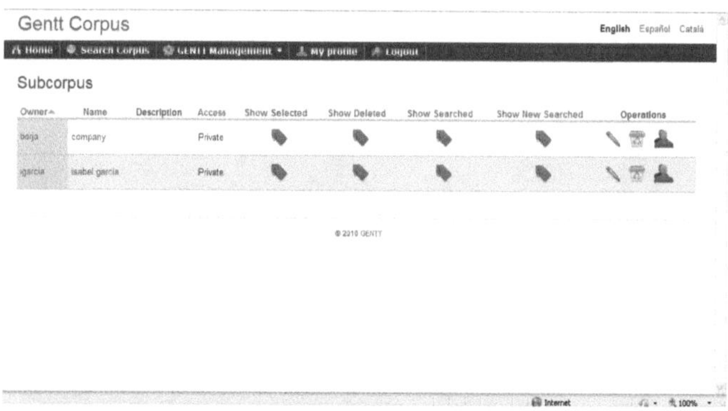

Figure 12 Subcorpus Management

Likewise, the system also makes it easy for the user to download the texts from the subcorpora, so that analysis tools that are external to the system can be applied (such tools include applications like Wordsmith, Freeling, TreeTagger, terminology extractors, Multitrans, etc.).

Lastly, the administrator can also manage the documents included within the corpus, together with the conceptual structures that act as the basis for the classification, as can be seen in the following screenshot. Thus, first there are the three broad areas being analysed (Medical, Legal & Technical), and the user can expand them one by one. By clicking on the cross on the left, the program will expand the different levels of the taxonomy (from the field to the macrogenre, genre and subgenre).

The administrator will also be able to use the buttons on the Toolbar to move some genres or subgenres (and therefore change the relation of dependence among them), as well as deleting or adding others if needed. Likewise, as can be seen on the right-hand side of the Toolbar, it is also possible to export the whole classification (see Figure 13).

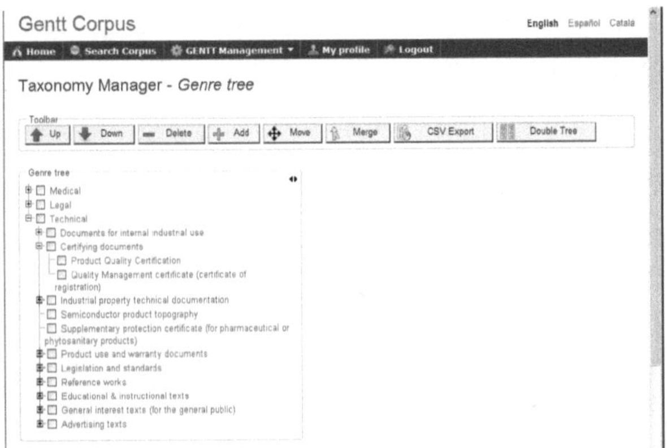

Figure 13 Genre Tree Management

In addition, the tool offers us the possibility of showing the Double Tree in the same window so as to allow us to establish matches between genres and subgenres. Once the trees have been expanded on screen, the buttons in the middle can be used to establish parent-child or synonymy relationships among genres that do not appear obvious at first sight. We can, for example, consider two or more genres that are dependent on the same macrogenre (or two or more subgenres from the same genre) as also being part of a genre system. In other words, they are related to the same communicative process, usually sequentially in time. This would be the case of genres related with the certification of a product, with legal proceedings or with a medical procedure (see Figure 14).

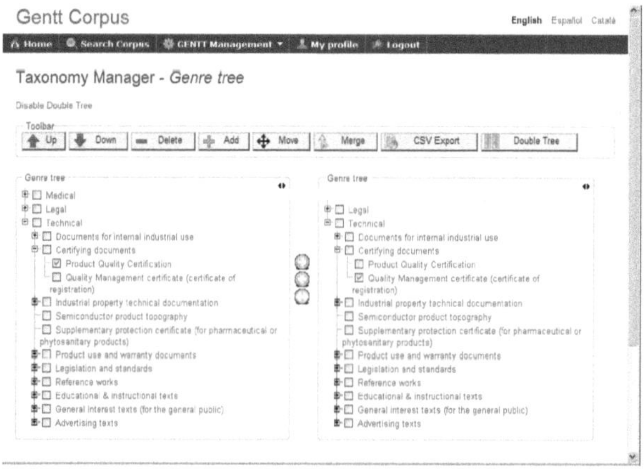

Figure 14 Double Tree

Similarly, from the conceptual structure each of the genres can be assigned a detailed description, which goes beyond purely linguistic aspects. As can be seen in Figure 15, clicking on the selected genre brings up a set of data fields on the right-hand side of the screen. In these fields we can include, together with the name of the genre, a detailed description of the communicative situation in which it is produced and its chief features in terms of its macrostructure, the way the information is organised and its formal characteristics. Additionally, the data fields will show how the genres are related to genres and subgenres from the same subject area and the same branch or macrogenre (which will automatically appear under the heading 'parents'). It will also reveal the relationships that exist between genres and genres and subgenres from other fields that we talked about earlier, for example, the obvious relationship between reports in the legal, medical and technical fields and relationships of synonymy (genres that, in certain contexts, can act as synonyms, for example, a poster providing a patient with information and a leaflet produced for the same purpose) or relationships that are determined by participation within the same system of genres, which are not always obvious, as we have seen (an abstract, research paper and a summary for patients; a hospital admission register, an informed consent document and a pre-anaesthesia report, and so forth).

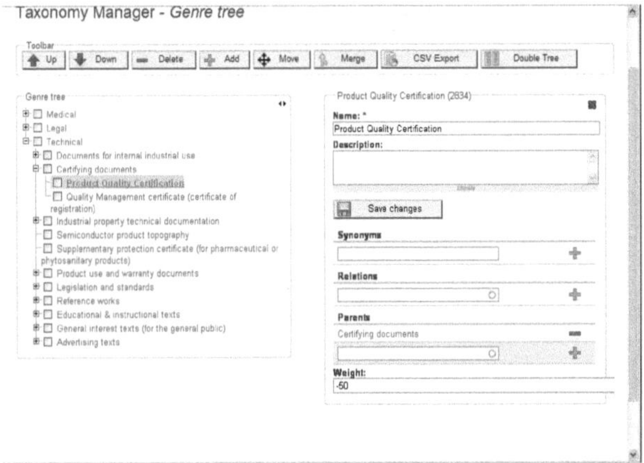

Figure 15 Genre Template

Lastly, the tool can also provide the administrator automatically with a report on the status of the corpus. As can be expected, the purpose of this utility is to allow the information to be monitored and managed. In fact, the administrator can use these reports to know details about the status of the corpus, including the number of documents that have been introduced. The system allows the information to be broken down according to genre, language or country, or any of the categories indicated by the headings (by means of Advanced Search) and, as can be seen in the image at the bottom of the figure, It shows it in the form of a bar graph. One of the main values of this first utility is that it allows the status of the corpus to be updated in an immediate and general manner. It is possible to know, for example, how many texts the corpus is made up of, what genres are the most commonly represented, what languages they are in, etc. This information can be used to make assessments about the need to change the strategies employed in gathering the texts, for example.

Furthermore, it also makes it possible to know what the status of the corpus is as far as the process of validation is concerned. This is essential at a time like now, when information is being migrated from the old system and we therefore need to check that all the documents have followed the right process and contain all the information needed to be able to work properly in the new tool (see Figure 16).

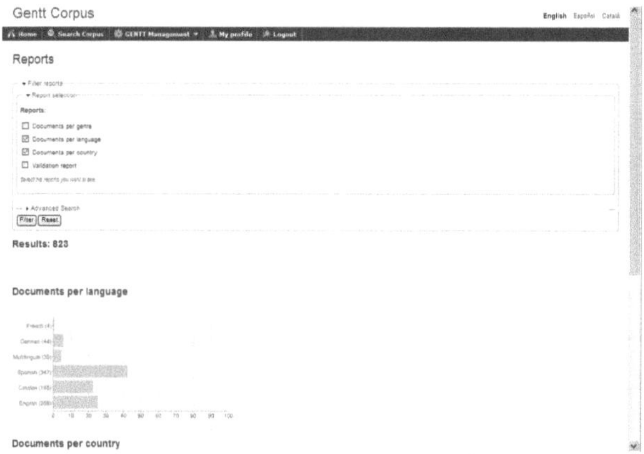

Figure 16 Corpus Report

5. Conclusion

In conclusion, it can be said that the study conducted by the Gentt research group confirms the need to consider the analysis of areas of specialised communication, and therefore the languages that are used as a vehicle for their discourses, from an interdisciplinary perspective.

With regard to the future of the research carried out by Gentt in the areas of specialisation focused on translation, two main lines can be highlighted:

a. From the qualitative point of view we aim to step up the contacts with organisations from the areas of specialisation under study (the Hospital Clínico; the TSJCV – High Court of Justice of the Valencian Community), the aim being, during the initial stage, to systematise the multilingual information that they generate.
b. From the quantitative point of view, we will carry out a more detailed exploration of the possibilities of achieving an automatic classification system; we will enhance the utilities of the management tool so that it can be used to write and translate the already-systematised genres discussed earlier; and we will also use it to start producing multilingual terminological dictionaries and glossaries by genres and genre systems.

In short, the research group aims to push forward in the design of an intelligent genre-based system for the management of multilingual specialised documents that allows the processes of retrieving, indexing, semi-controlled writing and assisted translation of professional texts to be carried out (semi-)automatically. At the same time it would also provide textual and contextual information about those texts that can be made available to the academic and professional community.

6. References

Alcaraz, E., 'La sociedad del conocimiento, marco de las lenguas profesionales y académicas', in Alcaraz, E., J. Martínez & F. Yus, eds, *Las lenguas profesionales y académicas* (Barcelona: Ariel Lenguas Modernas, 2007), 3–13.

Borja, A., 'Organización del conocimiento para la traducción jurídica a través de sistemas expertos basados en el concepto de género textual', in I. García-Izquierdo, ed., *El género textual y la traducción., Reflexiones teóricas y aplicaciones pedagógicas* (Berna: Peter Lang, 2005), 37–69.

——, I. García Izquierdo & V. Montalt, 'Research Methodology in Specialized Genres for Translation Purposes', *The Interpreter and Translator Trainer (ITT)*, 3/1 (2009), 57–79.

Cabré Castellví, M. T., and R. Estopà, 'Unidades de conocimiento especializado: caracterización y tipología', in M. T. Cabré and C. Bach, eds, *Coneixement, llenguatge i discurs especialitzat* (Barcelona: IULA, Sèrie monografies, 2005), 69–95.

Eggins, S., *An Introduction to Systemic Functional Grammar* (London: Continuum, 1994).

Fowler, A., *Kinds of literature* (Oxford: Oxford University Press, 1982).

García-Izquierdo, I., ed., *El género textual y la traducción., Reflexiones teóricas y aplicaciones pedagógicas* (Bern: Peter Lang, 2005).

——, 'Los géneros y las lenguas de especialidad', Alcaraz, E., J. Martínez & F. Yus, eds, *Las lenguas profesionales y académicas* (Barcelona: Ariel Lenguas Modernas, 2007), 119–127.

——, *Divulgación médica y traducción. El género Información para pacientes* (Bern: Peter Lang, 2009).

——, 'La investigación cualitativa en traducción especializada: una mirada a los ámbitos socio-profesionales', Proceedings of *IV Congreso Internacional de AIETI, 'Traducir en la frontera'* (Vigo: Universidade de Vigo, forthcoming).

——, & A. Borja, 'A multidisciplinary approach to Specialized writing and Translation', *LSP & Professional Communication* 8/1 (2008), 39–65.

—— & A. Borja, 'La gestión de la documentación multilingüe en entornos profesionales: propuesta de formalización', *LYNX. Panorámica de estudios lingüísticos*, Artículo inicial (2009), 1–27.

Halliday, M. A. K., & R. Hasan, *Language, Context and Text: Aspects of language in a social-semiotic perspective* (Oxford: Oxford University Press, 1985).

Hatim, B. & I. Mason, *Discourse and the translator* (London: Longman, 1990).

Hatim, B. & J. Munday, *Translation: An advanced resource book* (London & New York: Routledge, 2004).

Kress, G., *Linguistic Processes in Sociocultural Practice* (Victoria: Deakin University Press, 1985), 248–274.

Martin, J. R., 'Process and Text: Two aspects of human semiosis', J. D. Benson & W. Greaves, eds, *Systemic Perspectives on Discourse*, vol. 1 (New Jersey: Ablex, 1985).

Miller, C., 'Genre as Social Action', *Quarterly Journal of Speech, 70* (1984), 151–167.

Swales, J., *Genre Analysis. English in academic and research settings* (Cambridge: Cambridge University Press, 1990).

Trosborg, A., 'Text Typology; Register, Genre and Text Type', in A. Trosborg, ed., *Text Typology and Translation* (Amsterdam: John Benjamins, 1997), 3–23.

Vargas, Ch., 'El léxico especializado y las ontologías', in Alcaraz, E. J. Martínez & F. Yus, eds, *Las lenguas profesionales y académicas* (Barcelona: Ariel Lenguas Modernas, 2007), 41–53.

MIGUEL ÁNGEL CANDEL-MORA

8 Computer-assisted Translation and Terminology Management: Tools and Resources

1. Introduction

Until recently, the combination of the keywords 'interdisciplinary', 'languages' and 'IT' in the field of translation inevitably led one to think of the research and use of Machine Translation (MT). However, and despite the fact that MT is experiencing a rebirth with new advances in statistical machine translation, for the last ten or fifteen years the first thing that has come to mind is computer-assisted translation tools (CAT tools) and translation-oriented terminology management, as a new approach to the discipline and the professional practice alike. It is increasingly common for translators to use CAT tools and translation memory systems for different reasons, such as improvement in quality, speed, better return on investment or simply due to professional market impositions; translation buyers require the use of a specific tool hoping to maximise the functionality of these tools and increase productivity.

CAT tools have experienced considerable advances in the last five years, especially regarding the integration of these tools into the translator's workflow and simplification of their use. Nevertheless, there still seems to be a gap between researchers, translators and developers in the implementation of features, such as the communication between the different tools and the functions of these computer-assisted translation systems.

In principle, the question seems to be addressed equally from both parties – individual translators and language service providers – however, since this process is half-way between computational linguists, terminologists and translators and programmers who follow commercial or corporate criteria, it seems that the ideal of the translator's workstation (Hutchins 1998; Newton 1992; Somers 2003) is still far away.

The first part of this paper describes a general model of the process of professional translation and the context in which individual translators develop their business – in-house or freelance work – which will largely determine administrative and management factors, together with some of the reasons that lead translators to use CAT tools and in which contexts they may be more useful than others. The underlying principle of most CAT tools is that they allow the translator to reuse previously translated text segments. In short, the process is as follows: previously translated words and phrases are kept in a bilingual or multilingual database, and when those words and phrases appear again, the previous translation is automatically offered to the translator, who decides to directly place the translation in the text without changes, or edit and accept the changes to better accommodate the target text.

The second part reviews the evolution and current status of translation-oriented terminology management and its relationship with other disciplines such as applied linguistics, specialised languages and corpus linguistics with emphasis on the basic application of technical translation both from the theoretical and from the professional practice point of view and its use in the development of a terminology database, and further integration in the CAT tools workflow.

Translation-oriented terminology management is a fundamental stage in the process leading to the translation of a specialised text in that it provides and allows translators to organise linguistic and extralinguistic information which could not otherwise be accessed and will determine its subsequent translation work approach (Candel-Mora 2006). The development and management of terminology databases, 'Terminology Management', emerges as a working field within the discipline of Terminology to structure terminological data collection methodology, validation, organisation, storage, update, exchange and retrieval within a field of expertise. Currently these activities are unified in programs specifically designed for this purpose, the so-called management software or terminology databases, 'Terminology management systems' (TMS), that are applied to translation work in coordination with translation tools and translation memory systems.

2. Information technologies in translation

The widely used cliché regarding the influence of IT on translation is deemed to be valid in this paper and can be approached from a twofold perspective: on one side, due to the increased dissemination of information as enterprises continue to expand their operations around the world and understand the benefits of content translation and localisation, which results in a growth in the investment in translation. On the other, new technologies and the enhancement in computer storage capacity and processing speed has led to new tools intended to support human translators, to help increase translators' productivity, to assist them with mechanical tasks with a view to increasing productivity and giving support in producing accurate and consistent translations in less time.

What initially aroused interest among freelance translators, the hope that they would have to work less and be able to earn more, in a few years became a necessary investment in the everyday practice of the profession. Among the motivations for adopting CAT systems, the most frequently cited are that the market is no longer limited by geographic location, that they provide access to large sources of information and, as just mentioned, the hope of improving their productivity, quality and income, while retaining full control over the production of their translations.

2.1 CAT tools

Computer-assisted translation usually refers to computer applications that provide translators with resources and reference tools that help streamline the search for previously translated segments or terms in translation memories and terminology databases respectively, while integrated in the translation process itself. However, this technology does not yield the same results for everyone. For translators who do not work with repetitive texts, the main advantage of CAT tools is that, as they translate, the tool automatically compiles a bilingual database of translations – a translation memory – that can be consulted later on by means of the concordance function and the use of a terminology database that interacts during the translation providing a reliable quality assurance method to ensure consistency throughout the translation.

CAT tools have been used since the 1970s, although they have been commercially accessible on a large scale since the 1990s. Some authors (Hutchins 1998; Quah 2006) trace their origin to the research originally aimed at the implementation of machine translation systems which was recycled into computer-assisted translation tools.

2.2 *Criteria for selecting a CAT system*

Recent advances in information technology provide aid and tools to support the translator throughout the translation process, assist in terminology elicitation, term bank development, terminology retrieval, multilingual text processing, the provision of machine-produced raw translations, the identification of previous translations, and spell checks (Austermühl 2001; Oliver et al. 2007; Quah 2006). However, many translators have held back from employing CAT tools in their work because they were uncertain about what computer solution would be ideal in the long run. Translators should configure their approach within their own environments, bearing in mind the expanding possibilities of information exchange with other translators, institutions or within future projects and updates. It should be kept in mind that the profile of the technical translator depends on variables such as the specialised field of activity, working conditions, access to information resources, the IT tools used and individual skills and strategies. However, among the constants, time is one of the most important factors, since it usually limits the possibilities of extrapolating efforts beyond translation.

As mentioned above, among the advantages of using CAT tools, some of the most outstanding are that they offer the following:

- ensure reuse of previously translated segments,
- ensure consistency in translation,
- analyse translation projects and calculate budgets, deadlines, workload …,

- provide quality control,
- translate different file formats,
- automate repetitive processes,
- reuse the structure and format of the original document,
- provide uniformity of style and terminology in large volumes of documents.

Despite all of these advantages, in 2001 a study on the adoption of translation tools by freelancers in the UK (Fulford 2001) revealed some of the barriers that are still today present in discussions on the use of these tools. Some of the drawbacks suggested by individual translators are the negative effects on language style and linguistic creativity of this type of software. They point out that they reduce the importance of the linguistic and stylistic judgment and discretion of human translators; and the lack of time to create their translation memory and set up the system.

From the professional practice approach, in addition to current debates on copyright issues within regard to translation memories and pay-per-use of TM policies, the most frequently cited is that clients would be likely to derive most benefits from translation tools by requesting lower charges for previously translated text segments and by demanding shorter deadlines for translation production.

2.3 *Translation memories*

Translation memories are databases that store previously translated text segments with a series of attributes such as creation date, user name, customer, etc. They were originally designed for translating software, repetitive documents, or manuals with many similar or identical segments for industries that produce almost identical instruction manuals but with minor modifications for each model, or international institutions that publish a large number of documents in different languages and short timeframes. Although at first glance a major advantage for the professional translator may seem an increase in productivity, it should be emphasised that their main advantage is the quality and ease of searching for segments that have already been translated or incorporated into memory as a bilingual corpus to ensure consistency and quality for future translations. In fact, the main advantages of using translation tools, as they provide consistency in terminology and reuse previous work on a database of aligned segments, are the combination of increased productivity with greater monitoring of quality as the application can compare the new translation with the database of previous translations. Moreover, in larger projects, they promote teamwork and exchange of resources, project management and allow the use of different file formats without having to know how to use the native application.

Regardless of whether the translation memory system is a stand-alone application or a tool bar with macros that interact with a word processor, the basic features or components of the most common systems available nowadays are the following:

- Translation memory: a large database containing source segments and their translations into a number of languages, together with additional information, such as the date and time of creation, the user, the client, to mention just a few.
- Translation editor: the main interface that translators use to translate documents, fully configurable by the translator regarding the information to be viewed on screen, and depending on the tool, the capability to add translation comments, see the translation status, match information, have access to the terminology database, etc.
- Alignment tool: this feature allows the creation of translation memories by aligning segments from previous translations.
- Analysis feature: this function performs a word count or an analysis of the recycling potential of the stored segments, 100% matches or fuzzy matches.
- Concordance function, allows translator to perform searches within the database of bilingual or multilingual segments
- Terminology database, to access terminology management components
- Depending on the profile and working environment of the translator, other features such as automatic pretranslation, quality control verification and project management capabilities may be relevant for their workflow.

3. Translation-oriented terminology management

In essence, Terminology is conceived in an interdisciplinary way due to its especially close relations with linguistics, scientific knowledge and its applications, philosophy, information and documentation, corpus linguistics and knowledge engineering. One of the main difficulties reported by translators during their professional practice is the lack of reference material, especially in terms of validity and relevance of the terminology, linguistic expertise and type of information available. Therefore, this highlights the role of terminology in the translator's work, the process of developing a terminology database, its combination with software tools that facilitate the management of terminology, information retrieval, automation of the translation process and the consistency of the use of technical terminology, as well as the characteristics of the target text. Terminology management for translators takes for granted, in theory, problems of document guidance terminology (notional links in particular), management of linguistic terminology (recommended or preferred variants) and, above all, demands quite an elaborate linguistic analysis.

The view that terminology is the most relevant feature of a standard text, shared by several authors (Alcaraz 2000; Candel-Mora 2006; Hann 1992; Lerat 1997; Sager 1990), can be backed up further from the point of view of technical translation. The study of theories of terminology and their definitions of terms leads to the conclusion that the application of terminology to translation should not be restricted just to the compilation of a terminology database of reference in keeping with the goals of these theories, but also be closely related to the implementation of new technologies in translation, such as translation memory and terminology management programs. For translators, the elaboration of a terminology database is a hard and cumbersome task. However, in the long run it compensates these efforts since coherence in technical terminology is regarded as one of the most relevant quality parameters of a translation from both theoretical and professional practice approaches (Wright 2001: 490).

From the perspective of the profession, using a systematic database with the new computer-based translation tools facilitates decision making and guarantees lexical coherence. One of the key indicators of the quality of a translation lies in its intelligibility, which is based on the adequate use of specialised language (Wright 2001: 492). Professional translators first approach texts through terminology and so, in most cases, it will help guide them in the process of searching for reference material and parallel texts with which to capture the essence of the specialised language and the special characteristics of the text to be translated.

There is a vast body of literature on the different problems encountered by translators, who must convey the sense, cultural background, national features, tone, etc. Technical translators do not face such a wide spectrum of difficulties. However, problems in technical translation are not only restricted to the search for equivalents, since the total comprehension of the original text requires extralinguistic knowledge of the subject. Translators have to transpose the scientific information contained in the original document by using the appropriate terms as well as selecting the appropriate mode of expression according to the target audience, and the target language style. As Neubert and Shreve (1992: 14) point out:

> The translation of a technical text must be technically correct. This means it must correctly reproduce the technical content of the original document both in all its details and in its entirety. It must also be linguistically correct, which means specifically that the common language components must be correct, even phraseologically correct. The terminology must not only be correct, it must be applied uniformly throughout.

This text analysis stage provides the necessary insights for deciphering the texts to be translated, for compiling the database and for collecting parallel texts and documentation. Neubert and Shreve (1992: 15) conclude that:

> Translators have to deal with more than just individual technical texts from several or from many fields. They also have to cope with recurring text types, with manuals, research and development reports ... As soon as the translator recognizes which text type a particular document belongs to, he or she can concentrate on the specific special language more traditionally associated with that category.

The standards of textuality to take into consideration during text analysis include: intentionality, or interaction between the communicative purpose of a text and the reader's need for the information; informativity, the knowledge content of the text; acceptability, focused on the recipient, it deals with the compliance with the standards that apply to particular text forms; situationality, the conditions that describe the social and communicative context of the text, such as time, location of text, age, status and sex of the recipient; coherence, the logical relationships between information units in the text; cohesion, the expression of the semantic relationships and information structure of a text through linguistic means, lexical and grammatical elements; and intertextuality, the relationship between a text type and other instances of texts recognised by readers as being of the same type.

Taking Vázquez-Ayora 1977; Maillot 1997 and others into account, the overall task of the translator can be broken down into six essential components:

- The translation must be technically correct.
- It must be correct with respect to the language in general.
- It must be terminologically correct.
- It must represent technical language correctly in context.
- It must account for the text type.
- It must account for special characteristics of the target language culture.

The source language text, that is, the text to be translated, must be analysed, searching for difficulties and problems. Comparative analysis of the source text and the parallel texts becomes an essential component in the preparation stage for the translation process. The most natural tool to compensate for the inadequacy of currently available reference material is an original technical text in the target language, a text from the same subject field and, if possible, of the same text type. In addition to such parallel texts, we can also use texts from basic monolingual dictionaries, lexicons, etc. Text documentation is basic because the finished product anticipated from the translation process consists in language in context. Multilingual dictionaries provide only isolated orientation and control functions, not vocabulary in context.

The time-consuming task of compiling a terminological database will compensate translators. Therefore, the main reasons for technical translators to compile a terminological database are the following:

- Technical dictionaries generally fail to provide adequate phraseological components. However, technical collocations, fixed expressions and standard formulations play an especially significant role in technical texts, and frequently cause translation problems.
- Translators usually work in specific subdomains of subject fields. Custom-made glossaries are not usually commercially available.
- Large jobs are usually divided between several translators; however, the terminology used by the team of translators must be consistent throughout the whole project.
- Technology is constantly changing, and current terminology is needed.
- The terminological entry contains different types of information.
- Computerised terminology requires database management systems.

3.1 Terminology management in the translator's workflow

Auger and Rousseau (1987: 53) and Cabré (1993: 338) distinguish two types of terminological work based on the user's requirements: Ad hoc terminology, oriented to specific aspects, and systematic terminology management, which carries out terminological work within a field of a specialised area. Another classification of terminological work is based on the purpose of the terminology collected. Therefore, there are different methods depending on the approach: linguistic-terminological, standardisation (ISO, UNE, ASTM ...), language planning (Office of the French language of Quebec, TERMCAT), and translation. The other variable to delimit the method in terminology work is based on the type of user: specialist/terminologist, linguist, translator or language planner. The process for the establishment of the working method in translation-oriented terminology management presented here consists in carrying out an analysis of the main proposals in terminology work up to date, and combine them in order to select the most pragmatic and functional aspects.

Regarding systematic terminology work, Cabré (1993: 291) proposes the following six stages:

1. Definition and specifications of the work based on the subject, target users, functions, or dimensions;
2. Preparation of the work, collection of information on the subject, selection of advisers, selection of information, corpus design, structuring of the field, proposal of the working plan;
3. Elaboration of the terminology, term extraction, identification of terms, determination of their relevance to the conceptual field, elaboration of the extraction file, terminological file;
4. Presentation of the work, extraction, supervision, correction;
5. Supervision of the work, verify formal aspects of content and of the work of compilation;
6. Handling and resolution of problems, problem cases, conceptual aspects, denomination-concept relations, denomination issues, solutions, consultation of specialised bibliography, consultation of specialised lexicography, consultation of official standardisation bodies.

The other line of theoretical research on terminology is Standardisation. For example, Standard ASTM E1964–98: Standard for Practice Compiling and Writing & Terminology describes a systematic process for the compilation and elaboration of technical terminology in order to 'assist users in writing technical documentation for terms that are built on accurate and useful definitions' (ASTM E1964–98: 1). The main difference between the systematic models and the translation-oriented terminology work approach is marked by the inherent limitations of the nature of the work environment, especially deadlines and the planning of the translation project, which inevitably leads translators to carry out ad hoc terminology work aimed at the terminology problems detected during the initial phase of analysis of the original text. As Wright and Wright (1997: 148) point out, terminologists have the time and resources to carry out much more detailed work and maintain direct and permanent contact with the experts in the area in order to design definitions and systematic and exhaustive data collection, thus meeting the objective of representing the totality of the conceptual field of the specialised area.

On the other hand, from the point of view of translation-oriented terminology management based on the text to be translated, Wright and Wright (1997: 148), besides the time variable established for terminological problems, suggest that the other reason is that on very rare occasions a text contains all the examples that are represented in the conceptual field at hand, thus resulting in unproductive effort when trying to document the totality of terms associated with that field.

The type of information required in a translation-oriented descriptive terminology work differs to a great extent from the data required for systematic work. First of all, when considering the profile of the translator with expert linguistic knowledge, it is not necessary to include certain grammar aspects, except in cases of irregular uses. Secondly, this grammar information is better reflected in all the cases in the context included in each entry, thus simplifying the amount of information contained in traditional terminological entries, without limiting the information included in the entry.

3.2 CAT tools and terminology management

The Translator's Workbench Project (Kluger et al. 1995), a European-wide questionnaire survey is a good example in that terminology work is a requirement in translation. This survey indicated that terminological information is required throughout the translation process: during pre-translation editing to clarify the source language terms; in the translation process itself to identify and use target language terms; and during the post-translation edit phase to check the accuracy of target language terms.

It is terminology that provides translators with their first framework of reference within texts. Terminology analyses the corresponding terms and concepts of each sphere of knowledge to convey clarity in messages, which is an excellent means to establish improved communication between information professionals. Due to its importance, it is necessary to have useful elements for the development of terminological studies and their integration within technical language. Text documentation and comparative analysis during the preparation stage introduces the translator in a seamless way to the subject field. Sager's (1990:2) definition of terminology is expressed in terms of process, and directly associated with multilingual terminology compilation:

> The study of and the field of activity concerned with the collection, description, processing and presentation of terms, i.e., lexical items belonging to specialised areas of usage of one or more languages.

The overall process and guidelines for compiling terminology work applied to technical translation encompass the following steps:

- Checking existing resources. It should be checked whether terminology material for a particular subject field and the chosen languages already exists. A search for glossaries and dictionaries, either on paper, on disk or even online, is a task for which the Internet brought new possibilities.
- Collecting textual material for documentation purposes. Collecting textual material for subject specific knowledge acquisition and as a source for terminological information is one of the main tasks in terminography and is carried out primarily by traditional means, i.e., going to the library searching through catalogues and books, journals or articles, talking to subject field experts, or by contacting practicing individuals in companies or organisations.
- Analysing documents. Identifying definitions, synonyms and terms in documents.
- Structuring the specific domain (concept systems).
- Compiling terminology records (concept-related data, term related data, other types of information). It represents the core application of terminology management systems. This implies a standardised entry structure which means the use of a predefined set of data categories.
- Intralingual comparison: homonymy, synonymy.
- Interlingual comparison.
- Revision.

Sager (1990) adds to this list the need to distinguish between original and translated texts, that is, not original sources, and the use of running texts to ensure coherence and dating of terms, especially in fields like computer science, where technology is in constant change. Another important issue in terminology is standardisation. This can be seen from two points of view: on one hand, standardisation of terms. On the other, the different methodologies used, as well as the different terminology management systems used to organise and structure the terminology databases, which bar collaboration among peer practitioners by restricting compatibility of existing terminology compilations. Translation-oriented terminology management is thus a crucial activity in the flow of information between subject-field specialists.

The publications of international standards represent one of the most reliable and accessible sources of documentation for translators. However, it is easier to agree upon certain terms in one language than in two. This is the reason for taking into consideration the national standards documentation. Within the European Union linguistic projects it seems that there exists collaboration and willingness to compile technical terminology used among the associated countries. However, throughout the Spanish-speaking world the organisation, compilation and standardisation of scientific and technical terminology and of languages for special purposes has received little attention.

Unfortunately, the effects of this isolation in translation such as lack of standardisation, specialists' supervision and currency of terminology make the translation-oriented terminology process even harder. Translators have to deal with the specifications of clients, agencies and institutions without having solid arguments as to which terminology is preferred or more frequently used, which in the end, affects the quality of the text to be translated. For the establishment of a working method in translation-oriented terminology management, the starting point is the integration of different disciplines which have a clear influence on the translation process (Candel-Mora 2006). Therefore, the contribution of this proposal is not only the analysis of previous Terminology studies applied to translation, but also the application of the results of the different interactions between terminology and translation applied to the work of translators.

4. Concluding remarks

In conclusion, the desired translator's workstation or software interface for the translator to communicate, translate, manage terminology and perform searches in textual databases, send translated texts and managed accounts does not seem to be on the horizon of computer-assisted translation software firms. Thus, translators still need to be prepared to compensate this lack by enhancing their methodological competence and skills in relation to the use of technology tools and resources available.

5. References

Alcaraz, Enrique, *El inglés profesional y académico* (Madrid: Alianza Editorial, 2000).

Austermühl, Frank, *Electronic Tools for Translators* (Manchester: St Jerome Publishing, 2001).

Cabré, M. Teresa, *La terminología. Teoría, metodología, aplicaciones* (Barcelona: Empúries, 1993).

Candel-Mora, Miguel Ángel, *Propuesta de metodología para la gestión terminológica aplicada a la traducción profesional* (Valencia: Editorial Universidad Politécnica de Valencia, 2006).

Fulford, Heather, 'Translation Tools: An Exploratory study of their Adoption by UK freelance Translators', *Machine Translation* 16 (2001), 219–232.

Hann, Michael, *The Key to Technical Translation. Volume I. Concept Specification* (Amsterdam: John Benjamins Publishing, 1992).

Hutchins, W. John, 'The origins of the translator's workstation' *Machine Translation* 13 (1998), 287–307.

Kugler, M., Ahmad, K. and Thurmair, G., eds, *Research Reports ESPRIT, Project 2315 TWB Volume 1: Translator's Workbench – Tools and Terminology for Translation and Text Processing* (Brussels: ESPRIT, 1995).

Lerat, Pierre, *Las lenguas especializadas* (Barcelona: Ariel, 1997).

Maillot, Jean, *La traducción científica y técnica* (Madrid: Gredos, 1997).

Newton, John, *Computers in Translation. A Practical Appraisal* (London: Routledge, 1992).

Neubert, Albrecht, and Shreve, Gregory, *Translation as a Text* (Kent, OH: Kent State University Press, 1992).

Oliver, A., Moré, J. y Climent, S., eds, *Traducción y tecnologías* (Barcelona: Editorial UOC, 2007).

Quah, Chiew, Kin, *Translation and Technology* (New York: Palgrave MacMillan, 2006).

Somers, Harold, ed, *Computers and translation. A translator's guide* (Amsterdam: John Benjamins Publishing Company, 2003).

Wright, S. Ellen, 'Terminology Management and Total Quality Management' in Wright, S. E. y Budin, G., eds, *Handbook of Terminology Management, Volume 2. Application-oriented Terminology Management* (Amsterdam: John Benjamins Publishing, 2001), 488–502.

JOSÉ RAMÓN GÓMEZ-MOLINA

9 Developing Intercultural Communicative Competence through Video-web Communication in the NIFLAR Project

1. Introduction

Since Information and Communication Technologies (ICT) entered the field of education, language teaching has been set new challenges in the last decade, as is the case of virtual interactions. While technology is not an end in itself, it can be a powerful tool that enables, enriches and accelerates the learning process. In recent years, computer-mediated communication (CMC), a tool that enriches the learning environment as it enables distance collaboration between native and non-native speakers, has been applied in several foreign languages (Chapelle 2003; Belz & Torne 2006; Fuchs 2007; Jauregi y Bañados 2008).

Coordinated by the University of Utrecht (Holland), the Universities of Granada (Spain), Valencia (Spain), Coimbra (Portugal), Palacky (Czech Republic), Novosibirsk State Technical University (Russia) and Nevsky University (St Petersburg, Russia) are developing the e-learning content for Spanish, Russian, Portuguese and Dutch at different levels according to the Common European Framework of Reference (CEFR),[1] in the framework of Networked Interaction in Foreign Language Acquisition and Research (NIFLAR), an international project granted by the European Community, and with the collaboration of the Dutch consulting group TELL Consult (Technology Enhanced Language Learning).

1 Spanish (B1-B2-C1), Russian (A1-A2), Portuguese (A1-A2), Dutch (A2-B1).

The final goal of NIFLAR is to enrich and innovate foreign language teaching and learning processes developing different interactive tasks through video-web communication (VWC) and virtual worlds (VW, *Second Life*, *Open Simulator*); environments that enable synchronous interaction and distance collaboration, and enhance not only the educational context of foreign language learners at secondary and tertiary levels, but also the learning process of future teachers. By means of the combination and development of these innovative tools that facilitate synchronous communication and the appropriate pedagogical principles, the project aims to transform foreign language learning and teaching into a more attractive and authentic experience and, therefore, to increase motivation and achieve a higher degree of intercultural communicative competence (ICC).

The methodology is based on a socioconstructivist approach, as it encourages collaborative learning in real and authentic practice where learners maintain social interaction while performing tasks that favour the development of intercultural competence. Both the design of the interactive tasks and their evaluation have been accomplished according to common criteria previously discussed and established by all the teams involved in the project. In addition, audio-visual interactions are recorded for monitoring the speakers (native and non-native) as well as for researching educational and pragmatic aspects (adequacy of materials, development of interaction, the use of the chat tool, increase in communicative learning, conversational strategies, speech acts, non-verbal communication.)

The main purpose of this paper is to give an account of the e-learning experience of Spanish as a Foreign Language in which students from the MA in Hispanic Studies (pre-service teachers) from the University of Valencia and students of Spanish as a Foreign Language from the University of Utrecht (Holland) have participated using the virtual environment of video-web communication. We will discuss the role played by telecollaboration, how interactive tasks have been designed, how the interaction among participants is established as well as the research that is being performed in relation to quantitative and qualitative criteria so that it is possible to analyse the learning progress, the negotiation of meaning, the evaluation of tasks, problems and advantages that one might encounter in this communicative environment and suchlike.

2. Theoretical background

The objectives of the technological and educational innovation formulated by the project require a brief theoretical and practical presentation of the three key elements in its design and subsequent research: telecollaboration, intercultural competence and interactive tasks.

2.1 Telecollaboration

Accepting the approaches by Chapelle (2003), O'Dow (2006) and Lamy & Hampel (2007), the theoretical premise underlying the process of teaching and learning languages through virtual interaction indicates that bilateral interaction (two-way) influences the understanding of input, promotes a full negotiation of meaning and creates the conditions needed for the acquisition of language as well as adjusting the output. According to Belz:

> *Telecollaboration* involves the use of Internet communication tools by internationally dispersed language students in institutionalized settings in order to promote the development of (a) foreign language linguistic competence and (b) intercultural competence. (2003: 68)

O'Dowd & Ritter state that 'Telecollaboration refers to the use of online communication tools to bring together language learners in different countries for the development of collaborative project work and intercultural exchange' (2006: 1). Research on the potential of telecollaboration for the development of intercultural competence (skills and attitudes) continues to develop. One of the most interesting contributions is that of O'Dowd (2007), who evaluates the results of intercultural exchange through telecollaboration between groups with relatively similar characteristics to those of the participants in our project. His work shows three findings related to the development of online intercultural communicative competence: (a) the activities in telecollaboration favour the development of student's intercultural communicative competence (ICC) in a way that traditional materials for the teaching of culture would not be able to achieve; (b) telecollaboration can contribute considerably to the development of cultural awareness when it contains dialogues that involve explicit comparisons of the two cultures and a direct exchange of reactions with regard to the information given by the other speaker; and (c) telecollaboration can be the best support for the development of ICC when using a combination of different online tools.

Even though the term telecollaboration includes a variety of tools (chat rooms, web-based message boards, video conferencing, video-chat), we are now interested in one in particular: video-web communication. VWC is a digital, synchronous and collaborative environment where learners can engage in face to face communication, work together in pairs native/non-natives (in pairs or in group), store and display files (documents, pictures, videos, songs, etc.) as well as producing texts together. Therefore, the elements that were previously missing in electronically mediated communication are now present: context perception, parallel visual channels, direct eye contact which is similar to face to face communication, gestural information, mechanisms of dynamic repair in real time and, in general, the flexibility that is normally expected from participants in a conversation (see Figure 17).

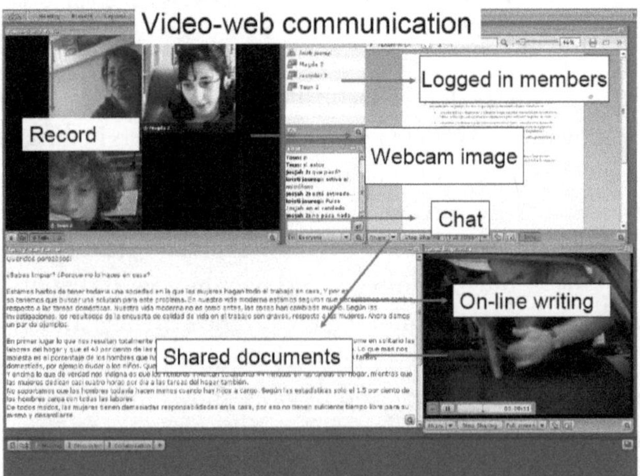

Figure 17 Adobe Connect platform

2.2 Intercultural competence

Another goal of the NIFLAR project is to improve the knowledge, skills, attitudes and intercultural relations of foreign language learners through appropriate interaction tasks that take place between speakers of different cultures (Byram & Grundy 2003; Müller-Hartmann 2006). According to the guidelines of the *CEFR*: 'The language learner becomes *plurilingual* and develops *interculturality*' (2001: 43), the main purpose is that the foreign language learner is able to relate his/her own culture with the new culture without causing a separation between them, thus contributing to intercultural awareness, skills and know-how.

While the idea of the intercultural dimension of language learning emerged in the eighties, whether as a cultural component of language learning or as cross-cultural pragmatics (Blum-Kulka 1989), it is at the end of the nineties when Byram (1997) and Byram and Zarate (1998) presented the final model of intercultural competence, a model that is influencing more and more researches since its inception.[2] For these authors, being intercultural is an activity; it is being able to interpret and understand the perspective of others as well as questioning one's perspective. Byram's intention was to add a dimension of reciprocity (*inter*) and socio-historical understanding (*culture*) to the notion of communicative competence since, according to him, learning a foreign language is something more than being able to convey a message in a clear, precise and appropriate way; it is even more than achieving a 'successful interaction' with native speakers; it is rather the ability to understand others in their national and historical specificity and come to understand oneself and one's own culture in the process.

If the process of teaching and learning foreign languages aims to help learners to communicate with native speakers in an appropriate way and to understand others and themselves, it is necessary to develop a competence that helps them to accept differences, to discover a new culture and

2 Byram's intercultural competence has attracted great attention not only in areas related to education in general and language teaching in particular, but also in the business world and politics.

to rediscover their own. Referring to intercultural competence, Byram (1997: 49–54) stresses skills, knowledge and attitudes other than on those which are primarily linguistic, and he proposes a return to the five factors integrated in real-time interaction (savoir apprendre/faire):

- *Attitudes*: curiosity and openness, readiness to suspend disbelief about other cultures and belief about one's own.
- *Knowledge*: of social groups and their products and practices in one's own and in one's interlocutor's country, and of the general processes of societal and individual interaction.
- *Skills of interpreting and relating*: ability to interpret a document or event from another culture, to explain it and relate it to documents from one's own.
- *Skills of discovery and interaction*: ability to acquire new knowledge of a culture and cultural practices and the ability to manage knowledge, attitudes and skills under the constraints of real-time communication and interaction.
- *Critical cultural awareness/political education*: an ability to evaluate, critically and on the basis of explicit criteria, perspectives, practices and products in one's own and other cultures and countries.

According to these premises, intercultural communicative competence includes the cognitive dimension (language and cultural knowledge), pragmatic competence (the competence to perform different speech acts) and the attitudinal domain (open mind and tolerance) in foreign language learning.

There are several authors (Wang 2007; O'Dowd 2007; Jauregi y Bañados 2008) who confirm that computer-aided intercultural collaboration – especially through video communication – develops an understanding of the cultural perspective and a vision of the world of the person with whom the interaction takes place.

2.3 Interactive tasks

According to the *CEFR*: 'Task accomplishment by an individual involves the strategic activation of specific competences in order to carry out a set of purposeful actions in a particular domain with a clearly defined goal and a specific outcome' (2001: 157). Hence, another goal of the project is the design of appropriate pedagogical tasks that encourage meaningful interaction in digital environments.

Interactionist theories (Long 1981) argued that interaction is the best way to learn and teach a language and that the activity should be directed to a communicative goal and ensure negotiation in the interaction through which learners play an active role; in this sense, communicative tasks are structured in a way that learners are encouraged to talk, share ideas and opinions in the process of collaboration towards achieving the target.

However, as Moonen, De Graff y Westhoff (2006) point out, in the field of second language acquisition there is no single definition of *task*. Thus, Willis (1996) considers a task as a communicative activity that involves the learner making use of the target language with a communicative purpose in order to achieve a particular result; Bygate, Shekan and Swain (2001) define a task as an activity in which students make use of the language by focusing on the meaning to achieve a goal. According to Ellis (2003), a task needs to convince the learner that what matters is the outcome and he identifies six criteria that respond to six dimensions: the perspective from which the task is seen, the field, authenticity, the skills required to perform the task, the psychological and cognitive processes involved in performing the task, and the outcome of the task. Finally, Nunan (2004) emphasises the power of the task as a source of understanding, expression and negotiation of meanings.

In order to design tasks, we have considered the principles of communicative and intercultural competence in L2 acquisition within the context of virtual interaction so as to enrich the interaction context (O'Dowd 2006; Jauregi y Bañados 2008; Thorne 2008). In order to promote intercultural competence we have applied the afore-mentioned factors stated by Byram (1997); and to promote communicative competence we have considered four components:

- *rich input*, that implies exposure to authentic, multimodal and contextually relevant language (Doughty & Long 2003; Westhoff 2004);
- *elicitation of meaningful and contextually appropriate language use* (Willis 1996; Ellis, 2003);
- *focus on language form alongside meaning* (Doughty & Long 2003; Ware & O'Dowd 2008);
- *convergent communicative outcome as a result of negotiation of meaning* (Ellis 2003; Doughty & Long 2003)

A final aspect is the choice of topics. Among the principles that guide this selection are the familiarity with the subject, the intrinsic interests and needs of the learners, as well as the relevance of the thematic content; that is to say, whether the learner will experience such situations in everyday life.

The tasks designed and carried out in the NIFLAR project are based on the principles described above (intercultural and communicative competence). The grid for intercultural communicative tasks in video-web communication shown in Table 7 has been used for task development and evaluation by all the researchers involved in the study.

The task exposes the learners to *rich* target language *input.* Does the task: • provide input that is authentic/unmodified, relevant/challenging and multimodal? • enhance interactional modification or negotiation of meaning? • elicit the use of authentic resources both before and during performance? • elicit the use of both predefined resources and resources provided by the interlocutors themselves?
The task elicits *meaningful* target language *use* *Meaningfulness*: Do the learners: • use the language pragmatically and communicatively? • use the language to engage in activities involving real-world processes of L use? • have a choice with regard to language to be used, that is, no linguistic forms are prescribed in advance?

Use: Does the task:
• involve some kind of gap (information, reasoning, culture)?
• have the right balance between language-demanding and content-demanding processing?
• promote learning by doing (processing and interaction)
• promote collaborative learning?
    o complementary roles, information, perspectives
    o two-way information exchange
    o convergent, goal-specific communication
    o positive interdependence
    o shared responsibilities
    o individual accountability

The task requires the learners to focus on *form* Does the task: • create a 'semantic space' in order to elicit processing specific L forms? • promote the detection and use of relevant chunks? • elicit feedback on form by the native speaker about the language of the learner? • provide opportunities to focus on form when learner need arises (negotiation, elaboration, recasts etc.)?
The task has a clearly defined communicative *outcome* Does the task: • have a clearly defined purpose that is relevant for all interlocutors? • have a clearly defined communicative end product? • elicit following a logical, relevant and challenging procedure? • provide instructions that meet the needs of all interlocutors? • aim at subjective, personal information exchange, related to objective, factual resources? • Is the task both open (not fixed, prescribed) and determined (goal-oriented)?

The task enhances *strategic* awareness on language learning and use
Does the task:
• elicit planning, feedback and reflection
    o on language use
    o on communication
    o on intercultural issues

The task enhances focus on *intercultural* linguistic competence Does the task: • require learners to focus on intercultural topics, beliefs, contrasts? • elicit focus on everyday, implicit cultural habits, and beliefs? • create intercultural awareness, but providing topics that contrast students' own beliefs and habits with that of their interlocutors? • elicit awareness and reflection not only regarding the target culture, but on the learner's own cultural habits and beliefs as well? General: • Are clear stages in task sequencing provided? o introduction o comparison/contrasting o construction/conversion o production/publication o reflection
The task takes the communicative and intercultural competence *level* of all interlocutors into account Does the task align with proficiency level on oral interaction and intercultural awareness: • with respect to task goal? • with respect to task topic? • with respect to task procedure?

The task makes effective use of the challenges and affordances of virtual worlds

- Is the virtual context sufficiently culture-specific/-focusing/-contrasting?
- Is the virtual context sufficiently relevant and attractive for the task goal?
- Is the virtual context sufficiently prototypical, without being caricatural?
- Is the virtual context used in a socially, cognitively, affectively, creatively and spatially effective and challenging way, e.g. by:
  - learning by exploring
  - learning by collaborating
  - learning by being (development of avatar character)
  - learning by building/constructing
  - learning by championing (focusing on strengths and successes)
  - learning by expressing
- Does the virtual context provide a safe environment (e.g., no other listeners/interlocutors are present at lower levels)?
- Is the number of interlocutors relevant for the communicative goals, topic and procedure?
- Is sufficient familiarisation provided with environment and technical aspects of virtual communication?
- Does the task trigger oral communication, that is, is intensive oral communication needed for successful task completion

Table 7 Intercultural communicative tasks in video-web communication

3. Development of the experience

As has already been mentioned, recent research (Belz & Torne 2006; Tudini 2007) has shown, on the one hand, that computer-mediated communication breaks down the barriers and inhibitions that often arise in the classroom and, on the other hand, that synchronous or asynchronous communication through various platforms (chats, blogs, videoconference, etc.) enriches language learning at different levels: grammatical, lexical, discursive and intercultural as it allows for the negotiation of meaning and the resolution of conflicts and misunderstandings that may arise in the interaction.

The video-web communication environment works as a meeting point for the interlocutors (natives ⟷ non-natives, learner ⟷ teacher), who are connected through the Internet, and experience a situation that commits them to authentic interaction. In addition, these interactions are recorded both for monitoring the speakers (natives and non-natives) as well as for carrying out research on certain teaching issues (adequacy of tasks, development of interaction, the use of the chat tool, the progress of fluency, accuracy and complexity, analysis and treatment of errors, etc.) and pragmatic aspects (conversational strategies, speech acts, non-verbal communication).

It goes without saying that to fully benefit from the contribution of telecollaboration in the development of intercultural communicative competence in foreign language learners, it its necessary that teachers and students receive explicit preparation for the activity. The process consists of carrying out tutorial sessions in order to explain how these platforms work, establishing the schedule of the interactions and organising previous informal meetings between native and non-native speakers in order to ensure the correct functioning of these tools before performing the interactive tasks.

The format of collaboration usually includes a native speaker, who may be a student or a pre-service teacher of the target language, interacting with one or more learners from different nations. There are times in which interactions are carried out in pairs (two natives and two non-natives) or one native interacts with two non-natives. The procedure used is as follows: both partners, native and non-native, prepare all the activities that integrate the intercultural task; then, they interact in the virtual sessions and, finally, they evaluate the task. In addition, all the participants in the project (native and non-native) fill in a pre-questionnaire and non-native students take a pre-test. At the end of each session, all the participants answer some questionnaires in order to evaluate the task and at the end of all the sessions they fill in a post-questionnaire. Additionally, non-natives take a post-test so as to measure the communicative progress.

The carrying out of a task consists of two phases: preparation and the session itself. In the first one, both the native and the non-native carefully prepare the planned activities. This involves developing their intercultural awareness and training in the skill that will involve interaction through collaboration. Moreover, in the case of pre-service teachers, it is necessary to understand the importance of the different roles that are their responsibility in the exchange process which makes up the session, that is, guide, organiser, problem-solver.

The interactive tasks are designed using an intercultural[3] approach and with communicative objectives adjusted to the learner's level (B1) and related to exchanges of information and opinion, reflection (oral and written activities, *focus on form*), negotiation of meaning and pragmatic value (*focus on meaning*). They also contain textual and audiovisual input that allows, in turn, a generated input by the speakers during the interactive sessions; all this facilitates real language use among the pairs or groups involved and makes a clear and specific communicative outcome possible (see Figure 18).

3 Five tasks have been created for the sessions: *Gente genial* (sharing a flat, going to the cinema/ visiting an art gallery/ going for a walk), *Gente y aventuras* (holidays, kinds of sports, organising a trip together), *Gente de cine* (celebration, actors and scenes), *Gente con corazón* (feelings, family relationships and friendship), *Gente y culturas* (different costums and habits of each country – gastronomy, traditions, work, ...).

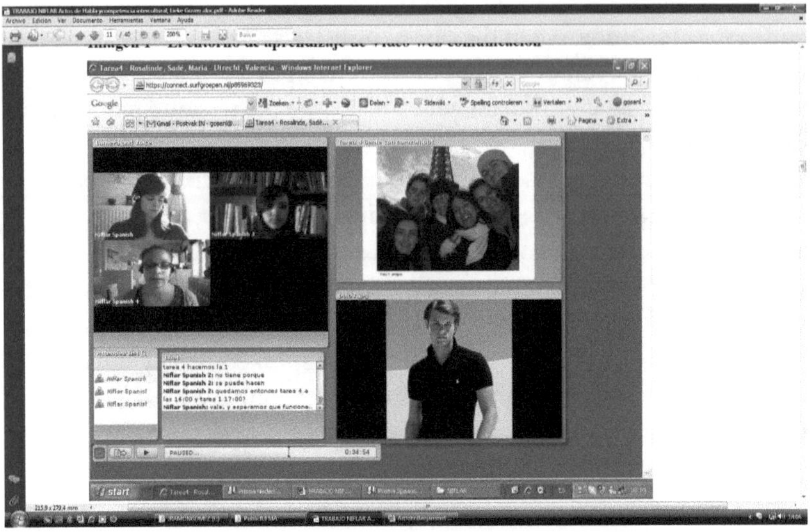

Figure 18. Carrying out the task *Gente con corazón*

The communication platform that is used in the project includes the Adobe Connect application, which uses broadband and enables simultaneous tasks, thus making it a sophisticated platform that allows more than ten students to be connected synchronously through their personal computers. It also allows students to participate, while being able to see each other, to chat and share documents (photos, videos, songs, oral and written fragments, power point documents). Moreover, it allows to debate, clarify doubts, solve misunderstandings, show understanding, agreement, disagreement, anger or other emotions, collaborate on shared documents and carry out collaborative writing. All this is carried out in real time, which commits participants to authentic interaction.

During the months of February, March and April 2009, piloting sessions were carried out. In these sessions 21 students of Spanish from the University of Utrecht (Holland) and 11 students from the University of Valencia (7 pre-service teachers and 4 Hispanic Studies Degree students) participated as language learners and as native speakers respectively. Pairs (native-non-native) and interaction groups (one native-two non-natives) were formed and all of them performed five one-hour sessions (one session per week). After this initial experience, a follow-up of the five tasks was performed during the months of February and April 2010. In this experience 16 students of Spanish from the University of Utrecht and 8 from the University of Valencia (5 pre-service teachers and three Hispanic Studies Degree students) participated.

4. Research results on the impact of video-web communication

The experience carried out to gauge the effect of video-web communication in the development of intercultural communicative competence gave us a set of results that allowed us, after the pilot stage (Jauregi, Gómez & Cantó 2010), to evaluate the designed tasks and improve them. After the follow up it will be possible to know whether the objectives have been achieved. At the moment, the recorded interactions of tasks are being analysed so as to investigate the added value of interaction with NSs through VWC in the development of the ICC of participants compared to traditional settings. Besides, we have established other research foci, such as the following:

- to describe what aspects of ICC are developed in interaction with NSs,
- to study the role different conditions play in the development of ICC (role of tasks, whether a specific technique works properly or badly, personal factors, role of pre-service teachers, ...) and
- the analysis of differences/similarities of ICC among the control group and the experimental group.

In order to study growth in general terms (pre-test with post-test and the interactions from the first session with those from the last session) and how to ascertain whether this growth is due to NIFLAR sessions, we have analysed different aspects:

- growth based on the *CEFR*: linguistic aspects (fluency, complexity, accuracy, lexical richness, ...) and intercultural aspects (pragmatic adequacy, speech acts, politeness, mitigation, attitudes, ...),
- language related episodes (negotiation of meaning – comprehension and production-, task sequencing, ...),
- culture related episodes (negotiations where cultural learning is taking place).

Once all the results on network interaction are collected and interpreted, NIFLAR teacher guides for (student) teachers will be created. On the one hand, these guides will focus particularly on the task design principles that (student) teachers should use for the development of networked language learning tasks as well as on the roles of teachers both as task implementers and as native speaker interlocutors in task completion with language learners. On the other hand, there will be organisational and technical specifications that teachers should take into account.

However, we already have some definitive results since participants from the University of Valencia and the University of Utrecht have answered a set of questionnaires and have been interviewed in order to evaluate the interaction, the technical problems they encountered, their satisfaction with the teaching and learning experience and the interest of the performed tasks. Table 8, 9 and 10 show some of these results obtained from post-questionnaires (answer options 1: *bad, negative, disagree*; 5: *good, positive, agree*).

Questions	Pre-service teachers (NSs)	Language learners (NNSs)
	Mean	Mean
Was it easy for you to communicate with a native speaker?	–	3.70
Was it easy for you to communicate with a foreign language learner?	4.38	–
Was it interesting for you to communicate with a native speaker?	–	4.70

Was it interesting for you to communicate with a foreign language learner?	1.88	–
Do you think that by speaking with a native speaker you can learn more?	–	4.85
Please, grade the fact that you had the same interaction partner for the sessions	5.0	4.30
Please, grade being able to see your speech partner during the interaction sessions?	4.90	4.62
Do you think that seeing your partner while talking facilitates communication?	5.00	5.00
Would you have preferred have a different interaction partner in each session?	1.20	1.10

Table 8 Evaluation of the interaction

It is clear that visual information enriches the communicative process due to the fact that it allows speakers to detect gestures and pragmatic features, as well as to promote the use of language in order to learn it and interpret a variety of meanings. Gestures are an important component for ASL in their dual role as a means of expression and meaning mediator; they are particularly important in intercultural communication as they are directly involved in the interactive process (turn taking, nodding for agreement or disagreement, laughs, etc.) and contribute to strengthening the relationship. Moreover, although it seems that anonymity may contribute to the building of self-confidence in shy students and, therefore, encourage their participation and communicative production, it is clear that if the purpose of the interaction is to strengthen interpersonal relationships and the negotiation of meaning, this is achieved more authentically in face to face interaction. On the other hand, changing interaction partners for each task makes it more difficult to get to know the other person well; if you already know her/him, the conversation will be more fluid and rich.

Questions	Pre-service teachers (NSs)	Language learners (NNSs)
	Mean	Mean
How do you grade the video-web communication environment you have used in the interaction sessions?	4.40	4.02
Do you think that the video-web communication project contributes to enriching the course you follow?	4.80	4.20
How do you grade the video-web communication project in which you have participated?	4.88	3.95
How do you grade the organisation of the project?	4.15	4.50
I would like to go on participating in this project	4.75	4.50
I would recommend that peers and future students to participate in the video communication project	5.00	4.92
What have you learned in this project?		
• how to use videocommunication tools for teaching	4.88	–
• to get familiar with criteria for developing effective tasks	4.75	–
• to be more conscious of my role as a teacher in interaction	4.63	–
• to analyse and evaluate the interaction sessions	4.63	–

Table 9 Evaluating the impact of video-web communication on motivation

The experience has been absolutely positive. Participants consider video communication an innovative and enriching procedure as it allows them to use language in authentic communicative situations, speak with more fluency and accuracy, improve their grammar and vocabulary, while offering a variety of educational applications. It has also been very productive in the training of future language teachers.

Questions	Pre-service teachers (NSs)	Language learners (NNSs)
	Mean	Mean
I found tasks motivating	4.63	3.92
I find tasks useful for my language learning process	–	4.02
Were the tasks you carried out useful to enhance the intercultural communicative competence?	5.0	5.0
What have you learned during the sessions?		
• to be aware of cultural contrasts and similarities	–	3.90
• to speak more fluently	–	4.27
• new words and expressions	–	4.00
• to use grammar more accurately	–	3.30
• to take more initiative in the conversation	–	4.80
• to be more motivated to talk	–	5.00
Comparing the first and the last session		
• I noticed an overall improvement in the communicative competence	4.50	
• The learners were able to talk more fluently in last session	4.12	–
• They asked more questions during the last session	3.75	–
• They enlarged their lexicon and use more adequate words and expressions	4.50	–
• They became more aware of cultural contrasts	4.63	–
• They were more motivated to talk in last session	4.25	–

Table 10 How do participants evaluate the interaction tasks?

These results show the adequacy of the interactive tasks in terms of encouraging participation from an intercultural perspective (topics and objectives), taking into account the learner's language proficiency as well as the development of their communicative competence (strategies and skills). The reasons given by O'Dowd & Ritter (2006) for failure in communication in telecollaboration exchanges, that is, problems with schedules, organisation of meetings, non-optimal attitudes towards interaction, curiosity, motivation, and unsuitable tasks, both for the selected topics and the intercultural focus do not occur in our study. This is due to the way the sessions were sequenced, their preparation and execution; academic organisation consisting of one task per week; schedule flexibility, which involved the participants agreeing on the date and time as there were available classrooms within the digital platform; and constant tutor supervision.

Along with the results from the questionnaires, interviews with pre-service teachers show these views:

- The possibilities offered by this environment are really varied, versatile and suitable for teaching purposes. All kinds of documents can be shared which helps to dynamise the communicative process. However, some problems existing with regard to the audio and video included in the task, which sometimes made understanding difficult.
- The five tasks have been successful thanks to the broad cultural content they contained. As regards to the duration of the session, they usually exceeded the recommended time.
- Interaction with the same partner during the five sessions helped to create a climate of trust that facilitated communicative exchanges and the learning process. Anonymity was thought not to favour the communication process.
- The experience exceeded the initial expectations. The pre-service teachers who took part in our study indicated that they would have been happy to continue developing tasks and be involved in more sessions.

5. Final considerations

Research on language teaching and learning through networks is in its second decade. The most studied aspects are the social dimension of learning, the negotiation of meaning and, more specifically, intercultural aspects. The main goal of the NIFLAR project is to enhance motivation of foreign language learners by providing challenging and authentic innovative learning by video-web communication, promoting (in addition to individual learning) collaborative learning, favouring experiences of enjoyment and success, supporting authenticity of learning and developing activities in collaboration with students, teachers and teacher trainees. All this represents a further contribution toward the synchronous use of technological tools that promote language learning through interculturality.

Once the pilot stage and follow up phases had concluded, it was confirmed that video-web communication is a multimodal environment that allows the development of intercultural communicative competence and encourages the reflection on aspects of both cultures through meaningful activities. Learners are given the opportunity to exercise their oral and written skills while being able to see each other (authentic and synchronous communication, exchange of opinions). They can also use the chat room as a complementary tool to aid conversation (to solve technical problems related to audio, the uploading of materials, etc.) and to upload multimedia content (videos, audio, texts, etc.).

In general, the comments of the participants (natives and non-natives) reflect positive attitudes (curiosity, willingness to learn about other cultures, self-criticism). They highlight the opportunity of getting to know social groups from other countries, their customs and habits of interaction, and recognise the opportunity offered by this environment to develop skills of interpretation (to prevent and improve the negotiation of misunderstanding), exposure, discovery and interaction.

This experience shows that video communications enriches the context of teaching and learning Spanish as a foreign language, as it serves as a motivator if accompanied by appropriate tasks. In our case, the tasks that were designed for the pilot stage and modified for the follow up, led to dynamic interaction among participants, which generated a clear exchange of information and views, many of which were of a cultural and pragmatic nature that contributed to broaden the cultural horizons of participants.

The final assessment is very positive. While there have been occasional technical problems related to slow communication or problems with sound quality such as echoes, and coordination problems, which are frequent in projects that use synchronous platforms of communication, the objectives that were set for the project have been achieved. Along with the motivation aroused in learners, the creation and development of educational materials involving the design, testing and evaluation of interactive and intercultural tasks, will allow us to develop guides for teaching and learning in this virtual environment that will benefit the e-learning of Spanish as a foreign language as well as teacher training programmes.

6. Acknowledgements

This paper describes the results of the pedagogical experience carried out in close collaboration with other NIFLAR members, but this would have been impossible without the cooperation of Dutch and Spanish students in their roles as learners and pre-service teachers, respectively.

7. References

Belz, Julie, A., 'Linguistic perspectives on the development of intercultural competence in telecollaboration', *Language Learning & Technology*, 7/2 (2003), 68–117.

——, and Steven L. Thorne, eds, *Internet-mediated intercultural foreign language education* (Boston: Heinle & Heinle, 2006).

Blum Kulka, Shoshana, and Gabriele Kasper, eds, *Cross-cultural pragmatics: requests and apologies* (Norwood, NJ: Ablex, 1989).

Bygate, Martin, Peter Skehan and Merril Swain, *Researching pedagogic tasks. Second language learning, teaching and testing* (Harlow, UK: Pearson, 2001).

Byram, Michael, *Teaching and assessing intercultural communicative competence* (Clevedon: Multilingual Matters, 1997).

——, and Geneviève Zarate, *Definitions, Objectives and Assessment of Socio-Cultural Competence* (Strasbourg: Council of Europe, 1998).

——, and Peter Grundy, *Context and culture in language teaching and learning* (Clevedon: Multilingual Matters, 2003).

Chapelle, Carol A., *Computer Applications in second language acquisition* (Cambridge: Cambridge University Press, 2003).

Common European Framework of Reference for Languages: Learning, teaching, assessment (Brussels: Council of Europe, 2001). <http://www.coe.int/t/dg4/linguistic/source/Framework_EN.pdf>.

Doughty, Catherine, and Michael Long, 'Optimal psycholinguistic environments for distance foreign language learning', *Language Learning and Technology* 7/3 (2003), 50–75.

Ellis, Rod, *Task-based language learning and teaching* (Oxford: Oxford University Press, 2003).

Fuchs, Caroline, 'Student Language Teachers as Intercultural Learners in CMC-Based Project Work', 2007. <http://www.immi.se.proxy.library.uu.nl/intercultural> accessed 11 September 2008.

Jauregi, Kristi, and Emerita Bañados, 'Virtual interaction through video-web communication: a step towards enriching and internationalizing learning programs, *ReCALL* 20/2 (2008), 183–207.

Jauregi, Kristi, Gómez Molina, José Ramón, and Silvia Cantó, 'Interacción virtual a través de la videocomunicación y mundos virtuales: dos estudios piloto', *MarcoELE*, 11 (2010), 1–17. <http://marcoele.com> accessed 2 October 2010.

Kramsch, Claire, 'Identity, role, and voice in cross-cultural (mis)-communication', in Juliane House, Gabriel Kasper and Steven Ross, eds, *Misunderstanding in social life. Discourse approaches to problematic talk* (Harlow: Longman/Pearson Education, 2007), 129–153.

Lamy, Mari-Noëlle, and Regine Hampel, *Online Communication in Language Teaching and Learning* (London: Palgrave MacMillan, 2007).

Long, Michael, 'NS/NNS Conversation and the Negotiation of Comprehensible Input, *Applied Linguistics* 4/2 (1981), 126–141.

Moonen, Machteld, de Graaff, Rick, and Gerard Westhoff, 'Focused tasks, mental actions and second language learning. Cognitive and connectionist accounts of task effectiveness', *ITL – International Journal of Applied Linguistics* 152 (2006), 35–53.

Müller-Hartmann, Andreas, 'The role of tasks in promoting intercultural learning in electronic learning networks', *Language learning and technology* 4/2 (2000), 129–147.

——, 'Learning How to Teach Intercultural Communicative Competence via Telecollaboration: A Model for Language Teacher Education'. <http://www.personal.psu.edu/slt13/589_s2007/mullerhartmann_AAUS2005.pdf> accessed 5 July 2009.

Nunan, David, *Designing Tasks for the Communicative Classroom* (Cambridge: Cambridge University Press, 2004).

O'Dowd, Robert, *Telecollaboration and the Development of Intercultural Communicative Competence* (Berlin: Langenscheidt, 2006).

——, 'Evaluating the outcomes of online intercultural exchange', *ELT Journal* 61/2 (2007), 144–152.

——, and Markus Ritter, 'Understanding and working with *failed communication* in telecollaborative exchanges', *CALICO Journal* 23/3 (2006), 1–20.

Thorne, Steven L., 'Transcultural Communication in Open Internet Environments and Massively Multiplayer Online Games', in S. Magnan, ed., *Mediating Discourse Online* (Amsterdam: John Benjamins, 2008), 305–327.

Tudini, Vincenza, 'Negotiation and intercultural learning in Italian native speaker chat rooms', *Modern Language Journal* 91/4 (2007), 577–601.

Wang, Yuping, 'Task design in Videoconferencing-supported Distance Language Learning', *CALICO Journal* 24/3 (2007), 591–630.

Ware, Paige, and Robert O'Dowd, 'Peer feedback on language form in telecollaboration', *Language Learning and Technology* 12/1 (2008), 43–63.

Westhoff, Gerard, 'The art of playing a pinball machine. Characteristics of effective SLA-tasks', *Babylonia* 12/3 (2004), 58–62.

Willis, Jane, *A framework for task-based learning* (Harlow: Longman, 1996).

VICTORIA GUILLÉN-NIETO

10 When Humanities and Information and Communications Technology Merge

1. Introduction

Before the 1950s '... the study of intercultural communication did not yet have a name', explain Rogers, Hart and Miike (2002: 8), 'its conceptualization at the intersection of culture and communication has not yet occurred ...' For many the story of cross-cultural communication begins at the Foreign Service Institute (FSI) where American social anthropologist E. T. Hall, in cooperation with other renowned anthropologists and linguists such as George L. Trager and Raymond L. Birdwhistell, worked out the conceptualizations which would give rise to the original paradigm (Khun 1970) for cross-cultural communication research in the 1950s. Many researchers are of the opinion that E. T. Hall should get the credit for having been the first scholar to use the term *cross-cultural communication* in his salient book *The Silent Language* (1973). Since the 1950s there has been an increasing interest in intercultural communication, which has probably been strengthened by the effects of globalisation in the last couple of decades. As a field of interdisciplinary research, in which intercultural communication plays a major role, intercultural business communication has attracted the attention of scholars from widely different academic backgrounds, namely social anthropology, cognitive and social pragmatics, linguistic and cultural mediation, translation and interpreting, foreign language teaching and training. It has also given rise to a great number of publications, the main purpose of which has been to explore the impact of culture on communication (Hall 1969, 1973, 1977; Clyne 1996; Scollon & Wong Scollon 1996; Pan, Wong Scollon & Scollon 2002; Spencer-Oatey

2004), organisations (Hofstede 2001, 2003; Trompenaars & Woolliams 2003; Trompenaars & Hampden-Turner 2004), global marketing and advertising (De Mooij 2004, 2005), and so on.

On the front cover of the North American business guru Frans Johansson's best seller *The Medici Effect. What Elephants and Epidemics Can Teach Us About Innovation* (2006), there is a quote from the *Entrepreneur Magazine* that reads as follows: 'If you can't read it and come up with at least a minor Mona Lisa or two you're not trying'. Persuaded by this eye-catching phrase, not long ago I read *The Medici Effect* and tried hard. The result was that, rather than a Mona Lisa, I came up with the seeds of the COMINTER-SIMULNEG research project (I+D HUM2006–12989) funded by the Ministry of Education in Spain for the period 2006–2009 the results of which I will present here. I was particularly fascinated by the way Johansson encourages breaking down barriers between disciplines and cultures to innovate. '... when you step into an intersection of fields, disciplines, or cultures', explains Johansson, 'you can combine existing concepts into a large number of extraordinary new ideas' (2006: 2). Johansson named this phenomenon *The Medici Effect* which originates in fifteenth-century Italy, particularly in the city of Florence which became a meeting point for artists, scientists, philosophers and business people. 'There', says Johansson, 'they found each other, and broke down barriers between disciplines and cultures. Together they forged a new world based on new ideas – what became known as the Renaissance' (2006: 3).

In line with the idea of interdisciplinarity, the renowned Dutch sociologist Geert Hofstede in his groundbreaking book *Culture's Consequences* draws on an Indian fable to illustrate the importance of crossing disciplines to gain a deeper insight into the nuances of culture:

> Social scientists approach the social reality as the blind men in the Indian fable approached the elephant; the one who gets hold of a leg thinks it is a rope, but none of them understands what the whole animal is like. We will never be more than blind men facing the social elephant, but by joining forces with other blind men and women and approaching the animal from as many different angles as possible, we may find out more about it than we could ever do alone. (Hofstede 2001: 2)

Interdisciplinarity is indeed a key strategic approach in the Information and Knowledge Society. A good example of the pervasive power of interdisciplinarity can be seen in the opinion article 'La innovación es cosa de Letras' by Fernado Casado Bergasa published in *Diario Información*[1] on 15 August 2010. Founder of the Alicante Institute of Knowledge Transfer and Application in 2008 and Chairman of the Industry Commission of the Chamber of Commerce, Industry and Navigation in Alicante, Spanish engineer Casado Bergasa argues that academics, more often than not, do research in watertight compartments producing knowledge that is uncreative and therefore, claims that academia should promote interdisciplinarity – *connecting brains* – in faculties as well as in research projects. 'This is innovation [my translation]', Casado Bergasa claims, encouraging academics from Humanities to work together with Information and Communications Technology (ICT) engineers to make real advances and innovate in their respective fields of research. Crossing disciplines in the field of intercultural business communication does indeed create a meeting point for social anthropologists, social psychologists, linguists, language teachers and trainers, and computer scientists among others, and fosters synergy, namely, 'the interaction or cooperation of two or more agents to produce a combined effect greater than the sum of their separate effects'.[2] Crossing disciplines is a *must* for the language researcher interested in exploring the impact of culture on language and communication. 'As soon as language is examined in its broader communicative context', argues Clyne (1996: 200), 'linguistics needs to synthesize its own insights with those of other disciplines'. In the COMINTER-SIMULNEG project, the insights of applied linguistics have been synthesized with those of social anthropology and ICT with a practical agenda in mind: (a) designing a pragmatic model for the analysis of intercultural communication between Spaniards and Britons in business settings; and (b) constructing a graphic adventure

1 1. 'La Innovación es cosa de Letras', *Diario Información.com* <http://www.diarioinformacion.com/opinion/2010/08/15/innovacion-cosa-letras/1035401.html> accessed 9 August 2010.

2 2. Compact Oxford Dictionary. AskOxford.com <http://www.askoxford.com/concise_oed/synergy?view=uk> accessed 23 February 2010.

for the purpose of developing intercultural communicative competence in business settings. In the next two sections we will look at the most salient results obtained in each of these two areas of study in further detail.

2. Designing a pragmatic model for the analysis of intercultural communication between Spaniards and Britons in business settings

Drawing on Hofstede's (2003: 4) social anthropological concept of culture as 'collective mental programming of the human mind' or 'software of the mind', the COMINTER-SIMULNEG research project explores the impact of cultural values on human interaction and communication at the micro level of interpersonal communication. In line with this inquiry, the reader of this discussion may find works by Wierzbicka (1992, 1997, 1999, 2003, 2006); Clyne (1996: 176–201); Pan, Wong Scollon & Scollon (2002: 1–26); Harris Bond, Žegarac & Spencer-Oatey (2004: 293–315); House (2005: 13–28); Prykarpatska (2008: 87–102); Loukianenko Wolfe (2008: 87–121), and so on.

The COMINTER-SIMULNEG research project is based on the main premise that culture permeates everything we do and say. Culture (Hofstede 2003: 3–4) refers to the particular ways in which universal basic bio-social problems affecting the whole of the human race have been negotiated and solved in each particular society. The collective level in human mental programming has been commonly portrayed as an onion (Hofstede 2003: 9). This metaphorical image depicts the different layers culture is made up of. Whereas the inner, intangible layers represent core values, basic assumptions, beliefs and attitudes, the outer layers correspond to the visual aspects of a culture, namely its heroes, its social institutions, its artefacts and products, the rituals and behaviour shared by its members, despite their different personalities, the individual values they may hold and their idiolects.

Three levels of analysis were distinguished in the proposed model for the analysis of intercultural business communication between Spaniards and Britons within the framework of our project (Guillén-Nieto, Pernías-Peco, Vargas-Sierra, & Williams 2009; Guillén-Nieto 2009a). I will be looking at each of them in turn in the following subsections.

Level 1: Selecting relevant value dimensions for the analysis of intercultural business communication between Spaniards and Britons

The concept of *value dimension* is a social construct that has been created to help the researcher in intercultural communication identify a number of basic social questions affecting all humankind but for which there are different answers. To begin with, eight basic social problems equally affecting human interaction and communication in all societies were selected. These were (Guillén-Nieto, Pernías-Peco, Vargas-Sierra, & Williams 2009: 342; Guillén-Nieto 2009a: 38):

- Time: It makes reference to people's concept of time and the use they make of it.
- Personal space: It considers the way people delimit their physical and psychological space.
- Context: It examines how people express and convey meaning.
- Identity: It concerns the relationship between the individual and the group.
- Hierarchy: It is related to the different solutions to the basic problem of human inequality.
- Gender: It is related to the division of emotional roles between men and women.
- Truth: It looks at how people in a culture cope with the unpredictable and the ambiguous.
- Virtue: It is related to the choice of focus for people's efforts.

Whereas for the selection of the first three value dimensions I drew on the cultural model of North American social anthropologist Hall (1969, 1973, 1977), the other five were borrowed from Hofstede's groundbreaking 5-D Model (2001). Each of the basic social problems proposed by Hall and Hofstede in their respective cultural models may be understood as a continuum between two opposite extreme value orientations, as shown below:

- Time: Monochronic vs Polychronic cultures.
- Personal Space: Non-contact vs Contact cultures.
- Context: Low context vs High context cultures.
- Identity – Individualism (IDV): Individualist vs Collectivist cultures.
- Hierarchy – Power Distance Index (PDI): Small power distance vs Large power distance cultures.
- Gender – Masculinity (MAS): Achievement-oriented vs Care-oriented cultures.
- Truth – Uncertainty Avoidance Index (UAI): Weak uncertainty avoidance vs Strong uncertainty avoidance cultures.
- Virtue – Long-Term orientation (LTO): Long-term orientation vs Short-term orientation cultures.

Level 2: Defining culture-specific value orientations in Spanish and British national cultures

As mentioned above, a value dimension spans a continuum along which cultural groups may show divergent or similar preferred strategic orientations, giving as a result a culture-specific value orientation, that is, a value which is at the core of a culture and hence, more resistant to change than other more peripheral cultural issues such as beliefs, attitudes, and thoughts which may change from generation to generation. In my view, value orientations may offer language researchers a set of cardinal points of reference like the ones on a compass by which to orientate themselves in the intercultural scenario, in our case, intercultural business communication between Spaniards and Britons.

As far as Hall's dimensions are concerned, we may say that Spain has been traditionally identified as a polychronic (multi-active, multi-focus, flexible), high context, contact culture. On the contrary, the UK has been recognised as a monochronic (linear-active, single-focus, rigid), low-context, non-contact culture. Unlike Hall's (1969, 1973, 1977) value dimensions, Hofstede's (2001) are based on empirically verified data. On visiting Itim International's webpage,[3] the language researcher may consult the scores calculated by Hofstede for the five value dimensions in 56 countries. Figure 19 compares Hofstede's value dimension scores calculated for the UK and Spain as regards Power Distance Index (PDI), Individualism (IDV), Masculinity (MAS), Uncertainty Avoidance Index (UAI), and Long-term Orientation (LTO).

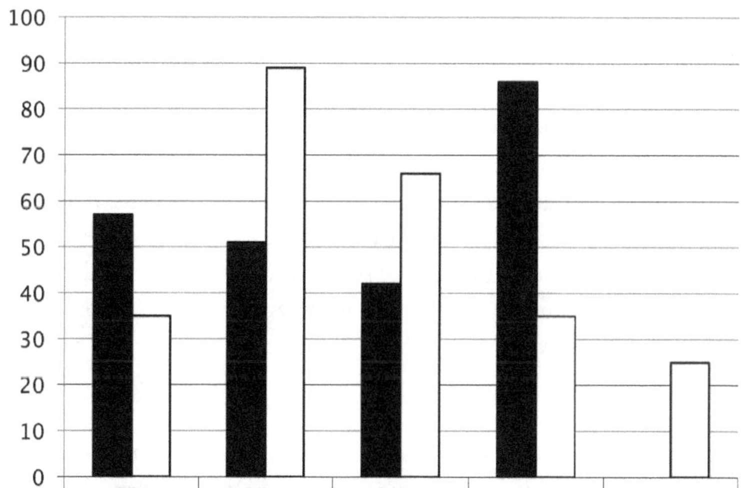

	PDI	IDV	MAS	UAI	LTO
■Spain	57	51	42	86	
□UK	35	89	66	35	25

Figure 19 Hofstede's value dimension scores for Spain and the UK

3 'Itim International, An International Consulting Organization Utilizing Prof. Hofstede's Concepts' (1967–2009) <http://www.geert-hofstede.com> accessed 9 September 2010.

As shown in Figure 19, Hofstede's empirically verified scores confirm that there are significant cultural differences between the UK and Spain. Therefore, we may assume that these two cultural groups have been mentally programmed at the collective level in different ways, that is, they have differing orientations as regards a number of value dimensions that have an effect on interpersonal communication. The above comparison between the preferred cultural orientations that are held at the collective level in Spain and the UK yields a relevant finding. The value dimensions that are likely to cause more friction between Spaniards and Britons are: Time, Personal Space, Context, Individualism, the Uncertainty Avoidance Index, and to a lesser extent the Long Term Orientation Index which curiously enough has no score for Spain.

Before moving on to considering Level 3 in the proposed model of analysis, two considerations need to be made as regards the study of value orientations. Firstly, one should be aware of the fact that the value orientations making up our mental programmes cannot be directly observed; what one perceives instead is the outer visible layers of culture, namely systems and institutions, artefacts and products, rituals and behaviour. And secondly, value orientations do not apply to single individuals. All in all, the mean of the scores calculated for each value orientation in each culture can be used to predict the degree of social integration of an individual into a particular community as regards the expected norms of non-linguistic and linguistic behaviour.

Level 3: Analysing how culture-specific value orientations have been negotiated into culture- and language-specific patterns of behaviour

Finding the intersection between language and culture is by no means an easy task. For some scholars it is certainly axiomatic that language reflects culture and gives shape to our thinking. In line with this thought, Hofstede argues in *Culture's Consequences*:

> Culture, as I use the word in this book, includes language. Language is the most clearly recognizable part of culture and the part that has lent itself most readily to systematic study and theory building. Language is very evidently a learned characteristic (not an inherited one) ... Language is not a neutral vehicle. Our thinking is affected by the categories and words available in our language. (2001: 21)

However, the relationship between language and culture is often faced with serious challenges. Wierzbicka (1992) in *Semantics, Culture, and Cognition* made this clear when she described her experience when giving a paper to the Sydney Linguistic Circle on linguistic differences between English and Polish and claimed that these reflected differences between Anglo-Saxon culture and Polish culture:

> My claims were challenged by Michael Halliday – not on empirical grounds but from a methodological standpoint. Is it justified, he asked, to link individual linguistic phenomena with non-linguistic aspects of culture directly? He acknowledged cases to the lexicon. As far as the grammar is concerned, he was more cautious. ... So at best, it is only some selected features of grammar which one might seek to correlate with something outside language. But how do we decide which linguistic phenomena can be legitimately interpreted as culturally significant outside language itself? Can it be done on a principled basis? (1992: 373)

During the international conference Eurosla 18 organised by the Université de Provence in Aix en Provence in 2008, I was kindly invited by Istvan Kesckes to participate in a workshop on *New tendencies in pragmatics research in SLA*. My paper on 'A pragmatic model for the analysis of intercultural communication between Spaniards and Britons' encouraged some lively discussion and was particularly challenged by two prominent linguists, Juliane House and Gabrielle Kasper, who seemed to be somewhat sceptical about the validity of my proposal. Their main claims were that individual differences rather than cultural differences are at the core of interpersonal communication and business people should be trained in dealing with such differences. I agreed with them that at the individual level of human mental programming there are differences between the speakers of the same linguaculture, because it is common knowledge that each individual has his own personality and a particular idiolect or idiosyncratic communicative style. But my counterarguments were swift: At the collective level, individuals have been culturally programmed to do and say things in a particular way. Being a member of a cultural and speech community involves sharing to a greater or lesser extent the same general preferred patterns of nonverbal and linguistic behaviour with the other members of the same community, otherwise one would be considered to be an outsider.

The above two personal accounts serve to point out the challenges one may come across when looking at the intersection between language and culture, and take me back to a major question posed by Wierzbicka (1992: 374): 'Is it possible to predict which areas of language are most likely to reflect the living culture?'. Her main conclusion was the following:

> Generally speaking, it is the pragmatic aspects of grammar which seem to be particularly culturally revealing. ... More specifically, among the aspects of language which would seem to be particularly revealing of social attitudes and of the style of social interaction I would single out the following four: (1) forms of address; (2) expressive derivation; (3) illocutionary devices of different kinds, such as interjections and particles; and (4) speech act verbs. (1992: 375)

In line with Wierzbicka's conclusion, I think that it is the pragmatics aspects of a language, namely rules of interaction, sociopragmatic conventions and pragmalinguistic behaviour, which seem to reflect the living culture more openly, though grammar and lexicon can also be characteristic of a culture. In this respect, the use of the personal pronoun 'I' in capital letters in Anglo-Saxon countries, traditionally depicted as highly individualistic, may be indicative of the importance that is given to the 'Self' in the Anglophone world. Similarly, the use of 'we' in tribalist countries such as Spain or collectivist countries such as China, highlight the significance of the group.

Relying on both the results of the empirical studies carried out in business organisations and settings within the framework of the COMINTER-SIMULNEG project and the research findings of other specialists in the field of intercultural communication – such as Clyne (1996: 176–201), Wierzbicka (2003, 2006), Prykarpatska (2008: 87–102) and Loukianenko Wolfe (2008: 87–121) – a hypothetical correlation of culture-specific values with language-specific behaviour was ventured, as shown in Table 11.

Value dimension	National culture	Culture-specific values		Language-specific behaviour
Time	Spanish	Polychronic		Multifocus High tolerance for interruptions High tolerance for simultaneous speech
	British	Monochronic		Single focus Low tolerance for interruptions Low tolerance for simultaneous speech
Personal Space	British	Non-contact culture		Promotes the use of independence strategies (negative politeness)
	Spanish	Contact culture		Promotes the use of involvement strategies (positive politeness)
Context	Spanish	Fairly high context		Promotes implicitness Relies on contextual cues and nonverbal codes
	British	Low context		Promotes explicitness Relies on symbolic language and the verbal code
Individualism index	British	Very high	89	Form of reference to self as an individual Uses independence strategies (negative politeness)
	Spanish	Average	51	Form of reference to self as a group Uses involvement strategies (positive politeness)

Power Distance Index	Spanish	Average	57	Honorifics Terms of address V/T forms
	British	Moderately small	35	Honorifics Terms of address Ø V/T forms
Masculinity Index	British	Moderately high	66	Task-oriented Instrumental
	Spanish	Average	42	People-oriented Expressive
Uncertainty Avoidance Index	Spanish	Strong	86	Turn-taking system is asymmetrical Long turns Low tolerance for silence Shows preference for digressiveness, circumlocutions, long explanations. long texts, and long sentences Needs to provide background information and context Purpose statement is postponed Thesis is delayed Indirectness in purpose statement Requires confirmation
	British	Moderately weak	35	Turn-taking is symmetrical Short turns More tolerance for silence Shows preference for linearity, short explanations, short texts, and short sentences Purpose statement is anticipated Directness in purpose statement

Table 11 Hypothetical correlation of culture-specific values with language-specific behaviour (Guillén-Nieto, Pernías-Peco, Vargas-Sierra, & Williams 2009; Guillén-Nieto 2009a)

The potential applications of the proposed model of analysis are varied, since it may enable language researchers in intercultural pragmatics to explain problems of miscommunication, misperception and misunderstanding; it may provide translators and interpreters with useful insight into the problem of mistranslation (Guillén-Nieto 2010); and it may be particularly useful for language teachers and trainers who aim at developing students' intercultural communicative competence (ICC) in general and in business settings in particular. At present different aspects of the above hypothetical correlation are being tested in two PhD dissertations in progress supervised by the author of this chapter, namely *Cultural Values and the Language of Business Web Pages in Spanish and English* by Francisco Miguel Ivorra-Pérez, and *The Impact of Culture on the Language of Press Advertising of Food and Beverages in Spain and the United Kingdom* by Miguel Ángel García-Yeste.

The research carried out in this first part of the COMINTER-SIMULNEG project resulted in the publication of a book entitled *Intercultural Business Communication and Simulation and Gaming Methodology*, vol. 83 in the Linguistic Insights series edited by Maurizio Gotti and published by Peter Lang (Guillén-Nieto, Marimón-Llorca & Vargas-Sierra, eds, 2009).[4]

In the second part of the COMINTER-SIMULNEG project, the crossing of social anthropology, intercultural pragmatics and ICT has given rise to the construction of the 'It's a Deal!' graphic adventure, to which I will refer in the next section.

4 The book was awarded the 'Enrique Alcaraz research award' by the European Association of Languages for Specific Purposes at the IX AELFE Conference held at the University of Hamburg, from 19 to 22 September 2010, for its originality, interdisciplinary nature, coherence, and innovative contribution to the field of research of languages for specific purposes.

3. The construction of the 'It's a Deal!' graphic adventure

The creation of a graphic adventure is not an easy task, partly because it is an interdisciplinary project and hence requires the joint efforts and coordination of two teams, namely the didactic team and the technical team, who need to reach compromise solutions as to the way the graphic adventure should be designed and work out discrepancies effectively throughout the creation process; and partly because an inventive venture like this is faced with technological and funding limitations. On top of this, the multifaceted nature of culture cannot be simply encapsulated in a series of episodes, scenes and screens. Therefore, the complexity that is inherent in real business necessarily has to undergo a simplification process (Guillén Nieto 2009b: 539–552). All things considered, 'It's a Deal!' graphic adventure has been created for the purpose of developing intercultural communicative competence (ICC) between Spaniards and Britons in business settings in which English is used as the lingua franca. It is important to note the significance of ICC in professional business contexts, since not being aware of the other party's cultural orientations and the way these are shown in human nonverbal and linguistic behaviour may inevitably give rise to cultural barriers, such as social distance and miscommunication (Guillén-Nieto 2006: 99–117). Unlike in the case of other simulation games involving intercultural encounters, in 'It's a Deal!' the focus is on the impact of culture on the rhetorical patterns of discourse and communication strategies in business English (Guillén-Nieto 2009b: 539–552).

Supported technologically by the General Foundation of the University of Alicante, 'It's a Deal!' is a serious video game designed using Visionaire, a tool for creating graphical adventure games. Figure 20 shows Visionaire's main screen that was used by computer engineer Alejandro Maldonado Fuentes to design the interaction between the characters, and the interactivity between the player and the characters and objects in the setting.

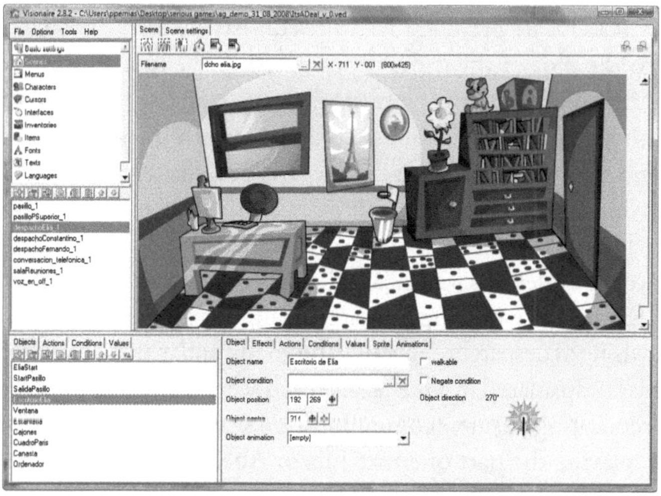

Figure 20 Visionaire's main screen. Setting designed by draftsman Facundo Ferré Luparia. 'It's a Deal!', 2010

In other words, 'It's a Deal!' is '... a mental contest, played with a computer in accordance with specific rules that uses entertainment to further ... strategic communication objectives' (Zyda 2005: 26), in our case intercultural communicative competence (ICC) in business English. More specifically, the graphic adventure uses a simulated experience to provide the targeted users, namely business English learners, with the opportunity to become aware that each culture has its own rules of the game, as well as to discover which rules apply in British culture and practise using these rules in the different stages encompassed in a business transaction. The didactic methodology employed belongs to the constructivist learning theory, since the user, motivated by the plot of the video game, explores the reality that surrounds him/her, discovers the right social interaction and communication strategies to be used in each business situation, adds them to his/her bank of existing knowledge and assimilates them as the correct response that should be given to similar communication problems arising in real business life (Guillén-Nieto & Pernías-Peco 2009: 6968).

The 'It's a Deal!' graphic adventure consists of seven episodes. In Episode zero the plot of the game is presented to the user so that s/he can become familiarized with the business setting and with the interactive devices that s/he will need to use to interact with the objects and characters, and solve puzzles. Once the user has become familiarised with the game setting and the interactive devices, six interrelated episodes will be presented to the learner one by one as s/he makes progress in the graphic adventure. Episodes 1 to 6 simulate the different stages involved in a sales transaction, namely making contact, asking for a quotation, placing an order, advising of despatch, delivering the goods, and making payment. Each episode is encapsulated in a scene, and each scene is divided into a series of screens replicating business communication situations. In these situations, the user, playing the part of either Elia or Abel, the two main characters of this graphic adventure, has to make decisions as to the most effective and appropriate way of accomplishing certain business tasks in English. The player will have to discover by himself/herself the actions that need to be performed, the rules of the game when doing business with Britons, and the most effective and appropriate way to communicate with them in English in the intercultural scenario. Figure 21 illustrates an animation involving part of a cross-cultural encounter between George Watts, the British sales manager at TAW Ltd, Elia Las Heras, manager of the export department and Abel, her assistant manager, in which cultural differences emerge dramatically. This activity yields a case study asking the user to help George Watts discover the factors that may have influenced the cultural shock he experienced on his visit to Las Heras Hermanos S. L.

Figure 21 Example of an animation. Setting and characters designed by draftsman Facundo Ferré Luparia. 'It's a Deal!', 2010

The following box exemplifies the draft of a didactic activity consisting of a cross-cultural dialogue in which the miscommunication problem between George Watts, the British sales manager at TAW Ltd, and Elia, the Spanish export manager at Las Heras Hermanos S. L., is not apparent. This dialogue gives rise to a case study in which the user is invited to reflect upon the cultural factors that may have had an effect on Elia's confusion and frustration on her visit to the offices of TAW Ltd in London.

The dialogue between George Watts and Elia continues on the screen as follows:

ELIA: Now if I could explain some of the details of our new business venture in the UK.
GEORGE WATTS: Why didn't you bring this up earlier?
ELIA: Excuse me?
GEORGE WATTS: I mean this is something we need to look at very closely. But I've got another ...
ELIA: Yes, of course. Now if I could just have one more minute or two.
GEORGE WATTS: Let me ask my secretary to put you on my calendar for Friday.
ELIA: Excuse me? (*perplexed*)
GEORGE WATTS: So we can continue then.
ELIA: You want me to come back?
GEORGE WATTS: Well, if you would like to talk about another project, you'll have to arrange another meeting with my secretary since it was not on today's agenda. Will Friday be convenient for you?
ELIA: Er ... I don't know. I'll have to consult with ... er ... first. I'd better send her an e-mail. Uhm ... Thank you very much, Mr. Watts. It's been a pleasure for me to do business with you.
GEORGE WATTS: It's been a pleasure for me too. By the way, you can call me George.
ELIA: Thank you. You can call me Elia too.
GEORGE WATTS: Elia, 'Check, check ...
ELIA: ... and double check. Always check'. I'll never forget that, George. Good-bye.
GEORGE WATTS: We'll keep in touch. Bye-bye.
Elia says good-bye to George Watts and takes a taxi to the city centre. She has plenty of time to walk around the shops before going to the airport. Her flight is leaving at 9 p.m.

After the meeting at TAW Ltd, Elia, on her return flight home, shows clear signs of confusion and frustration.

Draft of a cross-cultural dialogue. Didactic activity created by Victoria Guillén-Nieto and Judith Williams. 'It's a Deal!', 2010.

Figure 22 shows the scenario designed by draftsman Facundo Ferré Luparia for the scene in which the above cross-cultural dialogue takes place.

Figure 22 Elia and George Watts negotiating at TAW Ltd in London. Setting and characters designed by draftsman Facundo Ferré Luparia. 'It's a Deal!', 2010

In the 'It's a Deal!' graphic adventure each time the player performs an action or chooses an option, s/he will be given either positive or negative feedback. The user's recognition of the most suitable way to carry out such tasks in English is essential to achieve the specific didactic goals, that is, to develop awareness of a particular value orientation and how it affects specific language patterns of behaviour in business English. The following box illustrates the type of learning summaries included at the end of each Episode.

EPISODE 4
In Episode 4, you helped Elia to reflect upon the cultural problems encountered on her business trip to London and business meeting with George Watts at TAW Ltd. These are the communicative skills that were practised for the purpose of developing your intercultural communicative competence with the British in business English: 1. Using a formal register and the right dose of politeness when making contact for the first time. 2. Showing respect to the Other's space bubble in a business meeting. 3. Communicating with a direct, unambiguous, and polite communicative style. 4. Observing the interaction rules, e.g. speech turns, at a business meeting. 5. Using appropriate strategic language to solve communication problems and conflicts at a business meeting. 6. Identifying the communication problems that may arise between Spaniards and Britons due to their differing cultural orientations with respect to some visible and invisible aspects of a culture.

Draft of a learning summary. Didactic activity created by Victoria Guillén-Nieto and Judith Williams. 'It's a Deal!, 2010.

At the end of the video game, the learner will have overcome all the cross-cultural conflicts encountered in the different scenes by applying the right communication strategies. This is verified by means of a final evaluation report in which the user is asked to reflect on his/her performance and learning experience.

4. Conclusion

The discussion in this chapter has shown the advantages of crossing disciplines in the field of intercultural business communication research and training. These advantages can be summarised in two parts: (a) a deeper understanding of the way the cultural values at the core of a culture have an effect on intercultural communication between Spaniards and Britons in business settings, and (b) the construction of an innovative serious game, the 'It's a Deal!' graphic adventure, that uses interactive language learning in a virtual environment for the purpose of developing intercultural awareness and promoting ICC between Spaniards and Britons in business settings in which English is used as the lingua franca. Interdisciplinarity – *connecting brains* – has indeed helped the different agents participating in the COMINTER-SIMULNEG research project – social anthropologists, linguists, educationalists and computer engineers – make advances in the field of intercultural communication. This has resulted in a combined product that will hopefully prove to be particularly useful for academic and professional people in general and business people in particular who need to use English as the lingua franca in their daily activities, since it offers learners continuous communication training and feedback in a virtual setting.

5. Acknowledgements

The author would like to thank all the lecturers and technicians participating in the COMINTER-SIMULNEG research project. Special thanks go to Judith Williams (associate lecturer) for her thorough revision of the script and the didactic activities, and to Pedro Pernías-Peco (educationalist), Francisco Sanguino Oliva (screenwriter), Alejandro Maldonado and Rafael Torregrosa (programmers), Facundo Ferré Luparia (draftsman), Roberto Ruiz (sound technician), Marian Alesón Carbonell (junior lecturer) and Miguel Ángel García-Yeste (PhD student) who have greatly contributed to the creation of the 'It's a Deal!' graphic adventure.

6. References

Clyne, Michael, *Inter-cultural Communication at Work* (Cambridge: Cambridge University Press, 1996).

Compact Oxford Dictionary. AskOxford.com. <http://www.askoxford.com/concise_oed/synergy?view=uk> accessed 23 February 2010.

De Mooij, Marieke, *Consumer Behaviour and Culture. Consequences for Global Marketing and Advertising* (Thousand Oaks, CA: SAGE, 2004).

——, *Global Marketing and Advertising. Understanding Cultural Paradoxes* (Thousand Oaks, CA: SAGE, 2005).

Fantini, Alvino, 'About Intercultural Communicative Competence: A Construct'. < http://www.sit.edu/SITOccasionalPapers/feil_appendixe.pdf> accessed 15 April 2009.

Gudykunst, William B., 'Methodological Issues in Conducting Theory-Based Cross-Cultural Research', in Helen Spencer-Oatey, ed., *Culturally Speaking. Managing Rapport through Talk across Cultures* (London and New York: Continuum, 2004), 293–315.

Guillén-Nieto, Victoria, 'Understanding Social Distance in Intercultural Communication', in Mª Isabel González Cruz, ed., *Lengua, Sociedad y Cultura: Estudios Interdisciplinares* (Las Palmas de Gran Canaria: Universidad de Las Palmas de Gran Canaria, Servicio de Publicaciones, 2006), 99–117.

——, 'Crossing Disciplines to Make Advances in Intercultural Communication', in Victoria Guillén-Nieto, Carmen Marimón-Llorca, and Chelo Vargas-Sierra, eds, *Intercultural Business Communication and Simulation and Gaming Methodology* (Bern: Peter Lang, 2009a), 29–63.

——, 'Intercultural Communicative Competence in Business English: The Case of the "It's a Deal!" Graphic Adventure, in Estefanía Caridad de Otto, and Alejandro F. López de Vergara Méndez, eds, *Actas del VIII Congreso Internacional AELFE* (La Laguna: Universidad de La Laguna, 2009b), 539–552.

——, 'Lost in Mistranslation', in Theo Bungarten, ed., *Linguistic and Didactic Aspects of Language in Business Communication. Files of the 9th International Conference of the European Association of Languages for Specific Purposes (AELFE).* (University of Hamburg, Germany. Tostedt: Attikon, 2010), 1–12.

——, Carmen Marimón-Llorca, and Chelo Vargas-Sierra, eds, *Intercultural Business Communication and Simulation and Gaming Methodology* (Bern: Peter Lang, 2009).

——, and Pedro Pernías-Peco, 'Facing Intercultural Business Communication through a Serious Game: The Case of the "It's a Deal!" Graphic Adventure', in *ICERI2009 Proceedings* (Madrid: IATED, 2009), 6966–6974.

——, Pedro Pernías-Peco, Chelo Vargas-Sierra, and Judith Williams, 'Advances in Intercultural Communication Research and Training Based on Computer Simulation of Real Business Settings', in Reyes Gómez Morón, Manuel Padilla Cruz, Lucía Fernández Amaya, and María de la O Hernández López, eds, *Pragmatics Applied to Language Teaching and Learning* (Newcastle: Cambridge Scholars Publishing 2009), 337–361.

Hall, Edward T., *The Hidden Dimension* (New York: Doubleday, 1969).

——, *The Silent Language* (New York: Doubleday, 1973).

——, *Beyond Culture* (New York: Anchor Books, 1977).

Harris Bond, Michael, Vlad Žegarac and Helen Spencer-Oatey, 'Culture as an Explanatory Variable: Problems and Possibilities', in Helen Spencer-Oatey, ed., *Culturally Spaking. Managing Rapport through Talk across Cultures* (London and New York: Continuum, 2004), 165–190.

Hofstede, Geert, *Cultures and Organizations* (London: Profile Books, 2003).

——, *Culture's Consequences* (Thousand Oaks: Sage Publications, 2001).

House, Juliane, 'Politeness in Germany?', in Leo Hickey, Miranda Stewart, eds, *Politeness in Europe* (Clevedon/Buffalo/Toronto: Multilingual Matters, 2005), 13–28.

'La Innovación es cosa de Letras', *Diario Información.com.* <http://www.diarioinformacion.com/opinion/2010/08/15/innovacion-cosa-letras/1035401.html> accessed 15 August 2010.

'Itim International, An International Consulting Organization Utilizing Prof. Hofstede's Concepts' (1967–2009) <http://www.geert-hofstede.com> accessed 9 September 2010.

Johansson, Frans, *The Medici Effect. What Elephants and Epidemics can Teach us about Innovation* (Cambridge, MA: Harvard Business School Publishing, 2006).

Kuhn, Thomas Samuel, *The Structure of Scientific Revolutions* (Chicago: University of Chicago Press, 1970).

Loukianenko Wolfe, Maria, 'Different cultures – Different discourses? Rhetorical Patterns of Business Letters by English and Russian Speakers', in Ulla Connor, Ed Nagelhout, William V. Rozycki, eds, *Contrastive Rhetoric. Reaching to Intercultural Rhetoric* (Amsterdam/Philadelphia: John Benjamins Publishing Company, 2008), 87–121.

Pan, Yuling, Suzanne Wong Scollon and Ron Scollon, *Professional Communication in International Settings* (Malden, MA: Blackwell Publishers, 2002).

Prykarpatska, Iryna, 'Why are you Late? Cross-Cultural Pragmatic Study of Complaints in American English and Ukrainian', *Revista Alicantina de Estudios Ingleses* 21 (2008), 87–102.

Rogers, Everett. M., William B. Hart and Yoshitaka Miike, 'Edward T. Hall and the History of the United States and Japan', *Keio Communication Review* 24 (2002), 3–26.

Scollon, Ron, and Suzanne Wong Scollon, *Intercultural Communication* (Cambridge, MA: Blackwell Publishers, 1996).

Spencer-Oatey, Helen, ed., *Culturally Speaking. Managing Rapport through Talk across Cultures*. (London and New York: Continuum, 2004).

Trompenaars, Fons, and Charles Hampden-Turner, *Managing People across Cultures* (Chichester, West Sussex, England: Capstone, 2004).

——, and Peter Woolliams, *Business across Cultures* (Chichester, West Sussex, England: Capstone, 2003).

Wierzbicka, Anna, *Semantics, Culture, and Cognition. Universal Human Concepts in Culture-specific Configurations* (New York, Oxford: Oxford University Press, 1992).

——, *Understanding Cultures through their Key Words* (New York and Oxford: Oxford University Press, 1997).

——, *Emotions across Languages and Cultures. Diversity and Universals* (Australia: Cambridge University Press and Editions de la Maison des Sciences de l'Homme Paris, 1999).

——, *Cross-cultural Pragmatics. The Semantics of Human Interaction* (Berlin, New York: Mouton de Gruyter, 2003).

——, *English Meaning and Culture* (Oxford and New York: Oxford University Press, 2006).

Zyda, Michael (2005). 'From visual simulation to virtual reality to games', in *IEEE Computer* 38/9 (2005), 25–32.

Notes on Contributors

Editors

BARRY PENNOCK-SPECK is Senior Lecturer in English Language and Linguistics at the Instituto Interuniversitario de Lenguas Modernas Aplicadas (IULMA), Universitat de València, Spain. He has published articles in a wide range of fields that include discourse analysis, translation, contrastive phonology and grammaticalisation. At present he is the co-ordinator of the (MATVA) research group, which analyses British television commercials from a multimodal perspective. With regard to the field of teaching, at present he is co-ordinator for First Year in English Studies at the UVEG and also co-ordinates a Project financed by the UVEG to promote the use of communication and information technologies in English Studies (Anglotic). This project involves the creation of multimedia learning objects and the promotion of blended learning.

FRANCISCA SUAU-JIMÉNEZ is Senior Lecturer in English Language and Linguistics at the Universitat de València, Spain. She has published books and articles on specialised genres and translation, metadiscourse, discourse analysis and learning strategies, her latest being *La Traducción Especializada en inglés y español en Géneros de Economía y Empresa* (2010). At present she is the director of the Instituto Interuniversitario de Lenguas Modernas Aplicadas (IULMA) at the Universitat de València, a research and services institution that attempts to create a link between the university and society in matters related to modern languages. She is currently co-ordinating a corpus linguistics project with the University Abdelmalek Essaâdi in Morocco in order to create a database in English, Spanish, French and Arabic with the aim of making several bilingual dictionaries on Hotel Management. She has taught in the fields of discourse analysis applied to translation, semantics, lexis, business English and English-Spanish translation of science and technology.

Contributors

MIGUEL ÁNGEL CANDEL-MORA has a BA in English Studies from the Universitat de València, a MA in Translation from Kent State University and a PhD in Linguistics from the Universidad Politécnica de Valencia. For the last eighteen years he has worked as a translator actively involved in the localisation industry. He coordinates the UPV Translation and Interpretation Services translating and managing terminology and translation projects for different departments as well as for private and public institutions. His academic interests focus on translation-oriented bilingual terminology management, computational terminology, computer-assisted translation, information retrieval, corpus-based translation and text mining.

BEATRIZ GALLARDO-PAÚLS is Professor of General Linguistics at the Universitat de València. Her research focuses on pragmatics and, in recent years, its application to the field of language impairment, and specifically on ecological data from aphasia, Williams Syndrome and ADHD. She is also the editor-in-chief of '@tic.revista d'innovació educativa' and coordinates the Learning Innovation Unit at the Universitat de València.

ISABEL GARCÍA-IZQUIERDO is a professor in Applied Linguistics to Translation and Spanish for Translators at the Universitat Jaume I, in Castellón (Spain). From 2000, she is the director of the research group GENTT (Textual Genres for Translation) that focuses on the multilingual analysis of textual genres in the framework of specialised communication applied to translation. She has published several books as well as national and international articles related to her research. She is the author of *Análisis textual aplicado a la Traducción* (2000), and *Divulgación médica y traducción* (Peter Lang, 2009) and the editor of *El género textual y la traducción* (Peter Lang, 2005).

JOSÉ RAMÓN GÓMEZ-MOLINA has a PhD in Sociolinguistics and Language Teaching from the Universitat de València. He is a Professor of Spanish as a Foreign Language and Sociolinguistics at the Universitat de València and the director of several postgraduate courses: Acquisition of Spanish as a Foreign Language (1998, 1999), Communicative Competence (1999, 2001) and Teacher Training course of Spanish as a Foreign Language (1999–2010). He is currently a partner and the scientific leader of the Spanish part in Tempus, Lingua, Socrates and LifeLong Learning programmes.

VICTORIA GUILLÉN-NIETO has been a senior lecturer in the Department of English Studies at the University of Alicante since 1997. In September 2010, she was awarded the Enrique Alcaraz Research Award for the book *Intercultural Business Communication and Simulation and Gaming Methodology* (Peter Lang, 2009) at the IX AELFE Conference held in Hamburg. She has also patented the serious video game 'It's a Deal!', which has been created for the purpose of developing intercultural communicative competence in business settings in which English is used as the *lingua franca*.

VERÓNICA MORENO-CAMPOS holds a BA in Logopedy and a PhD in Psychology. She currently holds a research grant in the General Linguistics Department, Universitat de València. She is carrying out a research in pragmatic categories, aphasia and their application in the field of speech therapy.

MARÍA LUISA PÉREZ-CAÑADO is Associate Professor at the Department of English Philology of the University of Jáen, Spain, where she is also Vicedean of the Faculty of Humanities and Education. Her work centers on Applied Linguistics and has appeared in over sixty scholarly journals and edited volumes published by Elsevier, Peter Lang, Mellen Press, Multilingual Matters, Wiley-Blackwell, Routledge, or John Benjamins, among others.

FRANÇOISE SALAGER-MEYER was educated at the University of Lyons, France, and the University of Texas at Austin, USA. She is the author of numerous publications on written medical discourse, mostly from a diachronic, cross-linguistic and cross-generic perspective. In 1994 and 2004, she was awarded the Horowitz Prize for her works on the pragmatics of written scholarly communication. She was the section editor of the *Language and Medicine* section of the second edition of the Encyclopedia of Language and Linguistics and is currently coordinating the Multilingual and Multidisciplinary Research Group on Scientific Discourse Analysis.

DENIS SOCARRÁS-ESTRADA, PhD Candidate in Modern Languages, Literature and Translation, holds an MA in Intercultural Communication, Interpreting and Translation in Public Services and a BA in English Language and Literature. His research interests are the interpreter's cognitive processes and its methodological application. He has studied in Cuba, Belgium, Italy, UK and Spain, where he is currently teaching interpreting in health care settings at postgraduate level at the University of Alcala.

CARMEN VALERO-GARCÉS is Senior Lecturer at the University of Alcalá, Madrid, Spain, and the Director of the Postgraduate and Undergraduate Program on Public Service Interpreting and Translation. She is also the coordinator of The International Conference on Translation and Interpreting held at Alcalá since 1995 and the editor of the Proceedings. She is also responsible of the Research Group FITISPos® and a founder member of Red COMUNICA (Permanent Observatory of Communication between Languages in Cultures in Spain) as well as the author and editor of some books and articles dealing with interpreting and translating, cross-cultural communication, interpreting and translating, SLA and Contrastive Linguistics.

CHELO VARGAS-SIERRA is a Senior Lecturer in the English Studies Department, Universidad de Alicante and holds an MA in Terminology from IULA, Universitat Pompeu Fabra, as well as a PhD in English Translation and Interpreting. She has published several articles on terminology, specialised translation, computer-aided translation and corpus linguistics.

Among her most relevant publications in terminology are two specialised dictionaries: *Diccionario de terminos de la piedra natural e industrias afines inglés-español/español-inglés* (2005) and *Diccionario de términos del calzado e industrias afines inglés-español/español-inglés* (2006).

FRANCISCO YUS teaches pragmatics at the University of Alicante, Spain. He has specialised in the pragmatic analysis of media discourses and conversational issues. For instance, he has made two applications of pragmatics to characters in alternative comics (*Conversational cooperation in alternative comics*, University of Alicante, 1995; *El discurso femenino en el cómic alternativo inglés*, University of Alicante, 2001), proposed a pragmatic verbal-visual model of communication in media discourses (*La interpretación y la imagen de masas*, Instituto Juan Gil-Albert, 1997), and developed a pragmatic approach to Internet-mediated communication (*Ciberpragmática*, Ariel, 2001; *Ciberpragmática 2.0*, Ariel, 2010).

Index

5-D model 190

academic discourse analysis 113
ad hoc terminology management 48
Alcaraz 126, 132, 142, 143
alignment 53
ambient awareness 75
Amichai-Hamburger et al. 70
animation 201
Antia et al. 45
aptitude test 1, 2, 3, 5, 8, 17
Argentina 111, 114, 115
Arjona 9
Armbrust et al. 61
Arntz 50
assessment 1, 3, 7, 8, 9, 10, 17, 18
authentic texts 108

Bake 4
Baroni et al. 55
Belz 163
bitext 53, 56
blended learning 33, 38, 39, 40, 43
Blumler and Katz 70
Bodoff 71
Bolívar 113, 115
Borja, García-Izquierdo and Montalt 129, 143
Bowker 45
Bowker and Pearson 52
Brazil 108, 111, 113, 114, 116, 118
British national culture 190
browsing 71
Budin and Wright (1997) 55
Burkeman 83
business courses 113
business English 198
Byram 165, 166, 167

Cabré 52, 60
Cacioppo and Petty 70
Campbell and Hale 8
Candel-Mora 48
Carston 69
CAT tools 145, 146, 147, 148, 156
Central America 109
Celani 108, 109
Choo et al. 71
Ciapuscio 114
cloud computing 61
Clyne 185, 187, 188, 194, 206
cognitive effects 68
cognitive environment 66
cognitive rewards 70, 73
collaborative learning 162
collaborative software 61, 62
collaborative terminology 61
collaborative translation 61, 62, 63
COMINTER-SIMULNEG research project 186, 188, 194, 197, 205
communication strategies 204
comparable corpus 53
competences 3, 4, 5, 7, 8, 17, 21, 22, 24, 33, 38, 42
computer-assisted translation 145, 147, 148, 159
computer-assisted/-aided translation (CAT) 49, 51, 63

concordance 52, 148, 150
conditions of relevance 68
connectivism 99, 100, 101, 102
constructivist learning theory 199
context 189, 192, 195
corpus 47, 52, 53, 55, 60
corpus-based research groups 130
corpus linguistics 146, 151
cross-cultural communication 185
cross-cultural conflicts 204
cross-cultural dialogue 201, 203
cross-cultural encounter 2
Cuba 110, 111
cultural shock 200
cultural values 188, 197, 204
culture 193, 194
cyberpragmatics 66, 69, 75

Davis 72
De Mooij 186, 206
diachronic 114
Digital Literacy/Alphabetisation 89, 92, 100
digital natives 90, 91
digital competence 20
documentation 46, 47, 49, 52, 56
Downes 89, 99, 101

ECTS 20, 22, 24, 26, 29, 30, 32, 38, 39, 40, 41, 42, 43
EHEA 20, 21, 23, 24, 32, 33, 38, 40, 41
Ellis 167, 168
EMP 110
English as lingua franca 198, 205
environmental constraints 73, 74
ESP 107
European Master's in Translation (EMT) 6

final evaluation report 204
Friesen 94, 95, 97

Galinski and Budin 47
García-Izquierdo 127, 128, 143
García-Izquierdo and Borja 131, 132, 143
gender 189
genre (s) 109, 113, 114, 125, 127, 128, 129, 130, 131, 132, 135, 136, 138, 139, 140, 142, 143
Gentt 129, 130, 131, 132, 133, 141, 142
glossary 52, 53, 55, 60
graphic adventure 197, 200, 203, 205
Guillén-Nieto 189, 196

Hall 185, 190–191, 207
Harris Bond, Žegarac and Spencer-Oatey 188
Harvey 114
Hasan and Ahmed 72
hierarchy 189
Hofstede 186, 188, 207
House 188, 207
Hyland 112

ICT 20, 21, 22, 23, 24, 25, 27, 29, 30, 31, 32, 33, 34, 35, 37, 38, 39, 40, 41, 42, 43, 56, 57, 60, 61, 87, 91, 99, 100, 187, 197
identity 189
idiolect(s) 188, 193
Individualism Index (IDV) 190, 192, 195
Information and Communications Technology (ICT) 185, 187
innovation 22, 23, 33, 40
intercultural awareness 205
intercultural business communication 189, 190, 204
intercultural communication 185, 187, 189, 193, 194, 197, 204, 205
Intercultural Communicative Competence (ICC) 161, 162, 166, 175, 181, 197, 199, 205
intercultural communicative tasks 168

intercultural competence 162, 165, 166
intercultural pragmatics 197
interdisciplinarity 186, 187, 205
interface 72
internet 45, 46, 52, 57
interpersonal communication 188
interpreter 1, 3, 4, 5, 6, 7, 8, 9, 16, 17
interpreting 1, 2, 3, 4, 5, 8, 9, 10, 11, 12, 13

Johansson 186, 207, 14, 16, 17, 18

Khun 185

Latin America 107–124, 115, 116, 117, 118
Laviosa 53
learner-centred 21
learning summary 204
linguistic and cultural mediation 185
linguistic behaviour 192, 194
localisation 147
Long-Term orientation (LTO) 190, 192
LSP research 107
Loukianenko Wolfe 188, 194, 207

Machine Translation 145, 148
Management (Systems) 131, 132, 137, 138
Martínez 111, 112
Masculinity (MAS) 190, 191, 196
medicine 114, 115
miscommunication 197, 198
misperception 197
Müller-Hartman 165
mutual cognitive environment 66
Murphy et al. 79

national culture 195
Navarro 115
NECOBELAC 115, 116, 117, 118
Nicaragua 110
needs analysis 113, 114

O'Dowd 163, 166
oralised written text 71
Ortiz 114

parallel corpus 53
parallel texts 152, 153
personal space 189, 192, 195
phase 51, 52, 57, 58
post-translation editing 52, 59
Power Distance Index (PDI) 190, 191, 196
professional and academic languages 126
project management 150
Prykarpatska 188, 207

qualitative 23, 40, 42
quality assurance 59
political discourse 113
quality control 149, 150, 115

Ramirez-Polo and Ferrer-Mora 46
Ramos 108, 111, 113
reading skills 108
relevance 65
relevance equations 73
reliability 3, 5, 7, 17, 1
rhetorical patterns 198

Salager-Meyer 112, 114, 115
scientific writing courses 111
Scollon and Scollon 188, 207
Scollon and Wong Scollon 185, 208
SCORM 93, 94, 95, 98, 102
scroll factor 75
searches 58
serious game 205
shared cognitive environment 66
Siemens 99, 100, 101, 102
social anthropology 185, 187, 197
social distance 198
social pragmatics 185
social web / web 2.0 61

Spanish for Specific Purposes 112, 113, 114, 118
specialised language 146, 152
speech community 194
Spencer-Oatey 185, 186
Sperber and Wilson 67, 68
standardisation 154, 155, 158
Suler 76
Swales 112, 116, 126, 127, 143
synergy 187
systematic terminology management 48

technical terminology 151, 155, 158
technical translation 146, 151, 152, 157
Technology Acceptance Model (TAM) 72
telecollaboration 163
term base 46, 49, 53, 55, 56, 57, 58, 59, 62
Term Base eXchange (TBX) 56
term compilation 51
term extractor 47
term mining 55
terminology 45, 49, 50, 53
terminology database 49, 56, 146, 147, 148, 150, 158
terminology leverage 55
terminology management 45, 47, 48, 50, 145, 150, 154, 157, 158
terminology management system/TMS 46, 47, 51, 56, 58, 59
terminology retrieval 148
terminology work 46, 60, 62, 63
text analysis 152, 153
text deformation 71
Thompson 75
tourism 112
translation and interpreting 185
translation memory/TM 46, 49, 53, 55, 56, 57, 58, 59, 60, 62
Translation Memory eXchange (TMX) 53, 56
translation memory systems 145, 146
translation-oriented terminology 45, 48, 52, 60
translation-oriented terminology management 47, 49, 50
translator's workbench 45, 49
translator's workstation 46, 60, 145, 159
Trompenaars and Hampden-Turner 186, 208
Trompenaars and Woolliams 186, 208
truth 189
tweeter 82
tweets 82

ubiquitous web/web 4.0 61
Uncertainty Avoidance Index (UAI) 190–192, 196
underdeterminacy thesis 69
Uses and Gratifications 70

validity 3, 7, 9, 17, 18
value dimensions 189, 191, 195
value orientations 190, 192, 203
Vargas 47, 52
Vasconcelos 112
Venezuela 110, 114
video game 204
video-web communication 161, 175
virtual setting 205
virtual worlds 76
VLE 33, 38, 40, 42

Walker 50
web file downloader 54
Wilson and Sperber 65, 66, 79
Wierzbicka 188, 193, 194, 208
Wright and Wright 48

Yus 66, 69, 71, 75, 78, 79, 80, 83

Zanettin 53

CONTEMPORARY STUDIES IN DESCRIPTIVE LINGUISTICS

Edited by

DR GRAEME DAVIS, lecturer in the History of the English Language at the Open University, UK, and

KARL A. BERNHARDT, English Language Consultant with Trinity College London and for the London Chamber of Commerce and Industry International Qualification.

This series provides an outlet for academic monographs which offer a recent and original contribution to linguistics and which are within the descriptive tradition.

While the monographs demonstrate their debt to contemporary linguistic thought, the series does not impose limitations in terms of methodology or genre, and does not support a particular linguistic school. Rather the series welcomes new and innovative research that contributes to furthering the understanding of the description of language.

The topics of the monographs are scholarly and represent the cutting edge for their particular fields, but are also accessible to researchers outside the specific disciplines.

Vol. 1 Mark Garner: Language: An Ecological View.
260 pages, 2004.
ISBN 3-03910-054-8 / US-ISBN 0-8204-6295-0

Vol. 2 T. Nyan: Meanings at the Text Level: A Co-Evolutionary Approach.
194 pages, 2004.
ISBN 3-03910-250-8 / US-ISBN 0-8204-7179-8

Vol. 3 Breffni O'Rourke and Lorna Carson (eds): Language Learner Autonomy: Policy, Curriculum, Classroom.
439 pages, 2010.
ISBN 978-3-03911-980-6

Vol. 4 Dimitra Koutsantoni: Developing Academic Literacies: Understanding Disciplinary Communities' Culture and Rhetoric.
302 pages, 2007.
ISBN 978-3-03910-575-5

Vol. 5 Emmanuelle Labeau: Beyond the Aspect Hypothesis: Tense-Aspect Development in Advanced L2 French.
259 pages, 2005.
ISBN 3-03910-281-8 / US-ISBN 0-8204-7208-5

Vol. 6 Maria Stambolieva: Building Up Aspect. A Study of Aspect and Related Categories in Bulgarian, with Parallels in English and French.
243 pages, 2008.
ISBN 978-3-03910-558-8

Vol. 7 Stavroula Varella: Language Contact and the Lexicon in the History of Cypriot Greek.
283 pages, 2006.
ISBN 3-03910-526-4 / US-ISBN 0-8204-7531-9

Vol. 8 Alan J. E. Wolf: Subjectivity in a Second Language: Conveying the Expression of Self.
246 pages. 2006.
ISBN 3-03910-518-3 / US-ISBN 0-8204-7524-6

Vol. 9 Bettina Braun: Production and Perception of Thematic Contrast in German.
280 pages, 2005.
ISBN 3-03910-566-3 / US-ISBN 0-8204-7593-9

Vol. 10 Jean-Paul Kouega: A Dictionary of Cameroon English Usage.
202 pages, 2007.
ISBN 978-3-03911-027-8

Vol. 11 Sebastian M. Rasinger: Bengali-English in East London. A Study in Urban Multilingualism.
270 pages, 2007.
ISBN 978-3-03911-036-0

Vol.12 Emmanuelle Labeau and Florence Myles (eds): The Advanced Learner Variety: The Case of French.
298 pages, 2009.
ISBN 978-3-03911-072-8

Vol.13 Miyoko Kobayashi: Hitting the Mark: How Can Text Organisation and Response Format Affect Reading Test Performance?
322 pages, 2009.
ISBN 978-3-03911-083-4

Vol.14 Dingfang Shu and Ken Turner (eds): Contrasting Meaning in Languages of the East and West.
634 pages, 2010.
ISBN 978-3-03911-886-1

Vol.15 Ana Rojo: Step by Step: A Course in Contrastive Linguistics and Translation.
418 pages, 2009.
ISBN 978-3-03911-133-6

Vol.16 Jinan Fedhil Al-Hajaj and Graeme Davis (eds): University of Basrah Studies in English.
304 pages, 2008.
ISBN 978-3-03911-325-5

Vol.17 Paolo Coluzzi: Minority Language Planning and Micronationalism in Italy.
348 pages, 2007.
ISBN 978-3-03911-041-4

Vol.18 Iwan Wmffre: Breton Orthographies and Dialects: The Twentieth-Century Orthography War in Brittany. Vol 1.
499 pages, 2007.
ISBN 978-3-03911-364-4

Vol.19 Iwan Wmffre: Breton Orthographies and Dialects: The Twentieth-Century Orthography War in Brittany. Vol 2.
281 pages, 2007.
ISBN 978-3-03911-365-1

Vol.20 Fanny Forsberg: Le langage préfabriqué: Formes, fonctions et fréquences en français parlé L2 et L1.
293 pages, 2008.
ISBN 978-3-03911-369-9

Vol.21 Kathy Pitt: Sourcing the Self: Debating the Relations between Language and Consciousness.
220 pages, 2008.
ISBN 978-3-03911-398-9

Vol.22 Peiling Xing: Chinese Learners and the Lexis Learning Rainbow.
273 pages, 2009.
ISBN 978-3-03911-407-8

Vol.23 Yufang Qian: Discursive Constructions around Terrorism in the *People's Daily* (China) and *The Sun* (UK) Before and After 9.11: A Corpus-based Contrastive Critical Discourse Analysis.
284 pages, 2010.
ISBN 978-3-0343-0186-2

Vol.24 Ian Walkinshaw: Learning Politeness: Disagreement in a Second Language.
297 pages, 2009.
ISBN 978-3-03911-527-3

Vol.25 Forthcoming.

Vol.26 Shahela Hamid: Language Use and Identity: The Sylheti Bangladeshis in Leeds.
225 pages, 2011.
ISBN 978-3-03911-559-4

Vol.27-29 Forthcoming.

Vol.30 Francisca Suau-Jiménez and Barry Pennock-Speck (eds): Interdisciplinarity and Languages: Current Issues in Research, Teaching, Professional Applications and ICT.
234 pages, 2011.
ISBN 978-3-0343-0283-8

Vol.31 Ahmad Al-Issa and Laila S. Dahan (eds): Global English and Arabic: Issues of Language, Culture, and Identity.
379 pages, 2011.
ISBN 978-3-0343-0293-7

FSC
www.fsc.org
MIX
Papier | Fördert gute Waldnutzung
FSC® C083411

Kolibri 360 GmbH
Ferdinand-Jühlke-Straße 7
99095 Erfurt, Deutschland
produktsicherheit@kolibri360.de